THE MIGHTY FROM THEIR THRONES

Power in the Biblical Tradition

THE MIGHTY FROM THEIR THRONES

J. P. M. WALSH, S.J.

Wipf & Stock
PUBLISHERS
Eugene, Oregon

Wipf and Stock Publishers
199 West 8th Avenue, Suite 3
Eugene, Oregon 97401

The Mighty from Their Thrones
Power in Biblical Tradition
By Walsh, J.P.M.

ISBN: 1-59244-722-8
Publication date 7/5/2004
Previously published by Fortress Press, 1987

For
JANE and BILL

Contents

Editor's Foreword

On November 27, 1775, Abigail Adams wrote to John Adams that "power, whether vested in many or a few, is ever grasping, and like the grave, cries 'Give, give.'" Written at the dawn of both modern democracy and the nation state, her words sounded a warning for coming generations. As never before in human history the modern world has been characterized by struggles over issues of power. The carnage of two world wars and the nuclear cloud echo again the call from the grave, "give, give."

Less ominously, power has preoccupied contemporary consciousness. An eminent sociologist, C. Wright Mills, can describe the leaders in society as "The Power Elite." Volumes of psychological literature urge people to "take control" of their lives; theologians speak of "power to the powerless" and preachers laud the power of prayer as well as of "positive thinking." The language and images of power are likewise deeply embedded in the biblical heritage. A people, liberated from slavery in Egypt, sings "Thy right hand, O Lord, glorious in power, thy right hand, O Lord, shatters the enemy" (Exod. 15:6, RSV). The history of this people unfolds amid the struggles within the powerful empires of the ancient Near East. The Gospels portray Jesus as one who does "works of power" (Mark 6:2) that liberate people from demonic forces, and Paul proclaims the risen Lord as the "power and wisdom of God" (1 Cor. 1:24).

The Bible offers "a different vision" where power is understood in relation to justice and concern for the powerless, and where autonomy and dominance yield to trust, a vision that James Walsh seeks to unfold in this volume. After a phenomenology of the relation of power, selfhood, and society, he guides the readers through a pilgrimage of Israel's experience from its roots as *ʿapiru,* people on the margin of society, through its struggles to become a nation faithful to Yahweh and its challenge never to forget its history. Christians are summoned to be heirs of this history with its gifts, its pitfalls, and its challenges.

Though seeming to focus on concepts such as justice, judgment, vindication, and power, the work is far from a collection of word studies. Under Walsh's deft tutelage terms encrusted with religious solemnity or dulled by scholarly dissection will resound with new vigor and excitement. Words and concepts do not emerge from a vacuum, and Walsh lays bare the historical roots and cultural context of Israel's fundamental religious expressions. He draws on the research of George E. Mendenhall and Norman K. Gottwald as well as that of his mentor Frank Moore Cross to join sociological analysis and theological insight in a singular fashion. We are presented with a theology of Israel's historical experience, as it is handed on in the great blocks of tradition, which compromises neither history nor theology and which continues to challenge the way we think about our history and ourselves. The work offers a fundamental critique of any attempt to divorce theology from political reality. To hear God's Word is to walk in trust with God and with the human community in its struggles over issues of power and justice.

This volume bears the imprint of the author's pilgrimage. James Walsh did his doctorate at Harvard under Frank Moore Cross in Near Eastern Languages and Civilizations, and for the last dozen years has taught at Georgetown University (Washington, D.C.). He combines great technical expertise with a sensitivity born of listening to countless undergraduates whose library windows overlook the White House and the Lincoln Memorial. Issues of power and justice are never too distant. The author's lively style, cultural sensitivity, and range of interests make this Overture a real joy to read as well as a challenge to Bible and Theology.

JOHN R. DONAHUE, S.J.

Acknowledgments

Most of this book was written, during a sabbatical year and two summers, at Cove Cottage, Centreville, Maryland. I owe thanks to the Raskob Foundation, whose grant to the Jesuit Community of Georgetown University helped make Cove Cottage a place where writing could be done. Thanks also to my Jesuit brothers and to my colleagues in the Theology Department at Georgetown, for their friendship and interest. My teacher, Frank Moore Cross, has always been generous in his encouragement. I owe a special debt of gratitude to John R. Donahue, S.J. As an editor he is patient, appreciative, generous, and wise; as a friend he is even more so. Thanks as well to John A. Hollar of Fortress Press for his patience and his valiant efforts to rein in auctorial prolixity.

Finally, a word of appreciation to the reader. I have in this book left certain key terms in Hebrew, for reasons I explain in the text. From years of teaching college students I know that such a use of terms from the original language is most helpful, but I know also that it requires some effort to get used to. For making that effort, thanks.

Except where indicated, all translations of Scripture and of extrabiblical texts are my own.

Abbreviations

AB	Anchor Bible
AOS	American Oriental Series
BA	*Biblical Archaeologist*
BAR	*Biblical Archaeologist Reader*
BASOR	*Bulletin of the American Schools of Oriental Research*
BibOr	Biblica et orientalia
CBQ	*Catholic Biblical Quarterly*
CMHE	F. M. Cross, *Canaanite Myth and Hebrew Epic.* Cambridge: Harvard Univ. Press, 1973.
CTA	A. Herdner, *Corpus des tablettes en cunéiformes alphabétiques*
Dtr	Deuteronomistic History; Deuteronomistic Historian
EA	J. A. Knudtzon, *Die El-Amarna-Tafeln*
G	Greek translation of the Hebrew Scriptures (Septuagint)
HTR	*Harvard Theological Review*
Int.	*Interpretation*
IRT	Issues in Religion and Theology
JAOS	*Journal of the American Oriental Society*
JBC	*The Jerome Biblical Commentary*
JBL	*Journal of Biblical Literature*
JNES	*Journal of Near Eastern Studies*
JSOT	*Journal for the Study of the Old Testament*
KJV	King James Version
LXX	Septuagint
MT	Masoretic Text
NT	New Testament

OBT	Overtures to Biblical Theology
OT	Old Testament
P	Priestly writer
RSV	Revised Standard Version
SBL	Society of Biblical Literature
SBT	Studies in Biblical Theology

List of Hebrew Words

bᵉrît	treaty, covenant
'ēl/'El	god; God/El
ḥērem	setting apart; something set apart; destruction ("ban," "devotion")
ḥesed	covenant loyalty, "steadfast love"
mišpāṭ	"judgment"
naḥᵃmāh	consolation, comfort
nāqām	vindication, vengeance
nāzīr	nazirite
nepeš	throat; self, "soul"
qannā'	passionate ("jealous")
rāšā'	wicked
ṣaddīq	just
ṣedeq	"justice"
tᵉrū'āh	shout (in battle, in acclamation)
ṭôb	good, goodness
tôrāh	instruction, "Law"

The transliteration *š* represents the sound of English *sh;* the transliteration *ṣ* is conventionally pronounced *ts*. Hence *mišpāṭ* is "mishPAT" and *ṣedeq* is "TSEdek."

He puts down the mighty from their thrones,
and exalts the lowly.

Luke 1:52

CHAPTER 1

Introduction: Power, Selfhood, Society

Riding in a bus through a shabby section of Detroit one summer morning, I looked out the window and saw a man in a telephone booth, talking on the phone. The door of the booth was open, and a woman stood there listening intently. Both were middle-aged or even older; it was hard to tell because their faces were lined and they were stooped. They looked as if they didn't belong anywhere. The man was gesturing excitedly, his right hand chopping the air, as he talked into the phone. The veins in his neck stood out. I thought he was pleading with someone. I thought, "This is his last dime, and his last chance." He looked drained, as if he knew his pleading would do no good and it was only a matter of time till the conversation ended and that would be that. His companion stood by, tense but somehow slumped, staring into the gutter.

I thought: powerlessness. A man walks into his country club and you know, from his commanding air, that he belongs there. That is the look of power. Watch a news conference and listen to the clicking and whirring of cameras. That is the sound of power. Powerlessness has a look, too. Shabbiness, slumping, brow furrowed, a certain look in the eyes: haunted, anxious, pleading. You don't belong. You are there by someone else's say-so, and it shows in your face. That is what I saw that day in Detroit.

I also thought that I was seeing the destruction of two human beings. They were so helpless. They were abased. There was nothing they could do. Their humanity had been drained out of them.

"POWER" AND THE BIBLICAL TRADITION

The purpose of this book is to ask, What does the biblical tradition have to say about power? I have begun with an image that has stayed with me for seventeen years now. Other images—Ethiopian children with swollen bellies, refugees in Thailand, Jews crammed into cattle cars, peasants in Central America, blacks in South African townships—come to mind. The reader can supply others.

What light does Scripture shed on these scenes of powerlessness? What does it tell us about the possession and exercise of power? (There are rifles, and well-fed officials, somewhere in the background of all the pictures evoked above.) What does it say about power in interpersonal relationships, and in politics? What does Scripture say to women, to the poor, to racial and ideological minorities—and to those who dominate them? And how do these concerns tie in with theological concerns—divine omnipotence, human creatureliness? If "power belongs to God" (Ps 62:11, RSV), where does that leave us? Dietrich Bonhoeffer's familiar formulation about "man come of age" strikes a resonance in us: does it accord with biblical faith?

All these questions have more than notional importance for us. They come out of our experience. They attach to images which themselves act powerfully upon us. They are real questions. Now it would be easy to pull out of the pages of the Bible certain passages (Ps. 62:11; Deut. 8:17; 1 Cor. 15:24) that talk about power, or to assemble appropriate word studies *(kôaḥ, kratos),* but that would not get us very far. Scripture speaks not in the abstract but to specific readers or hearers, and what it has to say is filtered through what those readers bring to it: expectations, presuppositions, personal and communal experience, and above all certain ways of imagining reality and themselves. Without being aware of it, we "translate" Scripture into terms intelligble to *us,* as we are. So we have to attend to what we bring to its reading. We do well to try for clarity about how we see things. That is the purpose of this first, introductory chapter.

HAVING THE SAY

We like to have the say about things—colloquially, to "call the shots." Our sense of ourselves revolves around this ability to be "doers" and to put the world in order. "Having the say" involves not only our own efforts but also the collaboration of others. It is important to us that others go along with us when we determine that things should be thus and so. If they disagree with us or otherwise get in the way we take it amiss, very often with resentment.

In our dealings with family and friends and co-workers collaboration and conflict are face-to-face affairs, but in vast areas of our lives "the say" belongs to relatively impersonal organizations (governmental bodies, economic structures, and the like), and our role is limited by the ways those organizations work. Expressions of public opinion, voting, use of economic leverage are indirect means of influencing the way things go—of having, in however limited a fashion, the say.

Several things should be noted here. (1) "Having the say" is obviously at least part of what we mean when we talk about power. (2) Other people are essentially involved in "having the say," agreeing or disagreeing, going along or getting in the way. (3) "Having the say" is at the heart of our existence as human beings: we express and embody and affirm ourselves, and to that extent realize ourselves, in choice and action. (4) If we put together the last two statements it follows that our very selfhood is bound up with other people. Their affirmation of our "say" is affirmation of us; their rejection is rejection of us.

Finally, a terminological note. I have been using the rather odd phrase "having the say" because I know no other expression in English that comprises the various ways in which we make determinations and take action. We make determinations about what is to be done in a given situation; about what is right and wrong; about who is in the right, who in the wrong. We back up those determinations; we try to make them come true. That is, "having the say" is an undifferentiated notion that comprehends what in the political realm are called legislative, executive, judicial, and enforcement functions. The expression is lame, but it will have to do. There is no other handy way of putting the matter in English.

There is in Hebrew, though. As a matter of fact, what I have been calling "having the say" is a central concept in the biblical tradition (as the rest of this book will try to show). The Hebrew root is *špṭ,* and the noun derived from it is *mišpāṭ.* Unfortunately, the standard translation for the verbal form of *špṭ* is "to judge," and *mišpāṭ* comes out "judgment," renderings that bring to mind courtrooms and mišpat - to have our say over things

gavels. *Mišpāṭ*, though, takes in much more than the narrowly judicial activity suggested by "judgment." Other possible translations for *mišpāṭ* are "authority" and "rule," but they too are inadequate. I propose, then, that *mišpāṭ* be added to the repertoire of terms we take over from the original languages in our theological discourse, like *ḥesed* or NT *agapē,* and I will be using the word in the rest of this book.[1]

In summary we can say that *mišpāṭ* is central to our existence as human beings, both individually and societally: we seek to have the say about things, and others figure in that effort, especially as we participate in—or are excluded from—political structures.

"CONSENSUS"

There is another aspect of "having the say." How do we determine what is to be done? Why do others go along with what we say, or refuse to go along with it?

In answer to the question *why,* parents use phrases like, "Because I say so," and officials say, "That's the law," but that is an appeal to raw *mišpāṭ*. In fact, the parent and the official base their commands on a sense that what they have determined is appropriate, or right, or seemly, or fair, or just, or reasonable. People go against what is laid down for them out of a sense that it is wrong, unfair, unjust, unseemly, unreasonable. People go along with arrangements that seem sensible, fair, right, and so on. Where does this sense of things come from?

It comes from our "world." As we grow up we interiorize a vision of reality—of what is important or trivial, seemly or shameful, sensible or ridiculous. We are, as people say, inculturated into a sense not just of what is but of what matters. And that sense of reality shapes our sense of ourselves as well. We derive our identity from it. We get smiles or frowns, and react accordingly. Others tell us who we are and are to be.

None of this works on the level of propositions or principles, of course. I am talking about an unthematized sense of things, prior to reflection or analysis. I am talking about a shared sense. Let me use a shorthand term: "consensus." "Con-sensus": it is a sense or feeling about things ("sensus") that we have in common with others ("con-").

It is con-sensus, as well, in that it is concomitant with our perceptions and intentions and choices and actions. It shapes, and ratifies, them.

"Consensus" is what defines a community: a shared vision or feeling that underlies its common life, validating or legitimating what is done, communally and individually. It is expressed in laws, songs, stories, folkways, political and economic structures, language—all the works, procedures, and obligations that constitute the life of a polity or group or community. As those structures and customs embody consensus, so they mediate it to a new generation.

Not that consensus is a static thing. It is ever changing, in the dialectic of communal life. Laws or stories that embody consensus in one era may appear quaint or malign in a later one. That means that the consensus of the polity has shifted; the previous consensus is fossilized in the old laws, the old stories.

At the heart of consensus is that sense of what is right, just, fair, important, seemly, worthwhile. Is there a single English term for this? There is in Hebrew, I think. It is the word *ṣedeq* (or its frequent variant *ṣᵉdāqāh*). *Ṣedeq* is usually translated "justice," and sometimes "righteousness," but as with *mišpāṭ* those translations limp. "Justice" is overlaid with associations of distributive and commutative equity, Aristotelian virtue and Platonic forms; "righteousness" implies a personal moral quality, and it too has acquired barnacles (Pauline dialectics, Reformation polemics). No, *ṣedeq* means "rightness" (and can also mean *what* is right). Again, this term is central in the biblical tradition. For that reason, and because power derives from—or finds itself blocked by—people's sense of what is right, I propose to use the Hebrew word in this book.

We go along, then, with what we are told to do because it seems right to us. We accept someone's exercise of *mišpāṭ* because it seems to us to accord with *ṣedeq*. We resist *mišpāṭ* when it seems to us to go against *ṣedeq*. And that sense of *ṣedeq* is mediated to us by our participation in our community, as it also defines the consensus that holds a community together.

"VINDICATION"

Suppose someone acts in a way you judge to be wrong. What is your reaction? Say that a landlord, in the dead of winter, refuses to

"Vindication"
Naqam – Upholding Sedeq.
– Retribution for Mishpat Done wrong
– or Vindication

turn on the heat in his building, and a poor widow sits bundled up in front of the gas stove. She phones and writes to the landlord, and gets nowhere. She appeals to the city authority, and gets nowhere. A newspaper reporter writes up the story. You read about her plight and that of the other tenants. How do you feel? What do you want to do?

Our instinctive reaction is outrage, and a desire to see the wrong righted. If the city authority does nothing, we deplore its insensitivity. If the landlord gets only a judicial slap on the wrist we shake our heads in frustration and dismay. Our sense of *ṣedeq* has been offended. We want to have justice done. We want to see the person who is in the right (the widow) fairly treated. We want to see the person who is in the wrong (the landlord) receive his due.

This reaction is natural. It is deeply rooted in us. The widow's plight triggers our sense of what is right, fair, just, seemly, reasonable, and so on: our sense of *ṣedeq*. Our reaction has several aspects. There is our desire to stand up for what is right, to see *ṣedeq* vindicated. There is our desire to see the person who is in the right vindicated, as well. The two concerns—for what is right, for the one who is in the right—are inseparable. There is also our desire to see the one who is in the wrong be shown to be in the wrong, and to have something done about it. This side of our reaction usually involves strong feelings—so strong that we sometimes draw back from admitting them. Yet the feelings are there. They are a measure of our passion for *ṣedeq*.

In the example I gave, you instinctively identified with the widow, not the landlord. Suppose someone suggested that your reaction was misguided—in effect suggesting that your sense of *ṣedeq* is askew, or merely idiosyncratic. You would resist that suggestion. We *know* right and wrong. Someone who took the unscrupulous landlord's side, arguing that business is business, would appear cynically hardened or morally obtuse—simply in the wrong. This reaction reveals two further aspects of our sense of *ṣedeq*. (1) We are convinced that what is right is right in and by itself, irrespective of our individual say-so; and (2) this *ṣedeq*-in-itself is something we identify with strongly. We like to feel that we are in the right. So, in the example given, we identify with the widow: she is the one in the right. In our allegiance to what is right, and our sympathetic identification with the one who is in the right, we feel that we too are in the right.

So a sense of *ṣedeq* involves a desire to see it upheld. This desire, like *ṣedeq* itself, is central to the biblical tradition. The Hebrew term for upholding *ṣedeq* is *nāqām*. The word receives two translations: "vindication" and "vengeance." Standing up both for what is right and for those who are in the right is *nāqām* in its positive aspect: that is "vindication." Showing that those who are in the wrong are indeed in the wrong (most often by making them "get what's coming to them") is the negative side of *nāqām:* it is "vengeance."[2]

THE "JUST" AND THE "WICKED"

One further item of OT terminology is indicated here. One who is identified with *ṣedeq* is *ṣaddīq:* the one who is in the right, the "just" person. One who goes against *ṣedeq* is called (among other things) *rāšāʿ*, "wicked." Vindication *(nāqām)* is effected on behalf of the just against the wicked.

In sum, we have seen that (1) we get our sense of who we are and of what is real from the consensus of the society we live in. (2) This consensus centers on a shared sense of *ṣedeq*. (3) We identify ourselves with *ṣedeq,* and instinctively desire to see it—and therefore us, as being "just"—vindicated.

"CITIZENSHIP"

Let me make explicit some aspects of the relationship between *ṣedeq* and *mišpāṭ:* (1) What is right in a given situation has to be decided and carried out. That is, in concrete circumstances someone has to make *ṣedeq* a reality. Someone has to exercise *mišpāṭ*. (2) The "someone" for the most part will be a person or persons or bodies or instrumentalities of governance: king, queen, leader, official, council, elders, representatives, folkmoot, etc. *Mišpāṭ* can take many forms. Let us simply speak of "the established order." (3) Conversely, the established order and its ordinary exercise of *mišpāṭ* derive legitimacy from people's convictions about *ṣedeq*. If people judge that there is a contradiction between *ṣedeq* and *mišpāṭ,* the established order will be shaky. It will lose people's allegiance. (I should note that *mišpāṭ*—especially in the form of laws—is itself a powerful influence on people's sense of *ṣedeq,* as Orwell showed in *1984*.)

These are the dynamics of any political entity. In trying to show the central role *ṣedeq* plays, I have used the term "allegiance." Let me use another, overarching term: "citizenship." People who accept the legitimacy and dictates of a political entity are its "citizens."

Of course, "citizenship" is an analogous notion. We all belong to different polities: family, nation, religious community, political party, associations, clubs. There is a jostling between the demands of our participation in each, but we do not usually find any fundamental conflict in those demands: at most the occasional trade-off. E. M. Forster's famous quip can serve to show how such a conflict could arise, however. Faced with the need to choose between loyalty to his friends and loyalty to his country, he said, he hoped he would have the courage to side with his friends. The point is that we all have to respond to the requirements of various "citizenships." The sense of *ṣedeq* that defines one political entity can be in conflict with the *ṣedeq* of another, and then we have to choose.

IMAGINATION

In speaking of consensus I said that it consists of a shared vision or feeling or sense of things, centering on *ṣedeq*, that is deeply rooted in us as we are shaped by our whole life experience. Rooted where? In the imagination, I think. We may use abstract terms and generalized principles but what gives them content is a highly personal, concrete set of images and feelings, which amount to an all-encompassing vision of self and the world. Some people see the world as a dangerous place full of unknown perils. Some instinctively perceive others as competitors to be bested or neutralized. Some imagine reality as bleak and unyielding. Some see the world "charged with the grandeur of God." Whatever it may be, the way we imagine reality determines our perceptions and choices—what we attend to and go after, what we ignore or disdain.

Yet this fundamentally shaping vision is mostly opaque to us. It is, after all, second nature. What other people say and do gives away how *they* imagine reality, and we can see it pretty easily, but it is difficult for us to become aware of how *we* imagine it. Here is an example of what I mean. A man is writing to a friend:

> When I ask myself why I have always behaved honorably, ready to spare others and to be kind wherever possible, and why I did not give up being so when I observed that in that way one harms oneself and becomes an anvil because other people are brutal and untrustworthy, then, it is true, I have no answer.[3]

Overtly, the writer professes certain convictions he lives by: generosity, fidelity, and affection in human relations are to be esteemed and practiced, despite setbacks and betrayals. But see how he *imagines* reality. He is a white knight, standing alone in his integrity, kind and generous, judicious and reasonable. He is surrounded by monsters, "brutal and untrustworthy," who hammer him with cruel blows again and again. He is the only loving person among unloving, unlovable brutes.[4]

IMAGINATION AND STORY

How could this writer be brought to see the contradiction between his professed convictions and the affect surrounding them: between what he thinks he thinks and the self-image that so belies it? Is there an Archimedean point where he could stand and be brought to self-knowledge? Two stories may point the way.

A priest visits a family in Appalachia and notes that, though there is a well in their back yard, they travel miles to fetch water. Why don't they use their own well, he asks. "Rope's too short," is the answer. He buys them a longer rope. They are delighted. Life will not be so hard. On his next visit, some months later, the priest finds the family again fetching water from down the hollow. What happened to their own well? "Rope broke."

The family's experience of life had locked them in to a certain vision of things. They imagined the world as a place where nothing can change or needs to, where what is, is; and were therefore blind to other possibilities. They simply did not see what to the outsider—and to us, who in hearing the story identify with him—was so obvious. The key to changing the way we imagine reality, then, is the "outsider": someone who brings a different vision of what is and what can be. If we can be brought to share that other vision—to reimagine reality—we can change.

The second story is the familiar narrative about David and Nathan

(2 Sam. 12:1–7). David has gotten Bathsheba pregnant and contrived the death of her husband, Uriah. The prophet Nathan is sent to reprove him. This he does by telling David a story, about a rich man who takes advantage of a poor man. David gets caught up in the story, imaginatively identifying with one character (the "just" man), angrily condemning the other, the guilty man. That man, David says, deserves to die. "Thou art the man," Nathan says.

Nathan, the "outsider," succeeds in getting David to reimagine himself and his world. The story is what works this transformation. It wheels around and confronts the king, and he sees himself in its light. It even gets him to pronounce judgment on himself.

If someone were to play Nathan to me, he or she might well use the story about the Appalachian family, only it would end with the words, "You are that family." I would be taken aback. When I heard the story I identified imaginatively with the "outsider"—the one who sees everybody else's life more clearly than they can themselves, and who can solve all their problems for them. But that very identification proves the point. It shows that, like the family, I am locked into a certain way of seeing things, which keeps me from imagining myself any other way.

Such is the power of a story. It draws us out of ourselves, into itself, and enables us to reimagine ourselves and our world. The Archimedean point, then, is the imagination itself, engaged by story.

SCRIPTURE AND OUR CONSENSUS

Scripture can have that same power. It draws us in to another world, engaging our imagination. In crucial ways, as we shall see, the biblical tradition does hold out a different vision of human life than the one our culture has shaped in us. A word, then, on this.

Advertisers make lots of money, for themselves and their clients, by capturing our imaginations. "Have It Your Way." "Do what you want to do, be who you want to be, set yourself free with Stouffer's!" "Get control of your life: there's nothing you can't do!" (this from the maker of an aftershave lotion). "The best surprise is no surprise at all."

The vision of the human good these slogans express and appeal to can be put succinctly. Man is man to the extent he is free, and he is free to the extent he is in control. Man is shaper, mover, determiner, definer. The human good is mastery, of nature and of history. Autonomy is all.

The Canadian philosopher George Grant, in his book *Technology and Empire*,[5] has shown how these convictions are at the heart of the liberal tradition, and has traced the development of that tradition from the sixteenth century to modern times. Hobbes, Locke, Hume, Spencer, Marx, Freud all presuppose that man is defined by creative freedom and that freedom is control. Both technology and imperialism, as historically conditioned phenomena of modern times, are outgrowths of this conviction. It is at the heart of our self-understanding. We want to "have the say": to be in control.[6]

Grant's analysis is profound and rich but the sketch of his ideas I have given must suffice here to make the point: we are children of the liberal tradition. When we come to the reading of Scripture, this is where we are "coming from." It is connatural to us to want to be in control.

Yet I should anticipate some of the results of the survey we are about to undertake, if only briefly, by suggesting that the liberal emphasis on mastery and control contains anomalies. Its logic is the "master-slave" dialectic. If control is all, others pose a threat to my control of my own life. If I have to have the say about my own existence, I will treat others as objects of my own creative freedom. They have to "behave." The bonds of obligation, even of affection, are, precisely, bonds. At best I can limit myself by a free choice, but that must always be on my terms, no one else's. Promises and commitments therefore become unilateral, revocable by my sovereign freedom.

Above, I spoke of "man's" freedom as mastery. The sexist language is jarring but I intended it. As a matter of history, it has been the male who is seen as controller, shaper, dominator, and so as human: "man." Supposedly "male" qualities—active rather than passive, doing rather than contemplative—are precisely those identified with being-human. Woman, like nature, is the object of man's mastery. She has to be kept in her place.[7]

Notoriously, oppressed people take over the values—the *ṣedeq*—

of their oppressor. Even people who have suffered from the effects of the liberal consensus—women and minorities—have interiorized the same vision of being-human that has led to their oppression. One example: A woman talking on the radio about the trauma of pregnancy complained that men cannot understand what it is like (which is true), and fastened on one, to her central, aspect of being pregnant: "It's not *their* body growing out of control." Autonomy is all.

A DIFFERENT VISION

If this is the way we imagine reality (as that which is to be controlled) and ourselves (as the controllers), what is to keep us from simply reading this into Scripture? Two things. One is that Scripture gives voice to quite another consensus. It focuses on trust, obedience, living with insecurity and needfulness—conditions and patterns of choices that are contrary to what our culture holds as the good for "man." The other is that the heart of the biblical tradition is narrative: story. Story engages the imagination, and the imagination is protean. Scripture can draw us in and then turn and say to us, "Thou art the man." The imagination is a seedbed and the images and stories of the biblical tradition the seed. It yields fruit in its season.

CHAPTER 2

The Gods of Canaan

To enter the biblical world we must start where it did. Ancient Israel took shape as a people in a specific political and cultural setting, that bevy of city-states called "the land of Canaan," in the late second millennium B.C. The ways Israelites made their living, sang, fought, prayed, told stories, governed themselves—the whole complex of cultural and political forms that shaped their life as a people—came from the Canaanite world, at least by way of reaction against it. The reaction is what comes through most clearly in the biblical tradition, of course, in the strong opposition to everything "Canaanite" we find in the Pentateuch, the Deuteronomistic History, the prophets. Not just in its origins, then, but throughout its life in the land, down to the exile at least, Israel was locked in a kind of struggle with "Canaan." That struggle was in many ways a symbiosis. To understand Israel we have to understand Canaan.

THE WORLD OF CANAAN

How do we enter that world to find out what it was like? The biblical sources are instructive but rather colored. Extrabiblical data offer a way in, happily. Especially helpful are the abundant texts from the ancient Canaanite city-state of Ugarit, and, among those, the mythological writings, the stories about the god Hadad Baal.[1] Though written down toward the beginning of the Amarna Age, after 1400 B.C., the Baal myths seem to go back a good half-millennium earlier. They had a long run in Canaan. It seems likely that those stories said something important to people and were heard willingly.

We would be justified in thinking that they were "mythic," in the following sense.

"MYTHIC" STORIES, "MYTHIC" REALITIES

Some stories are interesting and some are boring. Among those that are interesting, some are fascinating, or terrifying, or profoundly moving. Among these, some seem to express what is most deeply true in life; they set forth conflicts and resolutions of conflicts that correspond to what the hearers know from their own most inner and determinative experience of life. There is a "resonance" between the characters and action of the story, on the one hand, and, on the other, the hearers and what they go through or have gone through, in their very selfhood and in their lives. They hear the story and feel, "That is *my* story." Such a story is "mythic."

Obviously, I am talking not of stories in themselves but in their relation to an audience.[2] A story is boring only because its hearer is bored; the same story might be "mythic" to another audience. What is crucial is the "fit" between the story and the hearers, in their self-understanding, their experience. Most often, the hearer is unaware of this relationship. All one knows is that one is caught up in, and deeply moved by, the story. "In itself," the story *is* shattering or profound or fascinating, and the fact that the story's power has its source within us—in the anxieties, needs, regrets, and desires that define us—is opaque to us. To college freshmen the writings of Kahlil Gibran can be mythic; years later they smile when they remember the hold his words had on their imagination, and realize how callow and self-absorbed they were. To a twelve-year-old, Judy Blume's characters are more real than her best friend and possibly even herself; the woman of twenty-two, rereading Blume, sees how emotionally needful her younger self was. In the same way, what is mythic to a given generation is merely quaint or puzzling to a later one. The figure of Napoleon was mythic to the nineteenth century, as Hitler is to ours; how will Hitler look to the twenty-first century? With time, or at least change, what an individual or an entire culture found mythic loses that power. If this is so within a given culture, how difficult it is for people outside that culture to understand, really, why its stories were mythic.

To understand Canaan, though, it seems to me indispensable to make that effort. Given the persistence and centrality of the figure of Baal in Canaanite life, the stories about him can reveal what people felt to be most important and "real" in life, what their experience was like. Mythic stories express a people's sense of reality and of themselves. They embody the "consensus" that defines a culture. Hence the myths of Canaan give us a way in to understanding the Canaanite world.

Two things should be noted here. One is that myths not only express but also shape that sense of reality and of self. The child growing up in Canaan, hearing the myths declaimed in (say) solemn assembly and seeing them taken seriously by parents and neighbors, learns to take seriously the vision of reality those stories embody. Myth is *paideia*. A caution, too, is in order. The same story is interpreted differently by different hearers. As it reflects their various kinds of experience it can "mean" various things. The meaning of a story is a function of the selfhood and the sense of reality it expresses. Myth is dialectical. It shapes a people's sense of reality and of self, and is shaped by them.

THE BAAL MYTHS

That all said, we must find a way in to the Baal myths. As they are products of the Canaanite imagination, the way in to them must involve our imagination. Owing to certain defining (and therefore, in their power over us, mythic) convictions our culture forms within us, those I sketched in the first chapter, our inclination is to seek a "mastering" sort of understanding: to distance ourselves, analytically and appraisingly, from the stories, and as it were to decode them. Thus, Baal would become to us "a personification of the power in and behind the storm, the principle of fertility and new life"—something like that. If, though, the figure of Baal was not allegorical to the Canaanites, but was known experientially, the way to understand Baal is to ask in what kinds of situation he was experienced.[3] His epithets and the imagery surrounding him provide a clue. He is "son of Dagon," hence—since Dagon was the god of grain—in effect "the grainy one." He is "Victor" (*'al'iyānu*, "'I-prevail'–er"). He is "the Rider on the Clouds," attended by a retinue of "clouds, wind, bolts, rains," by "Misty, daughter of light, Dewy, daughter of showers." Because of him "the heavens rain oil, the torrents run with mead." He "gives forth his holy voice, . . . the mountains quake." He is puissant:

> He loved a heifer,
> in the pasture a cow,[4]
> in the field of the shores of Death.
> He lay with her seventy-seven times,
> mounted her eighty-eight times.
> (*CTA* 5.5.18–21)

If we assume, with many scholars,[5] that Psalm 29 was originally a hymn to Baal, we can add to the Ugaritic picture some telling details: Baal

> 6 makes Lebanon dance like a calf,
> Sirion like a buffalo[6] . . .
> 8 Baal's voice makes the desert writhe,
> 9 Baal makes the hinds writhe.
> (Cf. Ps. 29:6, 8–9)

The god's thunderous voice causes a kind of manic dance: mountains, desert, hinds, all are awhirl. The mountains' quaking is the desert's stirring is the writhing—in copulation, in calving—of the hind. Baal's voice is fearsome and life-giving both.

Where in the life of a farming and pastoral people would the reality of Baal be experienced? I like to imagine an old woman sitting in the late-afternoon shade of her house in the oppressive airlessness of the dry season, noticing all of a sudden a breeze stir the crumbly soil, watching the western sky darken, hearing the roiling thunder, seeing the first fat drops of rain hit the dried clods and splatter. She knows that soon the green shoots will thrust tenderly up through the soil, and she recognizes the pledge of full granaries. She nods knowingly: "Baal." She might even mutter the words of the old story,

> Victor Baal lives,
> the exalted lord of earth *is*!
> (*CTA* 6.3.20–21)

MOT

This way of trying to understand the imagery of the Canaanite stories is fraught with the dangers of "subjectivism," of course, but something like it is indicated. We are dealing with products of imagination. We must begin in the imagination, and try to understand sympathetically, before going on to systematize. A certain playfulness is needed. And playfulness, in the form of gallows humor, is certainly at work in the depiction of "El's Beloved," the god Mot, "Death," when he says,

> I was out for a walk, wandering
> every mountain in the heart of the earth,
> every hill in the heart of the fields:
> my *nepeš* was in want, for the sons of men,
> my *nepeš* for the multitudes of earth.
> (*CTA* 6.2.15–19)

Death stalks the high places of earth; he describes it as a stroll. The *nepeš* (Ugaritic *napš*) is the throat and comes to mean the "soul" or self. All Mot's attention is focused on us human beings, as objects of his tender solicitude: his *nepeš* longs for us. Yet Mot would be king, whose task is, as we shall see, to

> fatten gods and men,
> satiate the multitudes of earth.[7]
> (*CTA* 4.7.50–52)

Since Mot is characterized by his voracious maw—

> one lip to earth,
> one lip to heaven,
> he stretches his tongue to the stars—
> (*CTA* 5.2.2–3)

his yearning for the multitudes of earth is, let us say, disingenuous. His realm is one of muck and mire and also one of desiccation; yet he would "satiate the multitudes of earth." Smiling Death is horrific.

YAMM

Playfulness becomes limitless unpredictability in the figure of Yamm, "Sea." It is hard, actually, to imagine him or the situations where he might be known. Very likely that is the point. Like his variant form, or allomorph, Lotan (biblical Leviathan), he is the "Twisting One," all restless and protean. Certain recurrent images in Israelite tradition[8] point to a conception of Yamm as surging and indomitable, illimitable and irresistible; this can safely be assumed to reflect the image of Yamm in Canaanite culture. He is never spoken of without the honorific titles *zabul* ("Exalted") and *ṯāpiṭ* ("Judge," one who exercises *mišpāṭ*). Yamm is authoritative. Perhaps we should imagine breakers destroying harbor and biting away shoreline, threatening to roll unstoppably across the coastal plain and envelop the mountains. For the rest, Orwell's Big Brother comes to mind.

THE DIVINE COUNCIL

Besides Baal, Mot, Yamm, and El, the head god, whom we shall meet in a moment, there were other gods. They are called the "sons of El," or "sons of god(s)" (the Ugaritic is ambiguous). The expression "sons of god(s)" simply means "gods"; a "son of god(s)" is a god, a divine being, a member of the genus "god."[9] These "sons of god(s)" are also "the Holy Ones" (literally, "sons of Holiness"). They are the stars, the hosts of heaven. They constitute the assembly of gods or divine council, which meets under the presidency of El. The important thing about them is that they are not so much individuals as they are a council. They act—or react—as a council. It is their massed activity that counts. Yet their plurality is important, too. The divine council reflects the multitudinous and competing goods and ends and purposes, the forces and movements, that are at work in the world and in our lives, and that pull us this way and that. These forces and goods make absolute claims on us; they jostle one another, insistently jockeying for position. In their absoluteness they resist compromise, yet inevitably there are trade-offs: now one, now another of them has the say about what we choose and do. The divine beings that stand behind and validate and move these goods and forces conduct themselves like big-city politicians. They speak for their several and competing constituencies. Their interaction is like the deliberations of a legislative assembly. Their competing claims have to be sorted out and mediated. They need a president to shape them up. That is why when they do manage to speak with one voice, that voice carries.

EL

Finally, above it all somehow, is El, "God." "Bull El" is the Compassionate One, Father of the sons of god, Father of man, Creator of creatures, Father of years. He presides over the council of gods, and as we shall see his decree is required for plans to become effective. It has often been noted that he seems abstracted from the concerns associated with the other figures we have been surveying; it has been thought that by the time our stories took form El had been superseded by the younger Baal. That may be, but perhaps El's remoteness reflects his role as "King of eternity," the timeless one, the ultimate arbiter: he is not tied to this realm of experience or that. Within limits he is safely ignored, but finally his decree of approval must be sought and gained.

THE GODS OF CANAAN

These figures were mythic because the realms they governed were of central importance in people's lives; that is why they were gods, "sons of god(s)." But they were mythic especially because of the conflicts in which they engaged. The struggles of Baal with Yamm and with Mot are not eternally perduring realities in people's experience. They had beginnings, middles, and ends. They were narrative. Events unfold, knotting in crisis and leading on to resolution, moved by the choices the actors make. As the listener is caught up in the action, hopes and aversions arise. The listener is configured to the conflict, feeling dismay at Baal's apparent defeat and his foes' apparent triumph, and finally relieved at being able to join in the gods' acclamation for Victor Baal. The action touches the hearers: their world is at stake. The story of Baal is "their" story.

BAAL VS. YAMM

The plot line of the Baal myth is well known but it will be helpful to go over it. The beginning of the story is lost; the first episode preserved describes how Yamm, through his messengers, demands of El and the divine council that Baal be given over to his power. Baal tries to arouse them to defiance—

> Lift up, O gods, your heads—
> (*CTA* 2.1.27)

but they capitulate:

> Baal is your servant, O Yamm,
> Baal is your servant, O River,
> the son of Dagon your prisoner.
> (*CTA* 2.1.36–37)

Baal is imprisoned "under the throne of Zabul Yamm." Kothar, the divine craftsman, gives Baal heart by promising him that he will capture "eternal kingship, the dominion which is for ever and ever," and he provides the means to do so. Kothar has fashioned two magic clubs for Baal. With these weapons, "Baal destroyed, drank Yamm, finished Judge River" (*CTA* 2.4.27). The goddess Astarte shouts an acclamation:

> Hail to Victor Baal!
> Hail to the Rider of the Clouds! . . .
> Yamm is dead indeed,
> Baal is king!
> (*CTA* 2.4.28–29, 32)

This is echoed by Baal's consort, the bloodthirsty Anat:

> Our king is Victor Baal,
> he is judge, none is higher.
> We all his chalice bear,
> we all bear his cup,
> (*CTA* 3.5.40–42)

as she intercedes with El to get for Baal

> a house like the other gods',
> courts like the sons' of Asherah.
> (*CTA* 3.5.46–47)

El's consort, Asherah, also lobbies the old god, and he decrees that Kothar should build a house for Baal:

Now behold let Baal make fertile with his rains
let him indeed make fertile with torrents and moisture.
Let him give forth his voice from the clouds,
flash to earth his lightning.
His house of cedar let him finish.[10]

(*CTA* 4.5.68–72)

Baal prepares a feast for the other gods to celebrate his kingship. Kothar puts a window in the house, despite Baal's misgivings, and no sooner does Baal "sit"[11]—that is, both take up residence and become enthroned—in his house than a new conflict emerges.

BAAL VS. MOT

The conflict is prefigured in Baal's boast:

No other, king or non-king,
on earth shall make his dominion dwell.
Tribute I will not send
to the son of gods, Mot,
homage to El's Beloved, the Hero.

(*CTA* 4.7.43–47)

Several lacunae in our texts make things unclear at this point but eventually Baal is told that he "will go down into the *nepeš*" of Mot, and he succumbs: "Your servant am I, who am yours for ever."

When Baal is "counted among those who go down into the earth,"

the olive tree is scorched,
the yield of earth withers,
and the fruit of trees.

(*CTA* 5.2.5–6)

El mourns him—

Baal is dead: what of the people?
The son of Dagon: what of the multitude?—

(*CTA* 5.6.23–24)

and so does Anat. A replacement as king is sought. Neither of the gods proposed is adequate to the job; the second candidate, Athtar, goes up to the heights of Baal's mountain Zaphon to sit upon Baal's throne but

> his feet did not reach the footstool,
> his head did not reach the headrest.
> (*CTA* 6.1.59–61)

Anat then takes direct action:

> She seized the son of gods, Mot:
> with a sword she sliced him,
> with a sieve she winnowed him,
> with fire she burnt him,
> with a mill she ground him,
> in the fields she sowed him.
> (*CTA* 6.2.30–35)

El has a dream; in his vision

> the heavens rain oil.
> the torrents run with mead. . . .
> For Victor Baal lives,
> Zabul, lord of earth, *is*!
> (*CTA* 6.3.12–13, 20–21)

But the dream is not yet a reality, for the fields are still parched: "Baal has neglected his plowing." Where is he? Sun goes out to seek him. After what appears to be a flashback, Mot and Baal battle, butting, goring, biting, kicking each other—like camels, oxen, serpents, stallions; the refrain goes

> Mot was strong, Baal was strong.
> (*CTA* 6.6.17, 18–19, 20)

When both have fallen, Sun shouts to Mot, warning him,

> How can Bull El your father not hear you?
> He will undermine the foundation of your "sitting,"
> he will overturn the throne of your kingship,
> he will smash the scepter of your judgment.
> (*CTA* 6.6.26–29)

Mot is terrified—and here the tablet breaks off. The final word is a judicial sentence of Sun's:

> Yours, O gods, behold
> Mot is yours.
> (*CTA* 6.6.47–48)

Each of these stories follows the same plot. To put it less simply, they are thematically isomorphic.[12] There is the enemy's claim to kingship, the handing over or abasement of Baal, his rescue (by the weapons of Kothar, by Anat's exertions), his victory over his enemy (not fully preserved in the second myth), and his assumption of kingship. In the Mot story, Baal's kingship is known by its exercise, in the restoration of food; it is already in place, and becomes efficacious once more. As we have these stories they have been "systematized," so that the second is no longer an allomorph of the first but dovetails with it. The window in Baal's house is what leaves him vulnerable to Death,[13] and this segues into Mot's challenge.

COSMIC *MIŠPĀṬ*

These are stories about *mišpāṭ*, "judgment." Who will have the final say about things? Will it be Yamm? Will it be Mot? Or will Baal be the one? What should our expectations of reality be? The question comes down to one of *mišpāṭ*, and the issue is cosmic. In the root sense of the word *cosmos*, ordering, the Baal myth is a story about what reality is. Is it immanently and inexorably subject to whim, limitless and chaotic unpredictability, unbridled destructiveness? Will that have the final say? Or will Death have the last word? If so, the future—what future there is—contains the certainty of desiccated hopelessness, starvation, "going down into the earth." That is how these things are ordered, in the real world, if Mot prevails. But if Baal defeats his enemies and wins *mišpāṭ*, then grain, wine, oil, and fertility, of field and womb, are assured. Survival is assured. Baal will have the say about what is and what is to be. Reality is as he orders it, and he is "cosmic" lord in a double sense, as orderer (effecting *cosmos*) and as orderer of all (the cosmos itself). One's sense of what is, and of what is worth taking seriously, and of oneself is determined by the knowledge that

> our king is Victor Baal,
> he is judge, none is higher.
> We all his chalice bear,
> we all bear his cup.

So the *mišpāṭ* won by Baal is the power to say what is and to make that stick. That in turn means that his concerns, his "agenda," are of central, absolute, and primary importance. Everything else is peripheral, conditional, and at most secondary. So the myth expresses the defining Canaanite conviction that survival transcends every other concern, as it also forms that conviction within its hearers, and validates it.

ROYAL *MIŠPĀṬ*

Baal's *mišpāṭ* can be specified further. It is actually kingship. In both stories that is the form of *mišpāṭ* in question. Canaanite conceptions of divine kingship feature certain motifs—house, throne, mountain, feast, acclamation by the gods—and those motifs are all present in the Baal myth, marking it as a story about kingship. In principle, other forms of *mišpāṭ* are possible. There could be *mišpāṭ* by town meeting or folkmoot. A vestige of this probably survives in the very old Canaanite conception of the divine council.[14] Or *mišpāṭ* could be exercised by the council and its president acting together. In fact, the beginning of the myth reflects this form of governance, though El and the gods simply wilt before Yamm's power move. Other variations are possible, but the *mišpāṭ* Baal achieves is monarchic: that is simply given. There will be a king: if it were not Baal it would be someone else. Kingship is the point of all that struggle.

I have been speaking as if kingship were an empty category, as if it were the case that Baal or Mot or poor Athtar could, in principle, fill the role and the only difference would be the policies of their respective administrations. One would provide food stamps, the other bombs. One would be desirable, the other disastrous. In fact, while *mišpāṭ* is an empty category, kingship is not. There is a job description, and it is pretty specific. In the "Keret" epic we hear a king being taken to task for not doing his royal duty:

> You have not adjudicated the case of the widow,
> you have not judged the judgment
> of the straitened of *nepeš*. . . .
> you did not feed the orphan, . . . the widow.
> (*CTA* 16.6.45–47, 49–50)

The point of the job is to provide food and ensure justice. Royal *mišpāṭ* comprises both functions.[15] Thus it is clear why not just any god will do as king—the job is "wired." It has to be Baal. Kingship and the power to ensure survival are essentially linked. This is what a king does, so Baal is king.[16] The *mišpāṭ* that Canaan longed to see effective in the ordering and governance of the cosmos—the way they wanted reality to be—was *mišpāṭ* that validated and ensured survival as "the one necessary thing." It was also the way they thought reality was. Baal is rendered powerless but ultimately triumphs; Yamm can be confined; Mot does not have the last word.

KINGSHIP AND EL

Let us note here the role of El. Without a house, Baal's kingship is incomplete,[17] and without El's decree he will have no house. Though El seems powerless to affect the outcome of things, the outcome that emerges needs to be ratified by him. He can

> undermine the foundation of "sitting,"
> overturn the throne of kingship,
> smash the scepter of *mišpāṭ*.

To that extent, Baal's kingship is not coterminous with cosmic *mišpāṭ*. It is relativized, in a way, because it is not self-validating. Its legitimacy—or something like legitimacy—comes from outside itself. It is conditioned.

Perhaps this duality reflects the historical development of monarchy in Canaan. Perhaps it reflects the nature of kingship itself, which once attained is not sufficient to itself but can be lost.

KINGSHIP IN CANAAN

The myth, in any case, does reflect the political realities of second-millennium Canaan.[18] Princelings ruled from fortified cities. They were vassals of Pharaoh but nothing limited their rule over the city and its surrounding lands. What the people produced was subject to expropriation, providing goods for trade and supporting the bureaucracy and royal army: the state extracted from the people the fruits of their toil. Professional warriors ensured security, both against rival dynasts and against the populace. All this was according to *mišpāṭ*. Baal ruled, and the king was his servant, participating as it seems in his divine kingship.

What comes through in the myths is the centrality of survival. This is the Canaanite "agenda." Everything else is subordinated to it. Though kingship is supposed to ensure justice for the powerless ("the widow and orphan") as well as bread, the question arises which of these goods would, in a crunch, take precedence. If survival—fertility, bread, wine, oil—is of absolute importance, surely justice and compassion are negotiable. First things first. The arrangements that ensure survival, the royal political economy, include centralized power and centralized distribution of goods. People enjoy the good things of the land so long as they "fit in" to the established order. It is by reference to that order that the efforts of the farmer and pastoralist yield produce. And that order is carried on through royal *mišpāṭ*. The Baal myth expresses and validates not only a vision of life but a specific set of political and economic instrumentalities that ensure that the goods central to that vision will be forthcoming.

Some details of this social order are reflected in the myths. Baal is helpless until Kothar crafts clubs for him: he overcomes the destructive dominion of Sea through the technological superiority those weapons afford. May we see in this detail the centrality of the professional military elite, with their horse and chariot, in the royal economy? And how is Death defeated? Anat, the survivor, sees to it that life perdures, even after the lord of life is swallowed up in death. W. F. Albright suggested an etymology for the name *ʿanat*: she is the "sign, indication of purpose, active will" of Baal, his alter ego or hypostatized selfhood.[19] If he is saved through her it is because she is an extension of him, an avatar, so to speak, of his reproductive power. In a sense he saves himself but only in the form of the eternal female. She can defeat even Death. To the extent that Anat tells the story of woman in Canaan, then, woman's story is that she is the vessel and pledge of new, ongoing life. She prevails. Or rather, Baal through her wins out. When survival is the agenda, everything else fits in. Woman is defined in terms of the guaranteeing of life. It would be unthinkable to see her in any other light. She shares in the divine power of Baal. "We all his chalice bear, we all bear his cup."

GOOD NEWS, BAD NEWS

If one grant that survival is *the* good, the Canaanite world view is not unattractive. The stories are both realistic, doing justice to the constant and seemingly inevitable possibility of disaster that hangs over us, and distinctly upbeat, offering assurance that, despite all, life will prevail. The stories are good news: "Lift up, O gods, your heads."

To me, though, the feeling dominant in these myths is anxiety. The dismay of the divine council, the fecklessness of El, the hopeless plight of Baal all bespeak a deep sense that "the one necessary thing" is at stake. This is not just dramatic effect, the result of artfully designed narrative, like the cliffhangers of our Saturday-afternoon youth. These stories embody the Canaanite's deepest sense of what really matters. They mean business. This is a matter of life and death. Competing visions of what matters are to be brushed aside. The anxiety is a measure of just how important survival is to people. It is so important that it validates centralized power and royal economic monopoly: those arrangements ensure survival. Anxiety makes what we would consider tyranny not just bearable but necessary; indeed, no other system is even imaginable.

CONTRADICTIONS

Yet the Canaanite vision of life (and, presumably, the Canaanite political system) contained certain contradictions. Royal *mišpāṭ* was conditioned by the decree of El. El was not immanently identified with this good or that value, but kept his distance. He did not stand for particular goods, like fertility and survival. He did not, so to speak, specify what reality was to be. Baal did that, as the story turned out: he had the say about things.[20] But Baal's "say," his *mišpāṭ*, needed to be validated by El. There was a power above and behind Baal's ultimate power. There was, in principle, an agenda besides the agenda embodied in Baal and his struggles and his victories.

Here is the contradiction, then, at the heart of Canaanite life. The "widow and orphan" were to be cared for. Kings who neglected justice were to be reprimanded. Yet the task of feeding the multitude required stringent exercise of centralizing power. Those royal granaries had to be filled. The story of Naboth, as we shall see,[21] suggests the tensions involved in carrying out the task of a king. Omelettes require broken eggs. It was difficult both to ensure plenty and to have regard for the powerless. But royal power depended on legitimacy, and legitimacy derived from that power's delivering on what was owed. The seal of approval represented by El's decree could be revoked.

Make survival primary, central, and absolute, and everything else is secondary, peripheral, and conditional. The potentialities of woman, the rights of the widow and orphan, justice, compassion—these become subordinate goods. Build into the way you imagine reality a concern for justice and compassion, involved somehow with the very power that validates the specific good of survival, and you have a potential contradiction.

The people of the land, then, were given a double message in their stories. What really matters is survival: that is absolute. But the god who ensures survival is subordinate to another, who is called "The Compassionate." It would be surprising if the concerns of the god who has the final say did not threaten to supersede the concerns of the other god. This is what happened when Israel began to be formed as "the people of Yahweh."

CHAPTER 3

The Origins of Israel

It might be helpful at this point to take stock, and show how what we have seen is connected with our theme of power. If power consists, at least in part, of having the say about things, the Canaanite world attributed it to Baal. "He is judge." To the extent that Baal's "judgment" needed to be validated by El, it was only provisional; but the old stories did not hesitate to assert that El's validation was granted, at the unanimous instance of the other gods.

Baal's cosmic *mišpāṭ* was exercised by the kings of Canaan. We might speak of the political consequences of the Canaanite myths, but that would be too simple. Because the myths embodied certain convictions, we should rather speak of the political consequences of those convictions. Perhaps we should see both the myths and the royal political system as expressions or outgrowths of the convictions which defined Canaan, two sides of the same coin. Even that, though, is too simple, too linear and undialectical. The convictions themselves were not only expressed in politics and myth, they were shaped by them. People professed Baal's kingly *mišpāṭ* because they lived under monarchic rule—and vice versa. That "vice versa" is indispensable in trying to understand the chicken-and-egg dynamics of consciousness and politics.

So power belonged to Baal, and more remotely to El, and most immediately to the kings of Canaan. Yet power also—and in many ways decisively—was exercised by the myths themselves. That is so, if my analysis of what is "mythic" holds water, almost by definition. Mythic stories not only embody our deepest anxieties and desires, they shape them, and they validate them. They have the say about who we are and what we take seriously.

Yet—again—their plastic power is a function of the needs and aspirations they embody, and so we come back again to what we have been calling "consensus." Consensus has the final say about things. And consensus comes down to *ṣedeq*.

MIŠPĀṬ AND *ṢEDEQ* IN CANAAN

Canaan, then, accepted the cosmic *mišpāṭ* of Baal, presumably because it corresponded to their sense of *ṣedeq*. What really mattered to the Canaanites was what Baal, "the son of Dagon," could deliver. His cosmic lordship was legitimate because fertility and survival are central in the scheme of things (and vice versa). Canaanites accepted the terrestrial *mišpāṭ* of kings, presumably because it corresponded to the same sense of *ṣedeq*. How did this work? Two models are possible:

(1)

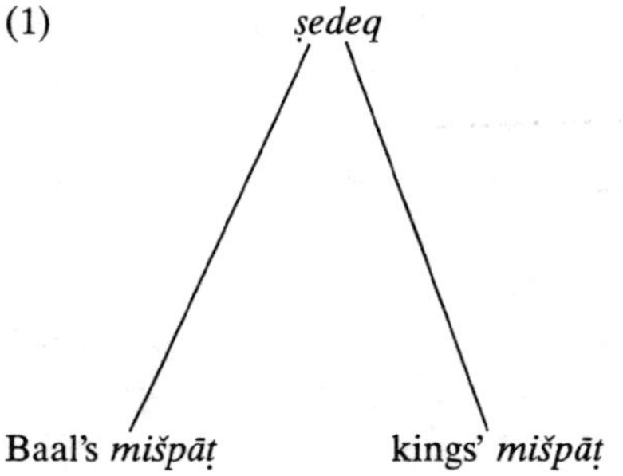

(2)

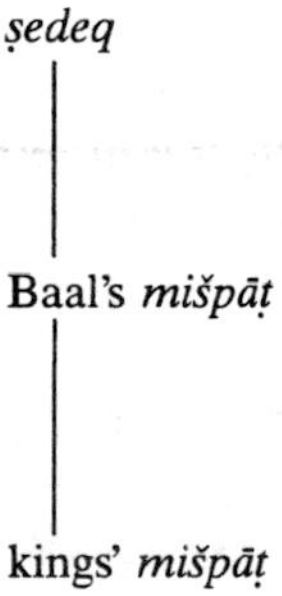

I think model (2) is the more helpful for understanding the dynamics of Canaanite life. The *mišpāṭ* of kings was legitimated because it was a participation in Baal's cosmic kingship. The king was a "son of god," a divine being,[1] as it seems, at least in terms of his royal function. His word was authoritative as a divine word is authoritative—unquestionable and per se efficacious. He had the say about things just as Baal did. Model (1), though, is also defensible, since it brings out the centrality of *ṣedeq* in the acceptance of both divine and human kingship. In either case, we are dealing with a package. The three elements were a systemic whole.

MIŠPĀṬ AND *ṢEDEQ* IN ISRAEL

A new consensus appears, around the turn of the twelfth century B.C., with the emergence of the new people Israel. Israel was the political entity that accepted the *mišpāṭ* of Yahweh, and people became members of that political entity—*bᵉnê yiśrā'ēl*, literally "Sons of Israel"[2]–by renouncing any other *mišpāṭ* and giving allegiance to Yahweh's. In accepting his *mišpāṭ* they were accepting his *ṣedeq* and renouncing any other *ṣedeq*, especially that by which Canaan lived, as the biblical tradition shows clearly. How did Israel differ from Canaan? How did *mišpāṭ* and *ṣedeq* work in early Israel?

In early Israel the *mišpāṭ* of Yahweh comprised both cosmic and terrestrial functions. "There was no king in Israel." People entered into a relationship with Yahweh called *bᵉrît*, "covenant," and accepted his "judgments"—*mišpāṭîm*—or, as they are misleadingly called, "laws." As the collection of *mišpāṭîm* in Exodus 21—23 shows, the kind of particular *mišpāṭ* Israel understood to be Yahweh's will had to do with the way people dealt with one another, especially in the economic and political sphere. His *mišpāṭ* mandated compassionate regard for defenseless people—the "widow and orphan," the *gēr* or resident non-Israelite—who would be easy prey for acquisitive and violent men. This interest in the dispossessed or "marginated" was backed up by Yahweh's passionate involvement. Compassion for the widow and the orphan was not just one option among many possible ways of arranging social relationships: it was what the acceptance of Yahweh's *mišpāṭ* operatively meant. And as he is not just the sovereign of the particular people Israel, but antecedently and definingly cosmic lord, as we shall see below, what he says as Israel's sovereign—his word—is normative not just for them, adventitiously or idiosyncratically, but is valid *in se*. It is given, built into the structure of reality. The god who hears the cry of the oppressed is lord of heaven and earth. His *mišpāṭ*, then, determines what is to be taken seriously, and his *mišpāṭ* commands that the weak should not be taken advantage of. This demand has cosmic force and validity. It is, concretely, what is meant by *ṣedeq*.

CANAAN'S *ṢEDEQ*, ISRAEL'S *ṢEDEQ*

In the two political entities, "Canaan" and Israel, then, there are competing visions of what is central, primary, absolute—of what should be considered just, right, good, fair, valuable: *ṣedeq*. Flowing from these competing visions are competing claims about which god has real *mišpāṭ*. Which has the final say about reality and about what kinds of choices one is to make? Is it the god who "satiates the multitudes of earth" or the god who "hears the cry of the oppressed"? Which divine agenda can claim *ṣedeq?* Acceptance of the one god's *mišpāṭ* entails royal political and economic monopoly and, in principle, unbridled rule. Acceptance of the other god's *mišpāṭ* entails a different kind of social order, which resolutely forbade taking advantage of the weak and powerless, and made compassion for them supersede any other consideration. In the one system *ṣedeq* means security and abundance. In the other, *ṣedeq* means . . . justice.

(We should note, then, two meanings of *ṣedeq*. *Ṣedeq* is "what is right," but what was "right" in Israel was equity and compassion for the powerless. When people nowadays speak of the biblical imperatives to "justice" they mean *ṣedeq* in the second sense, which I believe is really a specification of a more basic sense; but of course the biblical tradition unanimously identifies the two, as I am trying to show.)

ISRAELITE ORIGINS: CONTINUITY AND DISCONTINUITY

Who were the people, calling themselves "Israel," who professed this alternative vision of reality? And where did this vision come from? Two OT passages can orient us to an answer. One, Exodus 3, is set at the beginning of what Scripture presents as the long process of the formation of Israel as a people, from their deliverance in Egypt to their possession of the land of Canaan. The other, Joshua 24, comes at the end of that process.

In the burning-bush episode (and its parallel, Exod. 6:2–3) Yahweh identifies himself to Moses as the god of Abraham, Isaac, and Jacob—yet Moses has to ask what his name is! The tradition seems to reflect a consciousness that Yahweh is a new factor. In Joshua 24, the people who have just taken over the land of Canaan enter into the Israelite covenant with Yahweh; Joshua's recital of what Yahweh has done for them presents the recent "conquest" as continuous with, and the culmination of, what began in Egypt with the exodus. Yet another tradition tells us that of the original exodus group only two entered the land. This seems to reflect a memory that the people who were delivered from Egypt and the people who became Israel in the land were different groups. So much for continuity.

Yahweh is the god who first appeared in Egypt; yet he had guided "the fathers" in Canaan. He is the god who wrested the land from the kings of Canaan; yet that "conquest" is put into the context of the deliverance from Egypt, for people who have no living memory of it. There were the people of the exodus, and there were those in the land of Canaan who entered the covenant at Shechem, and the two groups are and are not related. The "Sons of Israel" came into the land; but somehow "Sons of Israel" had been there before. These dualities the tradition sustains.

To account for them I propose the following outline of the emergence of early Israel.[3]

CANAAN IN THE AMARNA PERIOD

Let us go over what we saw in chapter 2 about the social world of Canaan.[4] Pharaoh controlled Canaan, both through Egyptian officials appointed by him and, under them, vassal rulers. The power these native kings wielded was consolidated by the royal household, both officials (the king's "servants") and professional army ("warriors"). Through a system of royal landholding, forced labor, taxation in kind, and expropriation, the labors of farmers and pastoralists were at the disposal of the king and his "servants," used to supply the army and the bureaucracy and for commerce with other lands. It seems that the population was ethnically and racially[5] heterogeneous. They were, to borrow the biblical expression, a "mixed multitude" (Exod. 12:38, RSV).

The Amarna letters *(EA),* from the first half of the fourteenth century B.C., reveal tensions in this tidy world. Urgent requests to Pharaoh for military help and strenuous denunciations of various social elements show that the kings' power was not uncontested. Rival dynasts struggled, or jockeyed, for dominance, with the support of certain groups within the target cities. The established order was threatened. The liveliest examples of social unrest come from Byblos. Its beleaguered king, Rib-Adda, complains to Pharaoh that he is in need of immediate support against a neighboring ruler, Abdi-Ashirta, and his sons (especially one Aziru), and that Pharaoh has remained inactive while Abdi-Ashirta goes from strength to strength. "Who will love, should I die?" he reminds his suzerain (*EA* 114:68), using the political sense of the term "love": who will be a loyal vassal to Pharaoh, accepting his *mišpāṭ*?[6] The expansionist Abdi-Ashirta or Aziru will not "love" Pharaoh, or so Rib-Adda wants Pharaoh to believe. In any case his own people are withdrawing their "love" from Rib-Adda.

THE *ʿAPIRU*

There is a term used in these letters that to me seems central to understanding the origins of Israel. Rib-Adda refers to his adversaries as *ʿapiru* and as having the support of *ʿapiru*.[7] In applying this label he is not speaking of them as an ethnic group or occupational guild.[8] He uses it to call attention to their disloyalty to himself and to Pharaoh. *ʿApiru* are people who stand outside the established political order. They do not accept the *mišpāṭ* of the king.[9] In this rejection, or withholding of acceptance, of *mišpāṭ* they seem—certainly in the eyes of those who run things—to call into question its legitimacy, the *ṣedeq* on which it is founded. They constitute a rival political entity, but their standing apart from the established polity is not like the mere existence of other states. It is more dangerous, because by right they owe allegiance but withhold it. In George Mendenhall's happy expression,[10] they have "withdrawn." *ʿApiru* are *ʿapiru* precisely because they have "withdrawn" from the obligations and procedures of the established order. This "withdrawal" can be physical or it can be a matter of interior allegiance. It can be explicit rebellion or simply acts of lawlessness construed as equivalent to rebellion. In any case it represents a threat to the ruler, for it negates the foundations of his rule, *mišpāṭ* and *ṣedeq*. The *ʿapiru* therefore must be dealt with. If *they* get away with it, anyone can simply ignore the requirements of the political order, and all the king's horses and all the king's men will be powerless to put things together again. The *ʿapiru* have to be made an object lesson.[11]

The "Circle" of Ṣedeq

Imagine a circle, therefore, and label it the realm of *ṣedeq*. Those who overtly or effectively choose to stand outside that circle are *ʿapiru*. Inside the circle are those who identify with the established order, and of course those who rule: those who accept the legitimacy of the status quo. That *ṣedeq* must be upheld or vindicated. How? Why, by an act of *mišpāṭ*. Now, the act of *mišpāṭ* that seeks to defend the underlying *ṣedeq* of the established order has two aspects. From the viewpoint of the polity and its *ṣedeq,* it is vindication; from the viewpoint of those against whom it is directed, it is vengeance. That is, the appropriate response to *ʿapiru* is *nāqām*.[12]

Back to Rib-Adda

So Rib-Adda complains because his "circle" is continually shrinking. His rule is constantly being eroded. More and more neighboring cities are going over to Abdi-Ashirta. There is a relentless expansion in the "circle" of *ʿapiru,* those standing outside the circle of those who "love" Pharaoh and so keep faith with *ṣedeq*.

In Canaan of the Amarna period, therefore, there were *ʿapiru*. Things fell apart; the center did not hold. Of course, we do not know what moved people to "withdraw" from the circle of established *mišpāṭ,* and it is guesswork to try to figure out what was going on in their heads. It may well be that the partisans of Abdi-Ashirta did accept the established order but were simply interested in new management, a better deal than they could get with Rib-Adda as ruler. Or maybe desperation drove them into the arms of Abdi-Ashirta.[13] Rib-Adda is suspiciously emphatic: Abdi-Ashirta "has said to the people of Ammiya, 'Kill your leader and become like us; then you shall have peace.' And they went over in accordance with his words, and became like *ʿapiru*" (*EA* 74:25–29). "Why do you remain silent while the *ʿapiru,* the dog, takes your cities?" (ibid., 91:35). If "new management" was all that was in question, nothing fundamental was threatened. (This would explain Pharaoh's inaction in the face of Rib-Adda's panicky representations. Rib-Adda might fall but Egyptian *mišpāṭ* would perdure.)

Yet *ʿapiru* there clearly were in Canaan, and that is significant.

People withdrew their allegiance from those who exercised *mišpāṭ,* and in so doing presumably—in any case effectively—denied the *ṣedeq* of the established order. They were entering or forming an alternative political entity. Still, their existence as *ʿapiru* was not only withdrawal from but symbiosis with established political systems. Living in the interstices of established polities they sold their labor and military services to various princelings (that is the reason they turn up in the ancient documents). The *ʿapiru* "polity" was a mirror image of the "legitimate" social order. They were out-laws, and to the extent they defined themselves in that way their identity as political entity was based on what was already in place. They were people who lived outside the circle.

ʿAPIRU AND "HEBREWS"

This Amarna picture of monarchic *mišpāṭ,* squabbling dynasts, centralized power, and social restiveness provides the backdrop for the emergence of Israel in the land. That was the kind of social and political reality in which, 100 to 150 years later, the people Israel was formed. If we put the biblical data into this historical context, the origins of Israel appear something like the following.

Sometime in the late thirteenth century B.C., refugee slaves from Egypt (the "Moses group") entered the land of Canaan and brought with them good news. They had been delivered from the power of Pharaoh. They owed their deliverance to a god, Yahweh, who hears the cry of the oppressed and saves the afflicted. This proclamation had a transforming effect among the people of the land. The Canaanite "underclass" withdrew their allegiance to the established political order. They rallied to the banner of Yahwism. They were incorporated into a new political entity, whose nucleus was the exodus group. This new political entity was called "Israel." In the eyes of the rulers of Canaan, of course, the new polity Israel was *ʿapiru,* and they took out after it. The resulting wars of the kings against Israel and the kings' defeat through the power of Yahweh are reflected in the traditions preserved in Joshua and Judges. We call the process the "conquest."

This theory of Israel's origins—sometimes called the "Peasant Revolt" theory[14]—was proposed by Mendenhall twenty-five years ago in an article he punningly titled "The Hebrew Conquest of Palestine." The OT word we translate "Hebrew" is the biblical form of the familiar extrabiblical word *ʿapiru.* Since Israel lacked legitimacy, having been formed by renunciation of the "legitimate" authority of the kings, the Israelites were "Hebrews": *ʿapiru.* They took over the land, unseating the kings. This rebellion by the people of the land was, therefore, a "Hebrew Conquest."

"ELOHISTIC ISRAEL"

Between the Amarna letters, in the early fourteenth century B.C., and this emergence of Israel in the land, there was a century and a half. Of this period can anything be said, or is it a blank? The biblical tradition itself, of course, dates from a time after the formation of Israel; but does it give any clues about the time before—about those hundred-some years?

One useful suggestion[15] is that this period saw the formation in Canaan of coalitions of *ʿapiru* and other dispossessed people: that the social restiveness attested in the Amarna letters continued, and led to attempts at setting up political entities that were more than simply reactive to the oppressive rule of the kings. In this view, the emergence of Israel in the land was the culmination of other struggles to live free of the tyranny of centralized power. Indeed, it has been proposed that one such social formation called itself "Israel," and that the new Yahwistic entity that came together once the exodus group entered the land adopted the old name.[16] This forerunner of Yahwistic Israel, then, we would call "Elohistic Israel." (A terminological note: the members both of "Elohistic Israel" and of the Yahwistic exodus group in Egypt would then be referred to as "Proto-Israelites"; the names "Israel" and "Israelites" would be reserved for the people formed, in the land, from the coalescing of the newcomers and the native Canaanites.)

This reconstruction is intriguing and has much to recommend it, I think, though to some it seems merely speculative.[17] It represents an attempt to work backward, from the biblical accounts of the "conquest," and forward from the historical givens of the Amarna period, to try to understand what was the soil in which the seed of Yahwism was planted. Two things should be stressed. One is that Yahwism came into the land, with the exodus group, from the south.[18] Israel, the people Yahweh "redeemed," was led from Egypt to his holy mountain and there "planted" (Exod. 15:17): Israel qua Israel is not indigenous to Canaan. The other consideration has to do with the name "Israel," *yiśrā'ēl.* Bronze Age names are for the most part sentences (Niqmepa, "Vindication shines forth"; Rib-Adda, "Hadad contends" [?]). The grammatical subject in the name *yiśrā'ēl* is "El." The name of this Yahwistic people does not reflect the centrality of their god, Yahweh, in their life. It is true that "El" was an alias for Yahweh in the biblical tradition; but the absence of "Yahweh" in the very name of the people is suggestive.

GOING *'APIRU*

The formation of Israel in the land was the culmination of earlier movements of "withdrawal," those of "Proto-Israelite" groups in Canaan. But these Canaanite "Proto-Israelites"—who were they? What was their experience? Let us return to those Amarna *'apiru* and try to imagine their experience. Let us indulge in some guesswork.

We know what the establishment view of the *'apiru* was. They were *kalbu ḫalqu* (*EA* 67:17), a "stray dog": off the leash, belonging to no master, posing a danger to all, despicable. They were social riffraff. A biblical formulation from centuries later, describing a group that was for all practical purposes *'apiru,* is serviceable: there gathered to David "every man in distress and every man who was in debt and every man bitter of *nepeš*" (1 Sam. 22:2). The *'apiru's* withdrawal would have been construed as flight from social duty, and the withdrawers as people who could not "make it" in society.

Assume that this establishment view was shared, within the Canaanite world, by people in general. If that was so, there would be powerful social pressures—a strong centripetal force—keeping people within the circle of the established order. People knew what really mattered, and they knew right from wrong. They knew that accepting the *mišpāṭ* of Baal and the established order gave them standing in the scheme of things, so that they were assured that the central goods promised by the myths—abundance, fertility, survival—would be theirs. Becoming *ʿapiru* would lose them that assurance. They would be cosmic outlaws, clearly in the wrong.

Suppose, though, that those expectations of abundance were disappointed. Suppose yourself a Canaanite peasant, who found yourself unable to make ends meet, not because of famine but because royal officials took from you what you worked so hard to produce. You planted a vineyard and another enjoyed the wine—and this by royal *mišpāṭ*. Taxes in kind to the royal household left barely enough seed, say, for the next planting. Levies of produce and of labor were crushing. There was not only no abundance: sustenance was barely possible.

What do you do? One response is to identify more closely with the system than before—try to be a "better citizen," multiply sacrifices, increase your faith.[19] You have much invested in the Baalistic vision of the good. You would tend to affirm that vision more emphatically.

Just under the surface of this response, though, lies another. That is to feel the unfairness of it all. Here is a double bind indeed. You have always lived by the conviction that the only thing that ultimately matters is (to use a shorthand expression) Bread. Yet the more you struggle to attain that central good, believing the promise, the more life turns out to be toil and futility. That double bind would produce confusion and rage, or perhaps numb despair. Yet this disaffection would produce guilt. Your feelings are in conflict with everything you know to be right and holy and true.

Suppose, though, that conditions became intolerable, and frustration and need drove you off your land, and outside the established order, to make a living as best you could. Suppose there was no other choice. You make the break. You become *ʿapiru*. How would you feel?

At first you would feel yourself to be in the wrong. You are living outside the "circle" of what Baalism defines as *ṣedeq*. You would lack the agreeable sense of righteousness that comes from living according to *ṣedeq*, and indeed you would feel "unrighteous." You may have broken with the established order, but its moral claims—especially the conviction that Bread is central—still exercise their power over you. Hence, besides guilt, you would feel anxiety, even despair, about Bread. You can no longer look to Baal for sustenance. Becoming *ʿapiru* means both outlawry—"unrighteousness"—and radical insecurity.

Yet with time another reaction would set in. After all, within the consensus that defined Canaan there were other convictions than those associated with Bread. There was the conviction that the widow and orphan and those straitened of *nepeš*—the "multitudes of earth"—must be "judged." The king was supposed to look after these people. Yet the king and his servants were the ones who put people into straits. Something was wrong there.

Reflections such as these—drawing on the resources of the Canaanite consensus itself, taking bearings within the imaginative and moral horizon of that culture—would overtake your first reactions of "unrighteousness" and anxiety. The choice to become *ʿapiru* and the experience of *ʿapiru* life would lead to some surprising realizations. You are getting by. Anxiety that was previously focused on Bread now seems illusory. You are making a living, together with other *ʿapiru*. Now you have standing in a new community, where, at least in some cases, surely, *mišpāṭ* is not exercised by one person but is a matter of communal discernment and choice, a more "tribal" sort of existence than was known under the centralized rule of the kings. There are others to work with in making a living, to share the sense of outlawry and insecurity, and to help you see that there is a kind of *ṣedeq* to this new life, a *ṣedeq* centering on "justice" as the thing that most mattered. Acceptance of outlawry and insecurity, letting go of your standing in the moral universe you had inhabited, would bring other concerns into prominence.

THE GOD OF THE *ʿAPIRU*

These concerns attached themselves to the figure of El. He was the Compassionate One. He stood for older, or other, ways. He presided over the council of gods and dwelt in a tent, unlike the kingly Baal, who had his House and ruled alone. Baal was the focus of heavy-breathing anxiety about fertility and survival; El's interests were more catholic, or at least not so narrow and task-oriented, and more fundamental in the scheme of things. Indeed, El was capable of "overturning the throne of kingship, smashing the sceptre of *mišpāṭ*."

He was the primordial Creator of Creatures, who caused everything to be:

'Ēl dū yahwī ṣaba'āt	El who causes-to-be the hosts [of heaven]
'Ēl dū yahwī šamêma	El who causes-to-be the heavens
'Ēl dū yahwī 'arṣa	El who causes-to-be earth.

Something along those lines.[20] Which god, El or Baal, after all was to be taken seriously? Which had, finally, the say about things? And which god was better matched to these outlaws? Baal was the god of the kings; fine, they could have him. Now that the experience of insecurity and outlawry showed how illusory that all-consuming anxiety about Bread really was, people could see their previous craven dependence on Baal for what it was. Their worship of him had been (we might say) like putting a coin in a machine: a survival machine. It was a way of controlling their own destiny as that destiny had been defined for them by the tight world of Canaan. That was why Baal was so humorless: so much selfhood was invested in what he represented. Baal was solemn; El was serious, and therefore could afford to be whimsical. In the rigid world of monarchy, El even appeared a picaresque character. He possessed the animal cunning of the old. He could be exasperating, like King Lear, capable of the gratuitous—and therefore gracious—act. He had a genius *pour épater les bourgeois.* Like people who became *ʿapiru,* El was "marginated." Like them, he did not fit into the royal economy: he could "overturn the throne of kingship."[21]

CONTRADICTIONS REALIZED

Within the Canaanite world, therefore, there were these two possibilities of being, two "spirits" as it were, leading in different directions, shaping people's self-understanding and choices in different ways. What would have led to opting for one rather than the other? As always, it was people's "social situation," the concrete facticity of their lives within the social system: their experience. Though experience is structured and interpreted by cultural givens, it also reinterprets them. The convictions of one's culture validate one's experience, and vice versa. The convictions associated with Baalism—with its reflex political and economic system of centralized power, and its fundamental impulse to self-absorbed anxiety, manipulativeness, and need for security—produced one kind of experience. When that came apart, the vision of reality associated with El was there to help pick up the pieces. What led people from one to the other was, then, the concrete choices they made. We do not usually have things clearly laid out in a blueprint and choose accordingly. We react, and then look around for justification. I doubt that people chose to become *ʿapiru* because they had lined up ideological ducks in a row. It seems more likely that they were driven to that choice by simple need. Deprivation caused by the psychic and political tyranny they experienced forced them to let go of their standing in the order of things and with it their entitlement to what they needed so desperately. They chose "unrighteousness" and radical insecurity, because there was nothing else they could do. And they found that it worked, and then saw that the *ṣedeq* of it all had been there all along, in the figure of El.

I see the *ʿapiru,* therefore, as *lumpen:* people who do not know their right hand from their left, incapable of that clear-eyed, programmatic self-liberation that is the revolutionary ideal. *Lumpen* are the people scorned by the Lenins of history. Indeed, the self-regarding, self-dramatizing ideological purity and decisiveness of revolutionaries has much of the spirit of Baalism. It wants results, at all costs. It is solemn. It is ridden with anxiety, probably because the success of the whole project rests with one's own efforts and deserts. No, *lumpen* simply react to things. They do not control their own destiny. They are sheep without a shepherd. So they are thought despicable and given up on.

This reconstruction of the dynamics of becoming *ʿapiru* is, as I said, guesswork, and its chief merit lies in providing an occasion for a typology: the "spirit" of Baal and that of El. Yet it also accords with certain data in the biblical tradition. In the nature of the case we can have no certitude, of course. Social movements like that of the *ʿapiru* in Canaan do not erect monumental stelae. Yet they do tell stories, and in the biblical stories of the patriarchs are reflected many of the traits associated with life as *ʿapiru.* The figures whom later Israel regarded as their forebears in the land lived by their wits, constant prey as they were to the established powers. Their women could be taken, their wages withheld, and only a kind of "street smarts" enabled them to get by in their dealings with those in possession. That, and the guidance of El. The people who told these stories knew what it was to be "marginated" and to have no resource against The Man except a kind of giddy, and therefore savvy, trust—not in kings and princes but in the Creator of all. As we saw above, one of the hypothesized *ʿapiru* coalitions may have called itself "Israel." *Yiśrāʾēl:* does the etymology of the name in Gen. 32:28 preserve a memory of how El is associated with struggle—against gods and men—and how he causes his own to prevail?

Thus, while *ʿapiru* withdrawal as such is simple negation of the established order, the figure of El transforms their movement into something affirmative. Their existence as political entity becomes not merely a mirror image of centralized power but a matter of *ṣedeq.* There is a kind of *ṣedeq,* of course, in victimhood: resentment and a sense of grievance can be the center of a people's identity.[22] This may have been the case for some *ʿapiru,* especially those whose withdrawal sentenced them to a life of mercenary labor or soldiering in the interstices of the city-states. I suggest, though, that El got some *ʿapiru* beyond this stage. They became a people. El focused the *ṣedeq* that gave them their identity, and it was a positive identity. Statist oppression was not at the center of their self-understanding but something subsumed in their affirmation of equity and compassion. For the Proto-Israelite *ʿapiru,* El focused their sense of themselves as a people, and so enabled them to be more than *ʿapiru.* Their solidarity found new forms—ways of living, working, making decisions, defending themselves—that avoided the centralizing, security-obsessed tendencies of the city-state: associations of "families" and associations of such associations, or, to use the biblical word, tribes.[23]

Yet as the peoplehood of the new social formation differed from the "peoplehood" of the city-state, so El figured in their life in a way different from the way Baal focused the identity of the city-state. Baal was the city-state's tutelary deity. El, in contrast, was the "personal god" of the patriarchs. Thorkild Jacobsen[24] has described how in second-millennium Mesopotamian religion the gods were remote, engaged in the conduct of cosmic affairs, and the individual could hardly approach these exalted deities with any expectation of being taken seriously. Each person, however, had a "personal god," usually a minor deity, who would intercede at court with the major gods. The personal god cared about and cared for his client. To him the individual would bring troubles and needs. The god and his worshiper were on terms of familiar intimacy. Jacobsen has suggested[25] that this category might be useful in understanding the "god of the fathers" of Genesis. "The god of Abraham" (or Isaac, or Jacob) was his "personal god." Obviously there are differences. El was no minor deity but as we have seen the president of the council of gods, the Creator of all. But the affect or feeling associated with him was that characteristic of the worshiper's relation to the "personal god": the sense that the god is close to and cares for and has a special interest in those he makes his own.

FROM "WITHDRAWAL" TO PEOPLEHOOD: A TYPOLOGY

How did El care for the *ʿapiru?* What was their experience? We can distinguish two phases or aspects. One has to do with life in the "interstices," a mode of living reflected in the Genesis stories, where people have dealings with the established powers. In these encounters El protected them in the way I suggested above: in the canniness and good fortune that enabled *ʿapiru* to get by and even to get the better of the powerful, the Proto-Israelites experienced El's guidance. The second aspect or phase, though, is more difficult. This was managing to live not by sufferance or shrewdness but as a people on their own—not in the interstices but in their own "place," with their own lands for farming and grazing, their own systems of production and sharing of produce. But in the political and economic geography of southern Canaan in the late fourteenth and early thirteenth centuries B.C., where was such a "place"? How would people get by who had severed their links with economic systems? The land was all taken, material resources were controlled by the kings. According to the reconstruction I am following here, a way was found.

Pastoralists would have the easiest time of it. They are on the move, leading their livestock to upland or steppe pasturage according to the season. They are used to living on the fringes. They had always been in a position to evade the demands of centralized authority and, in principle, to break with it. That break, the *ʿapiru* withdrawal, would change their de jure relationship to authority, not so much their concrete situation. The livestock they shepherded may have been royal property; it was certainly subject to royal expropriation or taxation in kind. Withdrawal to the life of the *ʿapiru* would entail appropriation of the flocks and herds, changing the brand so to speak: what later ethicians called "occult compensation" (cf. Exod. 11:2–3a; 12:35–36).

Farmers, though, are tied to the land, and the land was the king's. Withdrawal to outlawry would mean that they could no longer farm, and so becoming *ʿapiru,* for them, would spell insecurity indeed. The only possibility for them was to take up the life of a mercenary. At some point, however, it became possible to cultivate the unpromising soil of upland Palestine. Methods of terracing were developed, and the discovery of slaked-lime plaster allowed the waterproofing of cisterns to collect and store rainwater for irrigation. Necessity is the mother of invention. Since in their necessity they felt themselves to be cared for by El those settlers in the hill country of Palestine must have seen his hand in providing them a "place" through the development of what moderns would call the "material base" of peoplehood.[26]

I project a typology of growth into peoplehood, therefore, consisting of three stages, from *ʿapiru* existence to life as "Elohistic Israel." First, and decisive, was the break with the established, "legitimate" order, the embracing of outlawry and insecurity. It was a matter of negation, of being defined, still, by the given order of things, but in opposition to it. Second, the choice and the experience of "unrighteousness" and insecurity led to the discovery of El's compassionate concern and the *ṣedeq* he provided. Now they were no longer illegitimate; they lived within their own "circle" of *ṣedeq,* according to forms of *mišpāṭ* we call tribal. Living in the interstices of the Canaanite political systems they experienced El's care and his confirmation of the way of life they had entered on. Finally, their peoplehood found its own "place," in the uplands, thanks to the new ways of cultivating the soil that were worked out there. This typology involves three oppositional pairs, in varying combinations: "negation," and positive *ṣedeq;* symbiosis with the established order, and autonomous existence; living in the interstices, and living in their own "place."

For a dialectic was at work. The break with the established order—entering into the state of outlawry and radical insecurity—meant that what had previously occupied all one's attention and efforts was now relativized. Giving up on agrarian plenty—Bread—as the center of one's life allowed a new spirit to emerge. Despair gave way to interior freedom, the kind we get when we burn our bridges. Innovation, solidarity, and a kind of playfulness would have characterized people's work. New things were tried. People carried off things they didn't know they could do. In hard times, discouragement would have made the old life seem attractive, predictable and familiar as it was, but the *ʿapiru* persisted. Their persistence came from the sense that this terror of freedom, the constant necessity of improvising, the day-to-day expenditure of effort without any predictable or assured outcomes was somehow *right,* and it involved the conviction that the old life was wrong. And because, against all expectation, things did work out, the rightness of this new life seemed to be confirmed. The dialectic I speak of, then, is that of *theoria* and *praxis,* each affecting the other. The choice to become *ʿapiru* forced people to the uplands, and successful cultivation of the soil there gave an experience of autonomy, and that experience confirmed the rightness of the new life. The choice led to a new life, and the new life validated the choice. So too for the pastoralist. Taking the risk of withdrawal—and what to the Crown would have seemed to be "rustling"—must have been formidable; but taking the risk worked out, and that confirmed the choice. We can imagine a ripple effect in Canaanite society, as the news got around of the new venture's success. Now there was a way out. More people became *ʿapiru* and were incorporated into the "tribal" associations. The established powers, too, would not have been slow to take alarm. The life of the Proto-Israelites must have put them in constant peril.

SUMMARY: ELOHISTIC ISRAEL, YAHWISTIC ISRAEL

One step remains in this reconstruction of the origins of Israel. We have seen the world of Amarna: the "circle" of established *ṣedeq*—derived from Baal, legitimating centralized royal *mišpāṭ*—and the

ʿapiru, outside that circle. We speculated about "going *ʿapiru*" and how that withdrawal from the established order—embracing outlawry and insecurity—would have shaped people's self-understanding: how it would have been focused in the figure of El. We followed out the suggestion that *ʿapiru* groups formed coalitions: new, "tribalizing" political entities (one of which may have called itself "Israel"). These postulated *ʿapiru* polities we call "Elohistic Israel," and we see something of their experience in the stories in Genesis.

The final step, then, is to trace the process by which the Canaanite *ʿapiru* groups became the people we know as Israel in the land. The catalyst in the process was the entrance into Canaan of refugee slaves from Egypt, proclaiming the good news of Yahweh. The people of the land would have recognized in Yahweh the god they knew as El, the god of the "marginated." With the exodus group, then, the *ʿapiru* coalesced, forming "Yahwistic Israel" in the land. Others, still adhering to the *mišpāṭ* of the kings, would have joined the new political entity, renouncing their allegiance to the kings and to the gods, especially Baal, who legitimated the kings' power.

The most unsatisfactory element in this reconstruction is the identity and character of the exodus group. The "refugee slaves from Egypt" remain shadowy, despite the circumstantial accounts of Exodus and Numbers. The reason for this is not difficult to understand. It is this: the story of deliverance from Pharaoh, proclaimed by those refugee slaves, became the story of deliverance from the power of the Canaanite kings. That is, the experience of exodus and "wilderness wanderings" (as we shall see below) was refracted through the experience of revolt against the kings and the taking of the land (and vice versa).

Is it possible to disengage from the traditions anything of what the exodus group proclaimed as the good news of Yahweh? I think so. I would argue that elements of that proclamation—even, perhaps, its core—are preserved in the Song of Miriam (Exod. 15:1–18).

THE SONG OF MIRIAM

The Song of Miriam, or "Song of the Sea," is not an account of the exodus event but a celebratory hymn.[27] Its hymnic character captures the exultant spirit of proclamation, and suggests that the news of the liberating god must have been astonishing. The refugees from Egypt had not just escaped. They had, miraculously, prevailed over Pharaoh and his force. Their god had overcome Egyptian military might with his strong right hand, using the power of sea to cast them down to the nether world. He had brought to his holy mountain the people he "fashioned" and "bought back." All the enthroned[28] and powerful ones of the neighboring nations looked on aghast at this divine act of deliverance. Panic seized them. The god who had done this was without peer:

> [11]Who is like you among the gods, Yahweh?
> Who is like you, awesome among the Holy Ones?[29]
> (Exod. 15:11)

His name was "He-causes-to-be the Hosts [of heaven]," *yahwī ṣabaʾāt,* or, to use its later form, *Yahweh ṣ*^{e}*bāʾōt:*

> [2b]This is my god: him I exalt,
> the god of my father: him I admire—
> [3]Yahweh the Warrior,
> Yahweh his name.[30]
> (Exod. 15:2b–3)

In this god of the "mixed multitude" from Egypt, the people of the land recognized the god of the *ʿapiru.* They knew him as El. But rather than being "marginated" and prevailing by wisdom, like El, Yahweh was a warrior god.[31] Indeed, he was *the* warrior god. Central to the defeat of the Egyptians was sea—

> [8]At the wind of your anger
> the waters were heaped up,
> the swells stood up like a hill,
> the deeps foamed in the heart of sea.[32]
> [10]You blew with your wind,
> sea covered them.
> They sank like lead
> in the awesome waters—
> (Exod. 15:8, 10)

but there was no hint that sea was anything more than Yahweh's inert instrument. There was no struggle with "Judge Sea, *Zabul* River." Yahweh worked deliverance through wind, and led his people in fire and cloud.[33] He was known in the phenomena of storm. Not only that, he ascended his holy mountain in victory, to the dais of his throne, to the sanctuary his hands established. The imagery—both in its specifics and in the pattern battle-ascension—is obviously reminiscent of Baal.[34] Against the background of Canaanite myth the associations are unmistakable. Yahweh is presented as cosmic lord, the Divine Warrior who defeats the foe and is enthroned in his holy place. In celebrating the victory over Egypt the Song of Miriam artfully transforms the old motifs of creation and divine kingship, appropriating them to Yahweh and tacitly, boldly denying any indebtedness to the cult of Baal. The original proclamation of the god of the oppressed managed to affirm Yahweh's cosmic *mišpāṭ* and, tacitly, the insignificance of Baal.

RESPONSES TO THE PROCLAMATION

Baal had been sole proprietor of the established order: the cosmos and, through his agents the kings, Canaan. *Mišpāṭ* belonged to him, him the gods acclaimed as king. Within this world, the *ʿapiru* had formed a kind of shadow polity. They lived in their own "place," thanks to their "personal god" and protector, El, while the realm of Baal continued to flourish in the city-states. That was the way things were: two polities, city and highlands; two gods, royal Baal and "tribal" El. They were used to coexistence. Now they saw a new face to the god they knew as their protector, and a new purpose. The news of Yahweh, the god who had overthrown the might of Egypt, whose *mišpāṭ* was incontestable, opened up previously unimaginable possibilities. *Yahweh ṣᵉbāʾōt* would take over everything. Baal would become a nonperson. The *ṣedeq* they lived by would displace and abolish the opposing *ṣedeq* of the Canaanite establishment. This expansion of the *ʿapiru*/Proto-Israelite experience must have seemed an audacious dream. Did some doubt or draw back? The armies of the kings had formidable skill and irresistible weaponry. "Strong is the people dwelling[35] in the land, and the cities are fortified and great indeed" (Num. 13:28). The status quo was not so bad. Better half a loaf. Leave well enough alone. Who could be sure of the outcome of such a venture? Perhaps it was not just the "enthroned" of the nations who felt panic at what was happening.

The same kinds of mixed feelings would have arisen in those who had not become *ʿapiru*, those who continued in servitude to the kings. Even if they were disaffected from the Baalist regime, Yahweh must have seemed a most pushy sort of god. Yet the claims made for him could plant a seed from which would spring both discontent with their lot and a readiness to live a new sort of life, the sort those others, those *ʿapiru*, had been managing to lead. What kind of soil would be receptive to such a seed? Certainly people who were anxious to remain safely within the circle of Baalist *ṣedeq* would hear of Yahweh with dismay. Those who were "making it" would find this new factor unnecessary and disruptive. That leaves the peasants who simply suffered, not resignedly so much as numbly, who had long since given up hope and certainly could not imagine themselves living any other sort of life than what they knew. The tradition tells us that Yahweh heard the cry of the oppressed. That cry comes from hopelessness as much as from pain. It comes from people who cannot "do" anything about their plight. It is a cry of absolute powerlessness. It may even be inarticulate, a silent scream, as the blood of Abel cried out from the ground (Gen. 4:10). Do those who thus cry out have a sense that their cry will be heard and, if so, of what kind of answer it will get? Perhaps the most they might have imagined was the status quo, only somehow better. To such people, the prospect that they would undergo the exodus experience—that they would be "led out" of oppression, that the kings of Canaan would suffer the fate of Pharaoh and his force, that those set free would be given the land, Yahweh's possession (Exod. 15:17)—would have been disorienting.

The news of the warrior god and his purpose, then, was unsettling to everybody. To the kings it caused panic. To those who experienced no discontent, it would be unnecessary. To the *ʿapiru* who had carved out a living and forged a kind of peoplehood, it would have seemed excessive, requiring as it did that they let go of their precarious autonomy. To those still suffering in hopelessness, it must have been terrifying. Yet it also represented a fulfillment of what had been begun in the land, with the Proto-Israelite movement and the social forces and sense of right that powered that movement. It was attractive, but people's instinct was to draw back. The salvation[36] offered was not only a gift but a demand. That is, it was available but not to velleity. Yahweh was serious. He was *'ēl qannā'* (Exod. 20:5), "a passionate god": serious, purposive, intense.[37] If his purpose is to be realized, there must be a corresponding seriousness of intent on the part of those he is to save. If the system is to be destroyed, a new system must be put in its place. The way people understand themselves and deal with one another must be transformed. There can be no half measures. Yahweh does not tinker with the status quo.

To accept this purpose and all its implications is to enter into a relationship called covenant.

CHAPTER 4

Covenant

The seed of Yahwism was planted in the soil of a certain kind of experience. It was an experience of oppression legitimated by the established order—both political and cosmic—and of withdrawal from that order. It was the *ʿapiru* experience: the centripetal pull of familiar if oppressive *ṣedeq,* and the centrifugal pull of another kind of *ṣedeq,* involving the call to insecurity and outlawry. At the end of the previous chapter I sketched something of the impact the Yahwistic proclamation must have had on the people of the land, both those who had gone *ʿapiru* and those who were securely within the circle of the established order. Now it is time to consider what kind of polity the people of Yahweh were to be. What did the *ṣedeq* of Yahweh entail? How was their life as a people to be lived out? It is time to go into the question of covenant. We begin with the narrative of Israel's constitution as a people, at Sinai, and, after this backtracking through the tradition, return to the point where we have just left off: the entrance of Yahwism into the land of Canaan.

SINAI

The long section of the Pentateuch from Exodus 19 to Numbers 10 is set at Mount Sinai. There, the covenant was made and various institutions (worship, Tabernacle and Ark, priesthood) and ordinances decreed. Only after a long sojourn does Israel resume its march to the land of Canaan.

Many scholars have wondered if the Sinai episode is not secondary. It interrupts the narrative of movement from Egypt to Canaan. It is not found in any of the summary recitations of Israel's history (Deut. 6:21–23; 26:5–9; Josh. 24:2–13) which Gerhard von Rad saw as containing the original story of Israel. Originally, it is argued, the story of Israel knew nothing of covenant making at Sinai.[1]

Where, then, does "Sinai" come from? The answer scholars give is: from the ongoing life of Israel as a people, generation after generation. In Israel's cult, generation after generation, there was an experience of covenant renewal. The cult comprised a theophany, the proclamation of Yahweh's sovereignty, the recitation of his laws, and the people's acceptance of that sovereignty, those laws. This liturgical experience was transmuted into the narrative we have in Exodus 19—24. The people's ongoing experience of covenant was "historicized" and inserted into the narrative of Israel's origins in exodus and wilderness wandering.

This is a question of how Israel's traditions developed, and it need not concern us here. But it is important to stress that link between "Sinai" and the experience of each subsequent generation in Israel. When people heard the account of "Sinai" they heard *their* story: not something true just of Israel-then but of Israel-now.[2]

LIBERATION AND COVENANT

Why, though, is "Sinai" placed where it is in the narrative? Why does covenant follow exodus? Because that sequence reflects Israel's historical experience—the experience of becoming a people. The slaves in Egypt could not be a people. They only became a people by being liberated, choosing and risking, undergoing a common experience. That liberation forged a common identity. And that identity had to be acknowledged; the implications, for the future, of what they had gone through had to be accepted. That acknowledgment and acceptance is at the heart of covenant. Just so, in the Book of Joshua, there is the "conquest," then the covenant at Shechem. The people ratify what has happened, both as past event and as something decisive for their future.

YAHWEH'S PURPOSE

They do not ratify only the bare event. At both Sinai and Shechem what people say yes to is the purpose of Yahweh, now fully known in their experience. As we have the exodus story there is a preliminary disclosure of that purpose. The burning bush episode anticipates Sinai. Yahweh tells Moses what he is going to do, and sends Moses to tell the other slaves what he is going to do. I think of a doctor, explaining to the patient at each step what is going to happen next, to calm the patient's anxiety and to secure cooperation. The early part of the exodus story (especially in the theologically explicit P passages) is trying to make the point that Yahweh knows what he is up to. He is not improvising. There is no stopping him from achieving his purpose: freeing the oppressed.

RESISTANCE

Yet the "patient" cooperates only reluctantly. The story contrasts the firmness of Yahweh's purpose with the fitful and changeable response of the slaves. They panic before danger and insecurity. They long for the familiar "house of slaves" and the fleshpots of Egypt. At the moment of liberation they "cry out" (Exod. 14:10) and say to Moses,

> 11What is this you have done to us
> in bringing us forth from Egypt?

Thus they echo the anguished regret of the oppressor:

> 5What is this we have done,
> that we have sent Israel
> from being our slaves?
> (Exod. 14:11, 5)

Oppressor and oppressed have the same kind of second thoughts.

To the complaints of the people–"It was better for us to be slaves to Egypt than to die in the wilderness" (14:12)—the only reply is "Be still":

> 13Fear not!
> Take your stand
> and see the salvation of Yahweh
> which he is doing for you today:
> the Egyptians you see today
> you will never again see, ever.
> 14Yahweh wars for you:
> You, be still.
> (Exod. 14:13, 14)

This answer offers assurance, but in so doing could well provoke even more anxiety. All it holds out by way of security is a promise and an exhortation, "Fear not."

So, according to the tradition, there was early and continuous disclosure of the divine purpose but people could not take it in. They resisted being freed. There was certainly no prior approval, on their part, of what Yahweh was up to. Though it was all announced beforehand people could not really imagine what was going to happen. The only "prior approval" came in the "cry of the oppressed." When that cry was heard and answered, it proved to be part velleity. Israel was led kicking and screaming out of slavery and into peoplehood. This the tradition insists on, and doubtless it reflects historical memory. The initiative lay with that pushy, passionate, willful god. If the slaves had had their way, and taken charge of their lives, they would have been slaves for good.

It all happened so quickly and confusingly. In a sense, there was no time for explanations, and what explanation there was people misunderstood or rejected. Hence the demand for security is sidestepped with the comprehensive but unspecific "Fear not," "Be still." Hence the need, once everything is over, for taking in what has happened. Now that they know what his purpose was, Yahweh has a few things to say about what is going to happen now. Now they can talk. This is what happens at Sinai, and that is why "Sinai" follows the exodus.

"NO OTHER GODS"

"Sinai," therefore, is an account of the experience, through acknowledgment and acceptance of Yahweh's purpose, of being formed as a people. In this experience—an experience, I stress, which every generation in Israel knew and took their identity from, in the cult—Yahweh is presented as cosmic lord. The storm theophany of Exodus 19 includes all the phenomena appropriate: cloud, smoke, fire, earthquake, and trumpet blast.[3] Finally, the introductions come (20:2). "I am Yahweh, your god, who brought you forth from the land of Egypt, from the house of slaves." The one to whom cosmic *mišpāṭ* belongs describes himself as the one "who caused you to go forth," *ʾašer hôṣēʾtîkā*. This is not simply a summary (necessarily brief) of their past dealings but a statement of who Yahweh is and of what he is all about.[4] This echoes the burning-bush story. There Yahweh disclosed his name, giving away his very self, in sending Moses to announce his purpose to deliver his people from slavery. In the tradition, the selfhood of Yahweh and his liberating activity are inseparable.

Then this liberating God asserts his sole *mišpāṭ.* Those who heard these words, especially people familiar with the ways of Canaan, knew the tyranny of other gods. To each god was a realm of competency and activity. Each god absolutized certain purposes and goods. They could make claims on people. People were thralls to the goods the gods stood for, and were tyrannized by the political and economic structures the gods legitimated. They had the say about people's lives. This whole draining realm of claims and competencies and legitimations of oppression, the whole cosmic politburo, Yahweh abolishes at a stroke, and thereby abolishes the power of that realm's terrestrial agents.[5] I, the liberator, am your god: you shall have no other gods besides me (or, over against me). The god who brings people out of slavery is the only one they are to take seriously.

We are likely to see this in terms of the psychic release it effects. Liberation indeed. Be free of the illusion that those other purposes and realms of experience and goods (like Bread) are central in your lives. Only my purpose, deliverance from oppression, really matters. In the real world, that's what counts. This is the way things are: Yahweh's proclamation is primarily an assertion of *mišpāṭ*. As such, it has to be accepted, affirmed, ratified, not just in the way we assent to the truth of what someone proposes as true but in the sense of making a commitment to live by it: letting it govern the way we see things, structure our sense of what is right, and have the say about how, in general and in specifics, we make choices. It has to be accepted as normative—as *ṣedeq*. And that acceptance will make the accepters a people. They will live within the circle of his *ṣedeq* and be ruled by his *mišpāṭ*.

"JUDGMENT" AND "JUDGMENTS"

What follows in the Sinai account bears this out. A series of "judgments" *(mišpāṭīm)*, in chaps. 20—23, spells out what Yahweh's sovereignty will mean in their life as a people. Then the people go through a ceremony of ratification. As we have the story, there is a sacrifice and a meal, and with their assent—"All that Yahweh has spoken we will do and hear" (24:7)—and with "the blood of the covenant," the freed slaves enter into the relationship that makes them a people. They accept Yahweh's *mišpāṭ* and his *mišpāṭīm,* the concrete ways in which his sovereignty is to be lived out.

These "judgments" and "words" are in many ways puzzling. It looks as though Yahweh expended vast efforts, using the full power of his cosmic lordship, so he could tell people what to do when their neighbor's ox got into their field. Historically, of course, the laws of Israel developed over many generations; when the Pentateuch was put together, the laws were incorporated into the Sinai portion of the historical narratives so as to show their connection with the foundational identity of Israel—as participating in the *ṣedeq* of the liberating god. Still, the awkwardness remains. How to understand these laws?

First, let us note that they fall into two sections. The Ten Words ("Decalogue") in 20:2–17 are spoken by God, as it seems, directly. The rest of these "judgments" (from the end of chap. 20 through chap. 23) are given through Moses while the people stand far off (cf. 20:18–21). Thus, the Ten Commandments have special authority. Second, the laws in chaps. 21—23 can be divided into two groups according to their form. One group (21:1—22:20) is a series of "case" laws. Each presents a case or situation ("When . . ."; "If . . .") and then gives the *mišpāṭ* for dealing with the case; the *mišpāṭ* is a procedure, determination of liability, remedy, indemnity, or punishment. The laws in the second group (22:21–31; 23:1–9) are markedly different.[6] They are short and uncomplicated. They do not specify a remedy or punishment for wrong done, like the case laws, but say *what* is wrong by commanding or forbidding something. "Do not wrong a stranger or oppress him . . ." (22:21). "Do not utter a false report" (23:1). "Take no bribe . . ." (23:8). Obviously, this is the form we find in each of the Ten Commandments: "Do not steal"; "Do not kill." This crispness in command or prohibition lends these laws a special authoritativeness, and this no-nonsense, categorical quality has led to their being called "apodictic."[7]

Case Laws

In the series of "judgments" of Exodus 20—23, then, some (the so-called case laws) obviously reflect the legal practice of Israel: how certain infractions were dealt with. Their placement in the context of Sinai gives them an exemplary character. If this sort of thing happens, this is the fair and equitable way to react. In some cases severity is called for. In other cases, do not go beyond what is fair, no matter how you might be inclined to act. (So, the *lex talionis*—"eye for eye, tooth for tooth"—moderates the retaliation the community may effect lest harm be done greater than the original harm.) Thus, they impart a sense of how conflict and wrongdoing are to be handled in the community of Israel; but their origins in the ongoing life of the people can be clearly seen in their specificity.[8]

Apodictic Laws

The apodictic laws, in contrast, are not so specific. They address the hearer as one who is to choose how to shape his or her life in those areas where the really important choices are made—those interactions where murder, theft, adultery, lying, oppression, cheating, and exploitation can occur. They warn the hearer from making ruinous choices in those situations. The apodictic laws are remarkably inclusive.

From that point of view, two things stand out. One is a formal characteristic of the apodictic laws, which I omitted to mention above. The commands and prohibitions are followed by what is called a motive clause. Do not oppress a stranger, "for you were strangers in the land of Egypt" (22:21; 23:9, RSV). Take no bribe, "for a bribe blinds the officials" (23:8, RSV). Honor your father and your mother, "that your days may be long in the land which Yahweh your god gives you" (20:12). These laws do not simply command or prohibit. They seem to be trying to persuade their hearer to do what they say. Now this is odd. Law requires, it does not exhort. Yet these apodictic laws make an appeal to the person they address. They do not "motivate" by stipulating a penalty (a ten-thousand-dollar fine and five years in prison) but by reference to one's own experience ("for you were strangers") or convictions ("for I will not put the wicked in the right," 23:7; "if you do afflict them, surely when they cry out to me, I will hear their cry," 22:23). They put themselves, and their hearer, into a larger context of human experience, feelings, sense of reality. Thus, they aim at formation of a right attitude as much as they aim at securing right behavior. It almost seems as if the list could be prolonged indefinitely. Precisely because these apodictic laws are inclusive, there are many other directives that could be given. There are many more areas, cognate with those that are dealt with, about which dos and don'ts could be given. The list of apodictic laws, however, suffices to get across the idea. It is not trying to be exhaustive. It is illustrative.

And this is the other thing that stands out. These laws have a metaphorical aspect. We have seen that the "widow and orphan" stand for the powerless. As the "stranger" has no standing, the widow and orphan have no one to enforce their rights. These three categories are representative of all members of a larger category. In the same way, what is commanded or prohibited in the apodictic laws is representative of an entire way of living. Make these sorts of choices; avoid those. Be the sort of person who does this; do not be like that. Suppose your enemy's ox or ass strays and you run into it: well, return it to him (cf. Exod. 23:4). This "law" can be violated—or kept—even if your enemy does not own an ox or ass. The saying uses the concrete universal of the situation to say, do not be petty or vindictive.[9] The best-known example of this "metaphorical" character of Israelite law is found not in Exodus 20—23 but in Deut. 25:4. "You shall not muzzle an ox when it treads out the grain." Again you do not need to have an ox to violate this injunction. All you need to do is be grasping and calculating.

Two more examples (note in each the form of apodictic law, the prohibition followed by motive clause):

> Do not remove an ancient landmark,
> and into the fields of the orphan do not come:
> for their Redeemer is strong:
> he will "contend their contention" against you.

The "ancient landmark" that can be removed is emblematic of a wide variety of situations and practices where opportunism can be active; so with "the fields of the orphan." Unscrupulous acquisitiveness should not think it can move in on weakness: there is a Redeemer (continuing the "property" image),[10] who will defend the right. Another example:

> When your enemy falls do not rejoice,
> and when he stumbles let not your heart exult:
> lest Yahweh see it and it be evil in his eyes,
> and he turn away from him his anger.

Again, the form: prohibition in second-person address, followed by motive clause ("lest . . ."); and the prohibition obviously is not aimed at behavior but at attitude. This is not surprising, since this "law" and the preceding example are both from the Book of Proverbs (23:10–11 and 24:17–18, respectively). The identity in form, in metaphorical applicability, and in their interest in attitude as much as in behavior shows how much the proverb and the so-called apodictic law have in common, and that suggests that some of the laws included in the Sinai covenant have a prehistory. As they stand, in the covenant context, they are the ways in which Yahweh wants his *mišpāṭ* lived out. In their origin, though, they are the kind of thing parents teach their children, handing on the clan's accumulated knowledge of life. Don't talk to strangers. Don't put off till tomorrow what you can do today. The conventional term for this kind of teaching, in the ancient world, is "wisdom."[11]

"Laws" and "Wisdom"

The "wisdom" affinities of what is presented as covenant law show through even in the present context. The effect is that Yahweh, whether addressing the people directly (in the Decalogue) or through Moses, comes off as a patriarchal figure, giving instruction in right and wrong. The god who frees from slavery, now that he has his own in a place apart and can talk to them, looks forward to their life together as a people and tells them what they should do if his purpose is to be fulfilled and they are indeed to be a people—and he tells them what, presumably, they already know. They know they are not to kill or lie or cheat. They also know, from bitter experience, that it is wrong to oppress the weak and take advantage of the powerless; but Yahweh pointedly insists on this, as if now that they are to be a people they might well begin treating others the way they were treated. "Do not oppress the stranger: you know the heart of a stranger, for strangers you were in the land of Egypt" (Exod. 23:9).

It is possible, then, to read at least the apodictic "laws" in these chapters[12] as "wisdom." Yahweh hands out good advice for the successful conduct of common life, with warnings and cautions and suasions—like someone who knows a route well, and gives prior warning about bottlenecks, potholes, speed traps, and detours, so that people traveling the route can avoid them.

There are some differences, however. This good advice comes from one who has the say about what is. He has special understanding of what most matters: as cosmic lord he is the one who set it all up. Further, the "advice" he gives is binding, not just in terms of the authoritativeness of the source, but as being given in the context of Yahweh's *mišpāṭ*—as the content, so to speak, of the relational structure being established in the covenant. Hence this traditional "wisdom" becomes the substance of politics.[13]

THE LANGUAGE OF POLITICS

I say politics not just because *ṣedeq* and *mišpāṭ* are involved but because the entire vocabulary in which Israel spoke of its relationship with Yahweh was derived from the realm of politics. To put it that way is misleading, however. It implies that there was some kind of bare "relationship" which then was dressed up in political clothes. In Israel the only way to talk about what we abstract as that "relationship" was to use the word *b^{e}rît*. We translate the word as "covenant," but *b^{e}rît* was the ordinary word for "treaty," a political arrangement between peoples or between rulers, involving obligation and *mišpāṭ*. One etymology for *b^{e}rît* derives it from a word that means "to bind": hence, ob-ligation.[14] Whatever its root meaning, the term *b^{e}rît* unmistakably and primarily referred to a political bond. It obliged the partners to deal with each other in certain ways, and the vocabulary for this is instructive. One partner undertook to "love" the other, "with all his heart," just as he would "know"—acknowledge, recognize—him.[15] He would "serve" him or be his "servant." He would "go after" him, be his follower.[16] He would "cleave" to him. He would "fear" him. He would "hear" or "listen to" or "obey" him.[17] The overlord would "speak" and what he spoke were his "words." His "words" spelled out what that love and service concretely meant. They specified or particularized the relationship between them.[18]

Thus, the one would "hear" and of course do the "words" of the overlord. This would mean "good" for the vassal: "good" was a technical term for both the substance and the consequences of the treaty relationship.[19] For his part, the overlord would defend, save, fight for, vindicate the treaty partner. All this was sealed with an oath, confirmed by a sacrifice and/or a meal.

In fact, these elements fall into a stereotyped pattern in the ancient Near East, the so-called treaty formulary. The overlord would present himself, recount the history of his and his predecessors' dealings with the present prospective treaty partner, lay down the obligation to unconditional loyalty, elaborate in concrete terms what that loyalty would entail, and then, in connection with the oath the partner was to take, invoke witnesses (the gods of the two partners) and sanctions (blessings and curses). There is also provision for storage of the copies of the treaty in a sanctuary and its periodic rereading lest its requirements slip out of memory.

This vocabulary of international relations is itself of course drawn from a more basic realm of human experience, that of friendship and family. The overlord who is to be "loved" is "father" to his partner "son," or sometimes they become "brothers."[20] Even in our day we speak of "friendship" between nations. Probably because of these interpersonal connotations of the biblical vocabulary, we tend to miss its primary, political import. We are so used to hearing that vocabulary in a religious context—as when the catechism, using good biblical categories, tells little children that God made them to "know, love, and serve" him—that we naturally assume that it is religious. It is not. It is political.[21]

Hence the Sinai story is a story about how Israel became a people. Yahweh "spoke" his "words" to them, as sovereign, as having *mišpāṭ,* and the people responded with an oath: "All that Yahweh has spoken we will do and hear" (Exod. 24:7). Thus, they swear to "love" Yahweh and "keep his commandments" (cf. Exod. 20:6), and to "serve" no one else (cf. 20:5).

We should be cautious, then, in imposing on the Sinai story our own categories of "religion" or "the relationship between God and man."[22] Exodus 19—24 tells us how Yahweh formed from a mixed multitude of the oppressed in Egypt a political entity, a people, called

"Israel." A political entity is defined by the *ṣedeq* it lives by and the *mišpāṭ* it accepts. That is what "Sinai" is about. That is why the story uses the terms *bᵉrît,* "love," "serve," "words," and so on, and why there is the oath, "All that Yahweh has spoken we will do and hear." There is no reason not to interpret the political language literally. This is an account of how a specific people, at a specific time in a certain place, was formed. The *ṣedeq* and *mišpāṭ* that defines that political entity is Yahweh's. No one else—no god or king—is to have the say over them. No consensus is to govern their dealings with one another except the sense of right imparted by the one who hears the cry of the oppressed. It is not the case that Israel is a people, alongside the other nations of the Near East, which happens to choose Yahweh as its god. That is backwards. Rather, there is a political entity called Israel, alongside the nations, only because people chose to live by a certain vision and a certain form of life. Those who became sharers in this political movement, by accepting that vision and form of life, did so by renouncing all other allegiances and instead acknowledging the sovereignty—the *mišpāṭ*—of Yahweh. They became a people by knowing, loving, and serving one ruler, Yahweh, rather than any other. "He only is our judge."

ISRAEL: A POLITICAL MOVEMENT

When we think of Yahwism entering Canaan, then, we should not imagine a missionary venture like that of Boniface or Xavier. It was a social movement. An image in the Song of Deborah is helpful:

> From the report of the recruiters,
> between drawings of water,
> there they repeat the justices of Yahweh,
> the justices of his peasantry in Israel.
> (Judges 5:11a)

The Hebrew is difficult and can be interpreted in several ways. This reading[23] pictures the news getting around, at places where people get together, about the *ṣidqōt Yahweh,*[24] the acts of *ṣedeq* effected by Yahweh on behalf of, and through, his peasantry against the kings of Canaan. Thrones are tottering. Pass the word. Join us.

Those serfs and pastoralists of Canaan were confronted with a hard choice, therefore, in hearing the proclamation of Yahweh's purpose to free from oppression. In some ways they were in the same position the Proto-Israelites in Canaan had been in. Like the *'apiru* groups who became Elohistic Israel, they were faced with the prospect of risk, insecurity, and outlawry. But with the coming of Yahwism, things were different. The Proto-Israelites had backed into peoplehood: they became a people through the experience of liberation, as a kind of byproduct of that experience. Even the *ṣedeq* that gave them their identity was so to speak discovered, through the changes within them that their embracing of insecurity had effected. That withdrawal from the established order had been chosen without any consciousness of a clear goal they were moving toward. There was no already-constituted people they could join. Now, though, with the arrival of Yahwism and its bearers the people of the land had a choice to make that involved both incorporation into the new social formation and acceptance of the *ṣedeq* that moved it and gave it its identity. That *ṣedeq* made its demand on them not as an option they might entertain at their leisure but as calling for a decision—and the decision was not just to choose Yahweh's *ṣedeq* and *mišpāṭ* but to become part of Yahweh's people. This was not "backing into" anything, nor was it merely "withdrawal" from the established order. It meant conscious revolt.

RESPONSES

The stories we have reflect a variety of responses to this proclamation. Some sided with Israel secretly: Rahab and her family (Joshua 2) can be seen as representative.[25] Some refused to join in the new movement—perhaps the puzzling "Meroz" of the Song of Deborah (Judges 5:23) reflects that response. The Gibeonites made a separate peace (Joshua 9).[26] Some city-states—notably Jerusalem—retained power, unaffected by the Israelite revolt. The catalogue in Judges 1 reveals that the movement's success was partial and piecemeal.[27]

Even where people did respond to the *ṣedeq* of Yahweh, and by accepting his *mišpāṭ* became "Sons of Israel," that response must have been piecemeal and partial as well. The old ways continued to have a hold on people's imaginations. The stories of the wilderness wanderings surely reflect the experience of the Canaanites who chose to enter the Israelite confederation: reluctance, discouragement, murmuring, incapacitating fear in the face of the kings' military power, second thoughts, anguished need for assurance, outright mistrust of the strange and passionate god who was wrenching them out of their familiar life.[28] Where did this response come from if not from the slave mentality of Baalism? The complaint of the Moses group says it all: "It was better for us to be slaves to Egypt than to die in the wilderness."[29] Yahweh promised liberation and abolished the claims of other gods and of the centralized power the gods legitimated, but there was no overnight transformation of people's self-understanding. Slaves always know where they stand. They have a kind of security, their hands always handling the familiar thing, their feet on the known track. Baalism embodied and fostered that security. Or rather, Baalism embodied and fostered a form of self-understanding that absolutized security. A sense of reality and of self shaped by the stories about Baal would include certain expectations: that the future is predictable, that things will work out just so, that there will be no surprises. Those expectations would attach to a sense of entitlement. The god who is "judge" has the say about the way things are and about what is to be, and his worshipers, because they are his worshipers, are entitled to have him deliver on what he stands for.

Such was the vision of reality of the Canaanite world: earnest, self-regarding, anxious, full of a sense of being owed assurance and results. These attitudes die hard. The new god, Yahweh, surely eluded them. The promise of victory and justice and peoplehood that Yahwism held out ran counter to their desire for certitude and to the expectation that they would always know where they stood. The stories of rebellion in the wilderness, again, show how incommensurable were this mind-set and Yahweh's way of doing things. Fear not. Be still. Trust. Implicitly Yahweh is saying, There is nothing you can do. The demand for proofs he answers with signs, and those are not really all that impressive.[30] What signs and wonders would suffice to satisfy that impatient, needful desire for absolute assurance? For Yahweh to accommodate himself fully to it would mean making himself Baal.

To accept the *ṣedeq* of Yahweh, therefore, was to accept not only his purpose to free from oppression but the demand for trust. It meant letting go of the cautious, servile obsession with security that people's entire experience had formed in them. That obsession was the real source of their oppression.

YAHWEH, THE GOD OF *'APIRU*

The stories of murmuring and rebellion, therefore, and the exhortations to "be strong" and "fear not," in their frequency and insistence, suggest a paradox. People who chose to live by Yahweh's *ṣedeq* and become part of Israel made themselves *'apiru* in the eyes of the kings of Canaan. They stood outside the circle of legitimacy. But in their own eyes as well (as we saw earlier) they must have seemed *'apiru*. If the old ways of thinking perdured within themselves, they too must have felt they were outside the circle. To choose Yahweh was to choose unrighteousness. That is one element of the paradox. The other element is that their choice of Yahweh was a choice they made as they were, formed by the Baalist consensus. As they were, they craved security and results, and found it difficult to let go of those expectations. Yet they were choosing one who demanded that of them. Radically unquiet people chose a god whose message was "Be still." Only by that kind of trust, though, could they truly accept his *ṣedeq* and live within the circle he defined. Precisely because in their anxious demand for certitude they did not trust, they put themselves outside his circle. Their rebelliousness amounted to a rejection of his *ṣedeq* and his *mišpāṭ*: vis-à-vis Yahweh they were *'apiru*.

The consciousness of illegitimacy, outlawry, and unrighteousness was central to being Israel, therefore. This is a theme we will keep coming back to. Suffice it for now to say that, in the double sense just explained, Yahweh is the god of the *'apiru*.

CHAPTER 5

Early Israel

To see what the tradition tells us about Israelite understanding of power, we have been tracing the development of Israel's existence as a people. We turn now from a study of Israelite origins (exodus and "conquest") to a look at their first generations as an ongoing political entity in the land of Canaan. This chapter will examine the institution of Holy War, and related matters, and then turn to the study of three very old poems—the Song of Deborah, the Song of Hannah, and the Oracles of Balaam—in order to get a sense of Israel's self-understanding, in those earliest times, as the people of Yahweh. But first a terminological note.

The canonical arrangement of the Books of Joshua and Judges has resulted in a certain way of thinking about the time before Israel had a king. First there was the "conquest" of Canaan, then there was the time of the Judges: "Early Israel." Two periods, distinct from each other, as Joshua is one book and Judges another.

The historical reconstruction I am following would call this schematization into question. Israel-in-the-land was not the result of an invasion or migration by a homogeneous people displacing the native population. It was the result of a social movement among the oppressed of Canaan, who heard the proclamation of Yahweh's "justices," chose to be incorporated into his people, and so renounced the *mišpāṭ* of the kings and of the gods who legitimated the king's power. One could even say that Israel-in-the-land *was* that social movement. In its formative period Israel was a people involved in struggle with the oppressive kings of Canaan and their professional warriors, "the nations round about." It was a people constantly increasing through the incorporation of other groups, whether as whole tribes or as elements of already constituted tribes.[1] Thus, Early Israel was a people constantly being formed, over the two hundred or so years prior to monarchy.

NĀQĀM AND HOLY WAR

The dynamics of this formation can best be understood, I think, in terms of *nāqām,* "vindication, vengeance." Israel was the people that chose to accept Yahweh's *mišpāṭ*. This choice made them *ʿapiru* in the eyes of the kings of Canaan. To vindicate their own power and legitimacy, and themselves, the kings had to take action against those who had withdrawn from the circle of royal *ṣedeq*. They had to effect *nāqām*.

Ironically, in so doing the kings of Canaan put themselves outside the circle of Yahweh's *ṣedeq*. They were defying the authority of the cosmic lord, by seeking to uphold their own, oppressive *mišpāṭ*. So Yahweh effects *nāqām*. He vindicates his justice and those who live by it. The fragment of ancient poetry preserved at the end of Joshua 10 is revealing:

> The sun stood still
> the moon stayed
> until he [Yahweh] had executed vengeance
> against the nation of his enemies.[2]
> (Josh. 10:13)

"BE STILL"

The tradition insists on this: Yahweh wars on behalf of Israel. But what is *Israel* to do? The tradition is clear on this, too: "Be still" (Exod. 14:13–14). If Israel relied on military might they would be arrogating *mišpāṭ* to themselves and rejecting the *ṣedeq* of Yahweh. They would be living by the same sense of *ṣedeq* that caused the kings to amass armies and multiply horse and chariot: of *ṣedeq* arising from, and validating, obsession with security and freedom from risk. For Israel to rely on power and strategy would mean rebellion against Yahweh.[3]

All Israel can *do,* then, is "cry out." In answer to that cry comes the assurance, Yahweh will war for you, and the word: Be still. As if the injunction to "be still" was asking too much, there is the alternative and more frequent exhortation *'al tirā',* "Fear not," or "Do not be afraid," as if to say: You are afraid, and want to do something, but the first thing to do is to stop being afraid; then, something can be done. You think you see the situation: the enemy has you in his hand. But you don't see the situation, really. In fact, Yahweh has put the enemy in your hand. That result is assured.

THEOPHANY AND PANIC

So in face of the panic that besets the people, there is a reversal. It is the enemy who should feel panic. They have Yahweh to contend with. We saw in the Song of Miriam (Exodus 15, in vv 14–16) how the leaders and the enthroned ones of the nations, when they see the procession of the people to Canaan, are overtaken by dread. Pangs of terror seize them. This was because they knew that what had happened to Pharaoh was about to happen to them. It was all over for them. This motif of panic is a constant in accounts of Holy War. What causes dread to come upon the enemy is the appearance of Yahweh. He goes forth, or "comes," with the heavenly armies, treading upon the high places of the earth. The mountains tremble and melt, cloud and fire attend his appearance. The imagery is that of the Divine Warrior: the god to whom cosmic *mišpāṭ* belongs.

That cosmic lordship is exercised on Israel's behalf. The *mišpāṭ* and *ṣedeq* Yahweh vindicates is not just foundational to his lordship over Israel but belongs to him as "god in heaven above and on earth below," to quote Rahab in Joshua 2:

> I know that Yahweh has given you the land, and that terror of you has fallen upon us, and that all the "sitters"[4] of the land totter before you. For we have heard that Yahweh dried up the waters of the Red Sea before you when you went forth from Egypt. . . . We heard and our hearts melted, and there arose no more any spirit in any man before you: for Yahweh your god—he is god in heaven above and on earth below. (Josh. 2:9–11)

The language is clearly Deuteronomistic, but the passage is helpful for showing how the tradition combined the *mišpāṭ* of Yahweh as covenant lord of Israel and his cosmic *mišpāṭ*, and for showing how the panic Yahweh produced was central in the taking of the land.

For its part, Israel goes forth also, in the train of Yahweh and the hosts of heaven. With the ark of covenant as the focus of Yahweh's presence, as he "goes forth before them,"[5] the Israelites march in his processional way. They replicate the phenomena of the storm theophany, with shouts, noise, lights, and trumpet blast.[6] It is this appearance of the Divine Warrior that undoes the enemy, causing them to flee in panic or turn their swords against one another.

THE SONG OF DEBORAH

These elements of Holy War can be seen in the very old poem we call the Song of Deborah (Judges 5). The introduction (v. 3), seemingly in the style of a bard entreating the attention of his audience, addresses "kings" and "princes": "Hear . . . give ear." The song does indeed have something to say to them, but the singer is no court troubador. These words sound a minatory note.[7] What follows shows why they should listen well. A series of quick vignettes impressionistically linked describes a battle against the kings of Canaan. First comes the Divine Warrior's march from the south:

> 4Yahweh in your going forth from Seir,
> in your marching from the highlands of Edom,
> earth quaked,
> 5mountains shuddered,
> before Yahweh, the One of Sinai,
> before Yahweh, god of Israel.[8]
> (Judges 5:4–5)

This description of the processional of Yahweh and his retinue starts the action *in medias res*. Unbeknownst to the kings, the warrior god is marching inexorably to effect "justices" for his own. The scene switches abruptly to the land, as if following the cinematic convention, "Meanwhile, back in Canaan, . . ." Trade (a royal monopoly in the feudalist political economy) is disrupted. Kings themselves are no longer secure. Something is brewing:

[6]Caravans ceased,
kings went by paths,
went by roundabout ways.
[7]The peasantry battened
in Israel, battened on spoil,
because Deborah arose,
because a Mother in Israel arose.
[8]Her force was chosen from raw recruits;
then it warred at the gates of the cities.
Was shield seen or spear
among forty contingents in Israel?[9]
(Judges 5:6–8)

"War was in the gates": the power of the kings was exercised from fortified cities. Social restiveness might flourish or have scope in the countryside, and guerrilla warfare be waged, but it was unthinkable to take on the professional armies of the kings in their strongholds, especially when they enjoyed a monopoly on arms. Despite the overwhelming superiority of the kings' warriors, the battle was taken to the very gates.

"Gates" has another connotation. Commerce, administration of justice, and other activities of public life were carried on "in the gates" of the city, and "gates" came to stand for the whole complex of what we might call the power structure of society, somewhat as in the United States "Wall Street" stands for the world of finance or "The White House" for the government. Hence, "gates" is shorthand for the established order and the class that runs it—what is sometimes called The Establishment.[10] Judges 5:8, therefore, celebrates the war of the unarmed peasantry against the military elite in their stronghold, the countryside against the city-state, and the dispossessed and exploited against the power structure that oppressed them; it can be translated ". . . warred against the gates."

Verse 10 echoes the ironic address of v. 3, in addressing "you riders on asses, you who sit in spacious houses," the wealthy and highborn, telling them to "muse upon those who walk upon the way." The ass was a royal beast of burden (cf. Zech. 9:9); the " 'sitters' in spacious houses" are those enthroned in their palaces. As we saw above, the people at the wells repeat the *ṣidqōt Yahweh,* the "justices" of Yahweh and of his peasants. The movement grows, as the news gets around (v. 11). Finally (v. 11), "down to the gates marched the people of Yahweh." Israel is a people, not a nation or nation-state *(gōy);* but the "people" is also his "army" *(ʿām).* Again, in v. 13: "the people of Yahweh marched down against the warriors."[11]

So far, then, the poem has described two sets of preparations. The tympani have been rumbling continually under the music. Yahweh is on the march from the south. The movement of revolt is spreading, and the people of Yahweh are marching down to the "gates" from the highlands, mustered according to their tribes (vv. 14–18). We expect to hear next how the heavenly army and the peasant army of Israel converge in attack upon the stronghold, but no:

> 19The kings came, they warred,
> then warred the kings of Canaan.
> (Judges 5:19)

"Come" is a technical term for going to battle (along with "go out" and "go up"). The chiastic structure with the repetition of "warred" and "kings" lends their appearance a certain solemnity in striking contrast to the skulking and darting of their last mention in the poem (v. 6). It is as if they take the initiative, or think that the outcome of events lies with them. There is a surprise for them, though. The heavenly hosts fight on behalf of Israel:

> 20From heaven warred the stars,
> from their stations they warred against Sisera.
> (Judges 5:20)

As with the battle against the coalition of kings in Joshua 10, the heavenly bodies collaborate with Israel against the enemy. Here there seems to be some kind of downpour causing the torrent *(wādī)* Qishon to wipe out the army of the Canaanite general Sisera:

> 21Wadi Qishon swept them away,
> Slammed into them, Wadi Qishon
> (Judges 5:21)

The onomatopoetic description of the chariotry—"Then hammered the hooves of the horses" (v. 22)—sounds ironically as the enemy's steeds gallop off in retreat.

Two further scenes bring the poem to a close. Sisera, the Canaanite general, on the run, seeks refuge in the tent of Jael. She gives him a royal welcome indeed, seducing him into death. His skull hammered, he lies where he went down (vv. 24–27). Abruptly the scene shifts. Sisera's mother stands at the window looking for her son's return, wondering why he is so long in coming, while in the room behind her the ladies of the court reassuringly murmur the inventory of the spoil they fancy will be brought home, a slave, a maidservant apiece, a kerchief of dyed embroidered stuff. . . . Freeze frame. The End.

The Song of Deborah is masterly and yet naive. It seems to exult in the defeat of the kings and the bloody, ignominious death of Sisera, but that feeling is not dominant in the poem so much as a kind of giddy surprise that the world is turned upside down.[12] The novelty has not yet worn off. The picture of Sisera's mother, and the address to those who "sit" in spacious houses, and the monition to kings and princes show that the old order is passing. "Justices" are being done, and must be celebrated. In this hymn we have a window into the upheavals Yahwism produced in the feudal political and social economy of southern Canaan in the twelfth and eleventh centuries B.C., and into the practice of Holy War in Early Israel.

"JUDGES"

The role of Deborah is noteworthy, too, in two respects. First, Deborah is "a Mother in Israel" (v. 7): whatever the precise meaning of this title, it is she who rallies the peasantry to take on the kings and their warriors. And it is another woman, Jael, who finishes the battle by dispatching the Canaanite general. In the new political entity, Israel, women have a different role than the Canaanite world (so far as we can tell) could ever allow or imagine. The world is turned upside down indeed.[13]

Second, Deborah's role is typical of the exercise of leadership in Early Israel. How do unorganized peasants get themselves together to fight against skilled mercenary forces? There are two problems. One is that the attempt to overthrow centralized, hierarchical power will be futile if the means of doing so merely replicate the old forms. A "strong man," pressing reluctant peasants into military service, ruthlessly organizing the restive population into disciplined cadres, and relying on force of arms, would be but an avatar of the kings who are to be overthrown. He will inevitably become one who "rides on an ass" (Judges 5:10). Nothing would really change. The other problem, as we saw above, is that such forms of social organization amount to the arrogation of *mišpāṭ* and in effect are rebellion against Yahweh. Foundational to the identity of Israel is the conviction that Yahweh is alone the one who vindicates the right and those who are in the right. "*Nāqām* is mine," says Yahweh (Deut. 32:25).

In the figure of Deborah and her co-leader Barak, and the other "Judges" of Israel, we see the Israelite solution to these problems. Our sources show the heavily theological editorial hand of the Deuteronomistic Historian (Dtr), who as we shall see has thought these matters through well. In Dtr, the leader is "raised up" by Yahweh. The "spirit of Yahweh" comes upon someone—like Gideon, like Jephthah—and in virtue of that afflatus the leader summons the people to war, reminding them of their covenant obligation,[14] and gives them heart by the exhortation "Fear not," and by the assurance, "Yahweh is with you: he has given the enemy into your hand."

The *mišpāṭ* of the leader in Holy War, therefore, is derivative, not something he or she exercises by personal title, and is purely ad hoc. Some Holy War stories (and those in this respect least marked by the hand of Dtr) even show the leader asking Yahweh, through divination, for marching orders. The people were not engaged in saving themselves by their own hand. They were engaged in what the Song of Deborah calls "coming, for Yahweh's help against the warriors." Yahweh was, of course, the helper.[15] The enterprise was his.

As if to underline this, the stories of how the Holy War leaders were called to office emphasize their inadequacy. In themselves the "Judges" lack the qualities that would recommend them for leadership. "How could *I* save Israel?" Gideon asks Yahweh's messenger (Judges 6:15): "my clan is the poorest in Manasseh, and I am least in my father's house."[16] Saul, too, is in one tradition a figure of fun: "How can this one save us?" (1 Sam. 10:27). But "the spirit of God came mightily upon" him (11:6, RSV) and there is a remarkable transformation. It has been suggested that these stories of call to leadership follow a convention of "demurrer narratives": "stylized, socially mandated self-deprecations."[17] Even so, the supposed genre reflects a conviction that power and position are not to be sought, which suggests a deep-seated mistrust of ambitioning *mišpāṭ*. This shows up in the theological assertion that it is only through "the spirit of Yahweh" that anyone is fit to exercise leadership. We are dealing with complementary traits in Israelite culture. One is mistrust of power-seeking. Another is the conviction that *mišpāṭ* belongs to Yahweh. And a third, mediating as it were between the two, is the conviction that the person best suited to be leader is the one who has no qualities of leadership in himself. Or rather, the one best suited to be leader is the one who is able to admit his need: that he is full of fear, and has no resources within himself to "save" anyone, himself included. Those who enter upon the office of leader in that spirit will not make the mistakes ambitious men make, of overreaching themselves, acting arrogantly, justifying themselves at the expense of others, proceeding as if the whole success of their projects depends upon themselves alone, and absolutizing their own *mišpāṭ* by identifying it with *ṣedeq*.

Ḥērem

Leadership—the "judgment" that the "Judge" exercises—comes from Yahweh, and to Yahweh belong the spoils of war. Here we come to one of the least attractive aspects of the practice of Holy War in Israel, the institution known as *ḥērem*. The Hebrew word means a setting apart. Something which is subject to *ḥērem* is put aside for some special purpose, and itself is said to be *ḥērem*. According to at least some of the stories in the tradition, what was taken in battle in Holy War was to be treated as *ḥērem*, something "devoted" to Yahweh or put under the "ban," to use the standard translations of the term. Spoils, chattel, and people were treated alike: they were destroyed. Hence, *ḥērem* for all practical purposes means the total destruction of the enemy and the enemy's goods.

Three things need to be said. One is that in Dtr, to be considered in chapter 7, *ḥērem* has a pronounced symbolic and theological meaning, so that (whatever was actually done in early Israel) the accounts of its practice should not be read literalistically. Second, the practice of *ḥērem* kept war from being an instrument of acquisitiveness. People fighting the battles of Yahweh were not looking to line their pockets. War is not to be a way of making yourself great and rich, or to acquire territorial or commercial advantage.[18] Third, if we understand the practice of *ḥērem* in the context of the peasant revolt theory, as Gottwald has tried to do,[19] it appears in a new light. The appurtenances of the kings and the royal establishment, the metals and material resources on which oppressive rule was based, are to be done away with. The destruction of the existing order is to be total. Otherwise, the new leadership will (so to speak) simply move into the presidential palace.

Celibacy

It seems that those engaged in Holy War practiced sexual abstinence,[20] and this accords with what we have just seen. To fight the wars of Yahweh required that one be wholly focused or centered. It required that one be *qannā'*, "passionate," as Yahweh is the *'ēl qannā'*, the passionate god. For this reason, all of the most central objects of human intention are to be put aside: building a home, raising a family, working the soil.[21] It is not that a "business as usual" attitude is inappropriate to the enterprise of Holy War or, more generally, to the fulfillment of Yahweh's purpose, though that is true. No, raising a family or planting a vineyard are not "business as usual." They are tasks that you must be wholly present to. You cannot be divided or scattered. The most general designation for the object of such focused intention, something that one has to be entirely present to, is the term "holy." By definition, therefore, you can only attend to one holy thing at a time. You are only one person.

The Nāzīr

Special dedication is the point of the institution of the *nāzīr,* or nazirite: one dedicated. The requirements of the nazirite vow are given in Numbers 6: one must avoid strong drink, ritual defilement, and cutting the hair of the head. The story of Samson (Judges 16:15–22) helps us to understand the meaning of these practices. When Samson was unfaithful to his nazirite vow he lost his strength, and the Philistines were able to subdue him. Originally, it seems, the *nāzīr*'s dedication was in function of fighting the battles of Yahweh.[22]

So the institution of *ḥērem* and, less centrally, the nazirite vow and the practice of celibacy indicate the seriousness of Holy War. It is important to place these matters in the context of Yahweh's identity and purpose as the *môṣî'*, the one who "brings forth" from slavery. This is what he is wholly centered on. That liberating social transformation supersedes all other concerns, even those that are most holy. Or rather, those other concerns, holy though they are, can only be realized if the foundational and central and defining reality of Yahweh's purpose and activity—his *ṣedeq* and *mišpāṭ*—is realized. He hears the cry of the oppressed, and is strong to save.

THE SONG OF HANNAH

Another poem is helpful to show how central to the self-understanding of Early Israel was the conviction that Yahweh's chief concern was freeing from oppression, and that the content of his *ṣedeq* was "justice." This is the Song of Hannah (1 Sam. 2:1–10). It is a hymn celebrating the "salvation" Yahweh effects, and how he turns things upside down. If we read it in the context of Early Israel it bears eloquent testimony to the overthrow of the oppressor and to the new social order Yahweh's "salvation" works. If we read it apart from such a context, however, it means something else, as we shall see.[23]

> 1My heart exults in Yahweh,
> exalted is my horn in Yahweh,[24]
> my mouth widens upon my enemies:
> I rejoice in your salvation.
> 2There is none holy like Yahweh,
> no rock like our god.[25]
> 3Do not go on so, speaking
> so haughty, haughty:
> outrage goes forth from your mouth.
> For a god of knowings is Yahweh:
> by him deeds are weighed.
> (1 Sam. 2:1–3)

The language and sequence of thought in the first three verses is already familiar to us. The mouth "widening" upon enemies uses the imagery of swallowing we saw in Exod. 15:12, where the Egyptians were swallowed into the nether world.[26] That Yahweh is incomparable amongst the gods, that no other god is like him (v. 2), is the burden of Exod. 15:11. And the monition to someone who "speaks" is, like the address of Judges 5:3, 10, aimed at a king or at someone, like a king, who "speaks" and whose "word" is determinative. Exploitative arrogance has consequences, for "a god of knowings is Yahweh." That is, not only does Yahweh "know" what happens,[27] he is faithful: he "knows"—recognizes, acknowledges, accepts, is faithful to—his own.[28] Just because people have the say about things they should not think they enjoy impunity. Yahweh "knows," and is active.

His activity is seen in a series of contrasts:

> 4The bows of warriors are crushed;
> stumblers gird on force.
> 5The satisfied for bread become hirelings;
> the hungry batten on spoil.
> The barren gives birth to seven;
> she who has many sons is bereaved.
> 6Yahweh causes to die and causes to live,
> to go down to Sheol and to go up.[29]
> 7Yahweh causes to be poor and causes to be rich,
> making low even those exalted,
> 8raising up from the dust the pauper.
> From the ashheap he exalts the poor,
> to cause (them) to sit with the nobles:
> the throne of glory he causes them to inherit.
> (1 Sam. 2:4–8a)

The weapons of the professional warrior are broken,[30] while "stumblers" become strong. The "stumbler" is one of whom no skill in fighting could be expected, no match for the "warriors"; yet he "girds on force," as if putting on, not armor,[31] but the might of the Divine Warrior (v. 4). Those who were satisfied[32] take any job they can just to eat, while those who were starving "batten on spoil" (v. 5a); the echo of Judges 5:7 is unmistakable. Those who enjoyed fullness of life go down to Sheol, while those whose lot was death are given life (v. 6). Those whose home was the dumps supplant the "sitters" on thrones (vv. 7, 8a). "Nobles" in v. 8a may be misleading as a translation of *n*^{e}*dîbîm*. The root *ndb* has to do with being generous. It occurs in Judges 5:2 and 9, referring to those who took part in the struggle against the Canaanite kings.[33] Here it may mean the same, and the poor then "sit"—are, ironically, enthroned—with those leaders. The language of kingship is obvious here: "sit," "throne," "inherit" *(nḥl).* In the Song of Miriam (Exod. 15:17) Yahweh makes a dais for his "sitting" on the mountain which is his *naḥᵃlāh,* his "heritage." The imagery can be traced back to the Baal myths:

ksu ṯbth	the throne of his "sitting"
arṣ nḥlth	the land of his heritage.
	(*CTA* 3.6.15–16)

In Exod. 15:17, these kingship terms are applied to Yahweh both as cosmic lord and as Israel's lord, "planting" the people he has "gotten" for himself (v. 16) on the mountain of his heritage, his sanctuary. Here in the Song of Hannah it is the poor and lowly who have as their "heritage" a glorious throne. The use of this imagery is ironic. It is as if those whom monarchy made and treated as nobodies now wander into the deserted throne room and take turns sitting on the seat of royal *mišpāṭ*. More to the point, the throne now is empty and unused. Anyone can sit in it.[34]

All this transformation of the social order is the work of Yahweh not just as Israel's god but as cosmic lord:

For Yahweh's are the straits of earth:[35]
upon them he set the world.
9The feet of his faithful he guards;
the wicked in darkness are immobile.
For not by strength is a man mighty.
10Yahweh crushes those who contend with him,
against them in heaven he thunders.[36]
Yahweh adjudicates the ends of earth.
(1 Sam. 2:8b–10a)

The reversals he effects are in conformity with the way he set things up. They are of a piece with the structure of reality. The wicked *(rᵉšāʿīm)* by their violence and injustices[37] involve themselves in opposition to the way things are; they do not live in the real world. Thus while those who know Yahweh's *ḥesed*—his *ḥᵃsīdīm*—move surely and without let, in freedom, protected by him, the wicked are like those trying to get around in darkness: they stand frozen, immobile, unable to take a step, for all their warrior's might (v. 9). They have taken on the one to whom governance of the world belongs.[38]

In discussing the contrasts of vv. 4–8a, I have omitted v. 5b. The pairing of the barren woman and the prolific woman does not seem to fit with the other, "societal" oppositions. Being rich or poor, exalted or lowly, hungry or starving, a warrior or a weakling all have to do with one's place in society, and the point of the poem is that Yahweh transforms the political order on behalf of the powerless. If the barren-fruitful contrast is taken as paradigmatic, though, the other contrasts become merely metaphorical for opposing extremes, a kind of merismus. The point of the Song of Hannah then would be something like: whatever happens is Yahweh's doing. He gives life, and he gives death. If you are rich, or if you are poor, that is because Yahweh has decreed it so.[39] He is boss. Far from being a celebration of his purpose and achievement on behalf of the dispossessed, the poem seems a grim statement of divine determinism, with at most a cautionary note included for those who would arrogantly rely on their own strength. Not only determinism: in his power, Yahweh upsets everybody's tidy world. If you're rich he will make you poor, and vice versa. A certain arbitrariness seems to characterize this divine economy. Omnipotence is all.

I cannot imagine a greater contrast betwen two ways of understanding the same text. A purely "religious" approach to the Song of Hannah would find the "omnipotence" reading congenial. The reading I have proposed—based on a certain reconstruction of the origins of Israel, and taking as central and normative in Israel's self-understanding the tradition's insistence on justice for the oppressed—seems to me to present a rather more attractive image of the Almighty.[40]

At that, the barrenness-fecundity contrast can be seen in economic and political terms. A large family has the advantage in agriculture and animal husbandry, and the prospect of numerous progeny is of a piece with the agrarian blessings promised to Yahweh's own. If the woman "many in sons" is taken, together with "warriors" and the "exalted," as a member of the oppressor class, bereavement fits in with the fate that lies in store for those "wicked" ones.[41]

This Song is placed on the lips of Hannah, as a thanksgiving hymn for the birth of Samuel, so its mention of the "barren" woman become fertile is appropriate to the narrative context (1 Samuel 1—2). Even so, it is not merely the case that an unfortunate woman's prayer has been heard. The child who is to be born is dedicated as a *nāzīr*

(1 Sam. 1:11). That is, his life, from the womb, is directed to the liberating purpose of Yahweh. That is why his conception takes place. "The hand of Yahweh was against the Philistines all the days of Samuel" (1 Sam. 7:13).

THE ORACLES OF BALAAM

There is one further piece of evidence about Early Israel in the old poetry the tradition preserves. The Oracles of Balaam (Numbers 23—24) purport to be the vision of a non-Israelite seer, hired by the king of Moab to curse Israel. They give us an insight into how Israel thought the nations regarded them and—what comes to the same thing—how they thought of themselves vis-à-vis the nations. Some specific passages are apposite.[42]

> [9b]Behold a people dwells apart,
> among the nations it is not reckoned.
> (Num. 23:9b)

"Dwelling apart" could be taken to refer to Israel's identity as Yahweh's particular people, a holy nation (Exod. 19:5–6). Some scholars—especially those who opt for an "infiltration" model of the Israelite settlement—might understand the phrase to reflect Israel's geographic position in the highlands of Palestine, away from the more densely inhabited coastal plain. I suggest, though, that the couplet reflects a consciousness that Israel's existence as a political entity was, in the eyes of the nations, illegitimate. They were not a properly constituted nation. They had no king, and no standing in the political life of the region. They were *'apiru*. For this reason, the verb in the second line should be translated "it does not reckon itself."

Yet Israel's existence is the work of El. This is the burden of the Oracles. There is no point in cursing or otherwise opposing Israel, because it is El/Yahweh who has formed this people and who, as their ruler, will protect them. Some few passages suffice to show this:

> [19]El is not a man, that he should lie,
> a son of man, that he should change his mind.
> Has he said, and will he not act?
> Spoken, and will he not cause (it) to stand?
> (Num. 23:19)

El "speaks": he exercises *mišpāṭ.*[43] And he is true to the "word" he utters. His "say" is efficacious. What he has spoken he "causes to stand," or "raises up." Despite the opposition of the nations—reflected in the narrative context and to some extent also in the Oracles themselves—Israel will "make it."

Now we come to the point. In six lines we have an epitome of the defining features of Early Israel. Yahweh/El started the whole thing by "bringing them forth from Egypt"; he is their ruler and protector; and this is a people in whose life oppression finds no place. Only, the poem has these items in reverse order:

> 21Iniquity is not beheld in Jacob,
> toil is not seen in Israel:
> Yahweh his god is with him,
> the shout of the King among them.[44]
> 22It is El who caused him to go forth from Egypt
> as the horns of a wild ox for himself.
> (Num. 23:21–22)

Iniquity and toil are not seen in Israel. The word I translate "toil," *ʿāmāl,* has the semantic range of the archaic English word "swink": hard labor, draining exertion, travail, misery (cf. Jer. 20:18 and Job 3:20). Given the parallelism with *ʾāwen,* "iniquity," *ʿāmāl* here means the hopeless toil associated with oppression. It is fundamental to their constitution as a people that oppression will not be "seen" in Israel: neither experienced nor countenanced. Yahweh is "with him." The phrase is suggestive of Holy War: "The Lord is with you." So also the *tᵉrûʿāh,* "shout" of battle and of acclamation for the king,[45] stands for the whole complex of Yahweh's involvement in Israel's battles. He wars for them, as their King, as he brought them out of Egypt.[46]

There is no withstanding this. It is futile to seek remedies:

> 23Surely there is no omen against Jacob,
> no spell against Israel.
> Surely now it shall be said of Jacob,
> and of Israel: "What has El worked!
> 24Behold a people like a lioness stands,
> like a lion raises itself up. . . ."
> (Num. 23:23–24)

Not only is Israel's very existence, and its existence free of oppression, and its existence "apart" from the nations the doing of Yahweh/El, the heavenly hosts are involved:

> The stars of Jacob prevail,
> the tribes of Israel stand.[47]
> (Num. 24:17)

That Israel will "stand" has been a theme in these oracles (23:24; 23:19, El causes his word to stand). The structure of this verse reflects the dynamics of that success. "Stars . . . tribes": the heavenly hosts fight on behalf of Israel (cf. Judges 5:20–21). As "the stars of Jacob" are (so to speak) in the ascendant, so Israel will succeed.

SUMMARY

The picture of Early Israel that emerges from the poetry and traditions we have examined is of a people "dwelling apart," "not reckoning itself among the nations," yet constantly beset by those nations. There is consequently a certain animus against the kings and "those who 'sit' in great houses." Yet that animus was not just the result of the wars Israel found itself fighting. The *ṣedeq* of Yahweh entailed the rejection of the oppressive Canaanite system. The rule of the kings was illegitimate. The choice to become "Israel" contained the seeds of conflict with the established order. Accepting the sovereignty of Yahweh and the political economy that embodied that acceptance was subversive of everything the Canaanite world took to be of ultimate importance. This was, in Canaanite eyes, an *ʿapiru* political entity. So the kings tried to effect *nāqām.*

Living within the circle of Yahweh's *ṣedeq,* Israel could not have recourse to the centralizing, "technocratic" means Canaan relied on to defend its sovereignty. More than particulars of warfare or of political and economic life, the tradition preserves certain central attitudes Israel was to live by. They should not be like the nations round about—the oppressive regimes they had so unexpectedly been freed from. They were to be free of anxiety about their future: "Yahweh has given the enemy into your hand." They were to be uncompromisingly intent on "the one necessary thing." Seek first the kingship of Yahweh and his *ṣedeq,* and all else will be added.

We would like to know more about those particulars of political and economic life. Norman Gottwald has mined the sources, using the tools of sociological analysis, to extract some understanding of the nature of Early Israel, and his description of the "tribe," "clan," "fathers' houses," and other divisions of the social order is illuminating, but this is not the place to go over those matters. The major point is that Israel was a political entity whose life as a people was made possible by a "decentralized" form of politics. There was no permanent central authority, and no privileged class. Economic and political relationships were based on equity and nonexploitative modes of exchange. This decentralization was possible only because *mišpāṭ* was Yahweh's. No one in particular had the ultimate say about things, because *mišpāṭ* did not reside in any officeholder in virtue of his or her qualities or hereditary position. No one's *mišpāṭ* was coterminous with *ṣedeq*. Power was relativized by being located with Yahweh.

The anomaly was that kingship language was used of Yahweh himself, discreetly but clearly nonetheless. The Divine Warrior imagery alone shows this. Add to this the references in the early poetry to Yahweh's kingship (Exod. 15:18; Num. 23:21; 24:7; Deut. 33:5) and there can be no doubt that Israel understood itself as being "the kingdom of Yahweh," or rather as living under "the kingship of Yahweh."

At the end of the Song of Hannah, however, there is a reference to the "anointed" of Yahweh. I omitted it above but now it is time to turn to that strange development in Israel's history by which the political entity born of the experience of *ʿapiru* withdrawal, and of being "brought out of the house of slaves," chose to be ruled by kings.

CHAPTER 6

Kings and Prophets

In a way it made sense for Israel to get a king. People knew what it was like to be led in battle by a "Judge"—one who exercised "judgment," *mišpāṭ*—and to be bound by the "judgments" of tribal officials. Even though the tradition is at pains to subordinate that authority to Yahweh's rule, for all practical purposes people's experience probably consisted simply in being given orders and in following them. *Mišpāṭ* was *mišpāṭ*, so they might not have made the distinctions the tradition insists on. They were used to having authority exercised by human beings. Then, too, the language of kingship survived (even if discreetly tempered) in the titles and imagery associated with Yahweh as Divine Warrior. If his *mišpāṭ* was monarchic, so in principle was the *mišpāṭ* mediately exercised by the Judges. The use of that kingly language in connection with Yahweh would have cleansed it of pejorative connotations. The kings of old, and those of the nations round about, might be tyrants; but kingship in itself might well have gotten more of a "good press" as the people of the land settled into being Israel, over the generations.

Above all, in the face of a threat to the very existence of the people monarchic *mišpāṭ* would seem to make sense. Philistine technology was clearly superior. Their military and political organization led them from strength to strength.[1] Countervailing measures were needed. All resources must be mobilized. The people's energies must be focused, and their activities coordinated. One person has to have the say, determining strategy and making the most efficient use of strength. When the Philistine threat emerged, then, it was natural for people to look for a strong man, a leader in whom all their hopes could be reposed and through whom all their anxieties could be allayed. Enter Saul.

CONTRADICTIONS

The theory of Israel's origins I am following would see contradictions here. Israel was the product of a decentralizing, "retribalizing" social movement. It represented a reaction against centralized control. The people's refusal to give further allegiance to the kings of Canaan and to be cowed by the kings' professional armies drained the established order of both legitimacy and the capacity to vindicate itself:

> They were melted utterly,
> the enthroned of Canaan.
> You made terror and dread
> fall upon them.
> (Exod. 15:15–16)

Further, this movement of "withdrawal" and "conquest" succeeded not despite but because of their lack of technology and military power. "Stumblers gird on strength." That success was attributed to the warrior god whose heavenly armies fought on behalf of the weak and oppressed. For Israel, their weakness was their strength. To rely, now, on strong, centralized leadership—"appoint for us a king to judge us like all the nations" (1 Sam. 8:5)—contradicted their beginnings and their identity as a people.

"BREAD"

The contrast is not just between two forms of political organization, one centralized and monarchic, the other decentralized and "tribal." The contrast is between two forms of consensus, two visions of *ṣedeq*. The centralized rule of Canaan embodied (and shaped!) certain fundamental convictions about reality: about what is and what is to be. The nonnegotiable good is survival ("Bread"). Nothing else signifies. This conviction animates and gives legitimacy to the king's rule, for his function is to ensure survival. Other desires, interests, goods are negated by or subordinated to that absolute good, and correspondingly all other fora, structures, and associations are lopped off in favor of centralized rule, or at best integrated into it. The political structure reflects the spiritual reality. The "one necessary thing" is monistically one.[2] Hence centralization is not just an accident of political organization.

"JUSTICE"

Israel had a "one necessary thing," too, but it consisted in "justice." "Justice," though, is a notion hard to get hold of. Clearly, it excludes certain things: oppression, exploitation, disregard for the weak—all the unhappy things that happen when people are subordinated to the attainment or maintenance of specific goods like Bread. Justice means a refusal to subordinate others in that way, and hence to allow any specific good to become absolute. Positively, it requires attending to the cry of those in need. It mandates what we might call an openness to the other: one is to "go beyond" one's private interests, to the other as other, imagining oneself in their place. "You know the heart of a stranger, for you were strangers in the land of Egypt" (Exod. 23:9, RSV). "Love your neighbor as yourself" (Lev. 19:18, RSV). As a norm of self-understanding and of choice, therefore, justice consists in an antecedent disposition, to "go beyond." Hence it does not lend itself to social blueprints. It works on a case-by-case basis. Its only positive "program" is to be aware of the neighbor's need and to act on that awareness. As a negative norm for economic and political schemes, however, it acts powerfully, and so, by neutralizing acquisitiveness, can determine the shape of a people's life. Yet this very quality—that it consists in a disposition, that this "going beyond" is realized in the here and now of the other in need, not in a utopian tomorrow nor in a macrocosmic There—means that justice as the "one necessary thing" of social existence brings about a social order of a certain kind. It is not something reserved for a few to practice, so that everybody else is absolved of obligation. It does not oblige only a leader or leaders, as if it could "trickle down" through the social system. It applies to everyone everywhere. This mandate to do justice—universal yet particular, applying to each one as to all together—will be reflected in the social structure. There will not be an elite, carrying out social tasks reserved for them, while everybody else, the *lumpen,* sits passively by. The social structure will not be centralized, nor stratified, nor manipulative. It will be egalitarian, decentralized, free. The political structure reflects the spiritual reality.

The Aniconic Law

An analogy suggests itself. "Justice" cannot be reduced to any specific good, like Bread. It cannot be "achieved" once for all, or "achieved" in any sense. It means going beyond. In contrast to the specificity of Bread, it looks almost like a vacuum at the heart of one's vision of reality. One cannot point and say, There, that's it, or, Now we have it, or, That's that. Just so, Yahweh cannot be reduced to any specific good. No representation is adequate to show what Yahweh is, no "likeness of anything that is in heaven above, or that is in the earth beneath, or that is in the water under the earth" (Exod. 20:4, RSV). Yahweh goes beyond any specific good. The aniconic prohibition and the command to do justice have a family resemblance.

Perhaps it is more than a resemblance.[3] Justice means that the other, the neighbor, the one in need, has an absolute claim on one's time and attention. Nothing else, really, signifies. One's self-understanding is involved with that other, as other. The tendency to focus one's selfhood on specific goods, and to make them absolute, and to fit the other into economic and political schemes, is to be counteracted by that absolute claim. Yahweh, too, makes an absolute claim. He is the one who causes us to go beyond. He, too, is other. He does not fit into any economic or political scheme. But, besides requiring that going beyond, Yahweh is the one we are to go beyond to. The openness to the other and the openness to Yahweh are the same. He is not only the god who hears the cry of those in need; he is the god who is known in their cry. To accept his *mišpāṭ* is to allow the other to have a claim on us. To hear the cry of one in need is to know Yahweh.[4]

What I have been calling openness to the other involves trust. By trust I mean a conviction about reality: the conviction that if one seeks first Yahweh's *mišpāṭ* and his justice all things else will be added; and I mean the readiness to make choices according to that conviction. To absolutize some specific good—like Bread—is to betray that conviction, because in seeking first Bread one is in effect accepting the vision of life embodied in Baalism, and accepting also, for all practical purposes, the cosmic *mišpāṭ* of Baal. It is to mistrust Yahweh, to look to another for one's salvation.[5] The choices that flow from that betrayal inevitably involve injustice and, so, oppression.

1 SAMUEL 8

This is how the story in 1 Samuel 8 sees things. There, the people's demand for a king is represented as "rejection" of Yahweh, and that rejection is said to entail tyranny. Why is that? Let us look at the story.

"Appoint for us a king to judge us like all the nations," the people tell Samuel (v. 5): the *mišpāṭ* they seek is to be centralized *mišpāṭ* like that of the "nations." Thus it represents an overthrow of the decentralized system of mediate *mišpāṭ* that has obtained from the beginnings of Israel. That overthrow affects the judge Samuel, of course, but more importantly it is the overthrow of Yahweh as well. "They are not rejecting you," he says to Samuel (v. 7), "they are rejecting me." Then he tells Samuel to apprise the people of what having a king will mean for them: "this will be the *mišpāṭ* of the king who will reign over you" (v. 11). Samuel lists all the innovations monarchy will bring in. Conscription: no longer will a militia be raised by levy from the tribes and clans; there will be a standing army, and Israel will rely on military power, "chariots and horse" (v. 11). There will be a professional officer class to run the army (v. 12). Corvée or forced labor will take people away from their own livelihood (vv. 12–13, 16). Land will be expropriated, and a landed aristocracy, the king's "servants," will arise (v. 14). The royal establishment will be supported by taxation in kind (vv. 15–17). Samuel's warning ends with the chilling declaration, "And on that day you will cry out because of your king, whom you have chosen for yourselves" (v. 18a). Israel began with the cry of the oppressed. Now they are getting themselves back, full circle, to their original condition, by their own choice. Things now will be different, though, in one tragic respect: "Yahweh will not answer you, on that day" (v. 18b).

Rejection of Yahweh entails tyranny. So the story has it. The key lies in the *ṣedeq* of the king they are choosing for themselves, and that *ṣedeq*—what legitimates his rule, what moves people to "hear and do" all his "words"—consists in their anxiety: their refusal to trust. In the king is reposed the intensity of their fears. Their need for assurance and security is projected onto him. Needfulness is "alienated," detached from them, taking on a kind of independent existence as an aura surrounding the figure of the king. It puts him on a pedestal. The dynamics are those of infatuation. And, as with infatuation, things soon unravel. There is an underlying resentment against the one onto whom the need is projected: he has power over us, power all the greater in that its source—our own need—is not recognized. We sense a loss of self to the other. The resentment must be denied, in adulation and obedience, lest we lose what is, after all, our only stay against needfulness. Needfulness denied thus feeds on itself, and grows: to the original need is added resentment, and a consequent panicky sense of impending loss. This basic, simmering resentment at the power the other has will come to the boil once he exercises that power. When he asserts himself, showing independent will, the adulation will turn to hostility. He has disappointed us. He is not "behaving." He has become other. The sense of disappointment and betrayal will be heightened, paradoxically, by a feeling that this "other" has no right to be acting the way he is acting. He is, after all, our creature. We made him, he is ours. Who does he think he is? The paradox is that the alienating, fetishistic process I have been describing so often includes that proprietary sense, and the contempt we feel for those who are thus our creatures. The other has power over us, because our need gives it to him, and part of us is conscious that without us he is nothing. "Without us": that is, without our needfulness, the very aspect of ourselves we are trying to exorcise by means of the other. Thus, he embodies our need, and so becomes an object of adulation: he has power over us. He embodies our need, and so becomes an object of aversion: we resent him.

I seem to be describing the emergence of monarchy in Israel as a love affair gone sour. In fact, it had to go sour. That *ṣedeq* could not last. It contained the seeds of its own dissolution. *Ṣedeq,* after all, is embodied in *mišpāṭ*. The people wanted a strong man. They got what they asked for. To do the things his *ṣedeq* mandated—to assure security and salvation from their enemies—he had to use strong-man measures. If the threat is to be removed, everything has to serve the war effort. A state of emergency exists. Mobilization is needed. Military resources must be beefed up. Horse and chariot must be amassed, and supported. Food and other materiel must be requisitioned from the people. Many acres must be devoted to providing food for the army and "the king's table." People have to be found to work these fields, the royal estates, and the estates themselves must be run by the king's "servants," the bureaucracy formed to handle all this royal business. The economy has to be planned around these military requirements.

To allay the people's anxiety, and ensure security, certain changes have to be made. But those changes will take people away from their lands, for military service, and will take land away from the people, to provide for the royal military and bureaucratic establishment. Every activity will be controlled from above. The people will have to pay a high price for their security. There will be resentment. Restiveness will set in. "You will cry out on that day because of your king, whom you have chosen for yourselves" (v. 18a). To ensure the success of Operation Survival—to ensure the continuance of his *mišpāṭ*—the king will have to put down the restiveness. His stern measures will cause further resentment and restiveness, and the alienation and repressiveness will grow in tandem.[6] Infidelity to Yahweh entails oppression. Q.E.D.

NEEDFULNESS

The theme of security and trust runs through the stories of Early Israel, from the exodus and wilderness wanderings to the beginnings of kingship. It seems to me that needfulness is central. The person in need "cries out." There is no alternative, if one is in need. One who is not in need does not cry out.

But what if one is in need and refuses to admit it? It is, after all, uncomfortable to admit need. We do not have the say about things. So we seek to get ourselves out of the need we are in, moving out of it in some way. We deny it. We take measures of our own devising, surefire means not to be in need. We act as if we are in charge. We try to manage events, to attain security, certitude, assurance. We trust in our own sense of the situation and our own measures to change it. We displace the anxiety onto "horse and chariot," the works of our own hands, and those products of our efforts are therefore invested with an aura of ultimate importance. We say to the works of our hands, "My God!" (Cf. Hosea 14:3). But, according to the biblical tradition, this is to find security in illusion. We miss out on the reality of Yahweh, the one who vindicates the powerless: "in you the orphan finds compassion" (Hosea 14:3).

Another form of the same illusion is numb despair. I am past hope and even past caring, so I do not "cry out." I am catatonic. There is nothing I can do. But this is not despair enough. The sense that "there is nothing I can do" is founded on the expectation that I should be able to do something. I have to despair of this expectation, of my own resources, of my secret conviction that I am in control.

For in the biblical tradition, it is the *lumpen* who cry out. That is all that they can do. They have no choice. They are "moved" by events and conditions, they are not "movers" of them. They have no resources. Far from being able to assure themselves of a successful outcome of events, they are convinced of their powerlessness. They have despaired of everything, even of despair.

The point is not so much powerlessness as willingness to be in need: to *be* what and where we are. "Crying out" is not a denial of need but its affirmation. It lets need be need, and us be need-ful. "Crying out" is letting go of the sense that we are in charge. That letting go opens us to amazing things. First comes the assurance, "Fear not: I am with you." "Fear not" is said to scared people. It makes no sense except to scared people. "I am with you" means "I am with you-as-you-are," full of fear and need, panicking, utterly despairing. The poet speaks of "magnanimous Despair": despair is magnanimous, "great-souled," because it brings us beyond the self-absorbed illusion of being in control, to the otherness of Yahweh. "Security" and "trust" are things that need-ful people experience.

This is a hard saying, but it is central, I believe, to the biblical tradition. According to the view represented in 1 Samuel 8, Israel, threatened by the Philistines, ought to have "cried out." Most likely, the strategic and tactical moves that would have come out of this choice would have been of a piece with the Holy Wars of the period of the Judges. What they should not have done, and did, was yield to anxiety and choose to be "judged by a king like all the nations." That was the Philistine victory.

A SUBVERSIVE STORY

But of course 1 Samuel 8 is not interested in imparting information about the origins of monarchy in Israel. It is in intent and effect a critique of monarchy, based on long familiarity with that institution. It describes what had become a kind of "second nature," something simply given in the life of the people, and characterizes it as innovation. The story takes the reader back to a time when "there was no king in Israel." It shows that monarchy was not only an innovation, but innovation based on infidelity to what makes Israel Israel. The choice of monarchy is rejection of Yahweh. Thus, the story offers a vision of what life in Israel should be like. The effect of 1 Samuel 8 is to say that in an authentic Israel, faithful to Yahweh and the covenant, there would be no standing army, nor aristocracy, nor forced labor, nor expropriation, nor reliance on "horse and chariot." Time was, the story says, Israel was not like that. It was egalitarian, classless, localized, free of intrusion by any central authority; people were able to work their own fields and keep their own flocks. Kingship and its exactions are by no means necessary elements of Israel's life as a people. Things could be otherwise: they once were. By relativizing what its hearers or readers knew as the given order of things, the story drives a wedge between what is and what both was and should be. 1 Samuel 8 is subversive.

PROPHECY

Still, the story has Yahweh accede to the people's request: "Listen to the voice of the people in all that they say to you" (8:7). In part this seems to be a case of letting people lie in the bed they have made. It also says that the change to monarchy is something not irretrievably in contradiction to Israel's peoplehood, only in tension with it. It is a problem, but not one that can't be handled.

The way to handle the problem is implicit in the very situation in which it is stated. Yahweh is speaking to Samuel, the Judge. When

Yahweh tells him to appoint a king Samuel ceases to be a Judge and becomes something else. He inaugurates an office whose functions include designating and anointing a king, and, as we shall see, reproving and even deposing a king. The office is symbiotic with kingship. It is called prophecy. That is how the problem is to be handled: to have someone there who will speak for Yahweh and give utterance to his *mišpāṭ* and *ṣedeq,* someone who will be a "servant" (official) and "messenger" (representative) of the true ruler of Israel. That person is called a "prophet."[7]

This could be looked at in a number of ways. The reason people desire to have a king and are willing to obey him—the *ṣedeq* that underlies his *mišpāṭ*—can be good or bad. Anxiety about survival, as we have seen, could motivate people to have and obey a king but that *ṣedeq* is contradictory to Yahweh's *ṣedeq*. On the other hand, a king could govern according to Yahweh's *ṣedeq,* "judging the poor" (Isa. 11:4), for example, so that there is no contradiction with Yahweh's *ṣedeq:* the king's *mišpāṭ* could be instrumental to it. The king could be the agent of Yahweh's *ṣedeq*. Yet even where there is no fundamental contradiction tensions could arise. The king could ascribe *ṣedeq* to himself, claiming ultimate authority for his own *mišpāṭ,* so that his *ṣedeq* is not derivative but, as it were, self-generated. What is needed is an instrumentality to rein in the human tendency to claim ultimacy for one's own decisions, to relativize them, to discern among them. The role of the prophet is to provide just such relativizing and critical insight. More than insight, really: what the prophet announces is Yahweh's "word," an authoritative declaration of Yahweh's sovereignty.

This can cut both ways. It can be uncomfortable for a king to have an alternative source of authority on the scene. He would always be looking over his shoulder, conscious that his "Thus says" can be countermanded by another "Thus says" which supersedes his own, and even that his very position can be undercut. People might not feel bound by what he says in this instance or that, or at all.

On the other hand, if this other source of authoritative utterance confirms what he says, the king's say-so becomes irrefragable. It would be worth keeping a prophet on the payroll to have such a source of validation. If only the prophet can be made to behave, the king's will would be Yahweh's will.

SAUL'S REJECTION

How uncomfortable the king's position could be is seen in the stories, found in 1 Samuel 13 and 15, about Saul's insubordination to Yahweh and Yahweh's consequent rejection of him from the kingship.[8] In both stories, Saul acts—well, like a king. He takes matters into his own hands. He acts masterfully. He is unable to wait. He takes measures guaranteed to bring events around to how he has determined they should turn out (1 Samuel 13). In reserving captured livestock for sacrifice to Yahweh (1 Samuel 15), he both violates the law of *ḥērem* and shows himself disposed to "use" ritual, and Yahweh, for his own purposes. The decisiveness he manifests is really manipulativeness, and betrays a failure of nerve. Taking matters into his own hand, however piously he pretends to be acting, he proves himself unfitted to exercise kingship as it is to be exercised in Israel. "Because you have rejected the word of Yahweh, he has rejected you from being king" (1 Sam. 15:23). Even though he is called king, his task is to carry out Yahweh's "words."[9] *Mišpāṭ* still lies with Yahweh.

In sum, kingship in Israel is anomalous. By divine designation and legitimation the king has the say but cannot exercise it on his own terms. To do that is to exercise *mišpāṭ* according to a false *ṣedeq*. The king's *mišpāṭ* is instrumental to carrying out Yahweh's *ṣedeq*. It must be in accordance with that *ṣedeq*. Trust is central to that *ṣedeq*. The only security available is Yahweh and his *mišpāṭ*, the passionate involvement of the *'ēl qannā'*.

DAVID

That a king can exercise *mišpāṭ* in accordance with Yahweh's *ṣedeq* appears from the stories about David, and is reflected in some other Davidic traditions as well. David is youthful, and not particularly impressive. He is "meek." Saul's armor encumbers him. His weapons are those of Yahweh of Hosts (1 Sam. 17:45–47). The story in 1 Samuel 24 and 26 shows how when he is persecuted by Saul he does not seek to effect his own *nāqām*. Saul has treated David as one who stands outside the circle of *ṣedeq*: David has been made *ʿapiru* (1 Sam. 22:1–2). Saul seeks to effect *nāqām* against David. In thus treating David unjustly, of course, Saul is himself outside the circle of *ṣedeq*. Saul must be shown to be in the wrong, and David in the right. *Ṣedeq* and David must both be vindicated. When David has the opportunity to effect his own vindication, however, he refuses: David says to Saul,

> [12]Let Yahweh judge between you and me,
> and vindicate me from you.
> [15]Let Yahweh be adjudicator
> and judge between you and me,
> and see, and "contend my contention"[10]
> and judge me from your hand.
> (1 Sam. 24:12, 15)

"Judge me from your hand": exercise *mišpāṭ* so that I am no longer in your power. The *mišpāṭ* involved means determining who is in the right, and acting to carry out that determination. David lets Yahweh have the say. Thus, David shows himself a true Israelite, giving wholehearted allegiance to Yahweh's *mišpāṭ* and Yahweh's *ṣedeq*.[11]

In the story of Abigail and Nabal (1 Samuel 25) David shows himself capable of murder and vengeance, but he is prevented from "saving himself by his own hand" (vv. 26, 33).[12] Here, as we shall see below, a characteristic emphasis of Dtr is easy to see, but David's readiness to play God also appears clearly. No less than Saul, David could take matters into his own hand. Unlike Saul, he did not.

David was thus a man "after the heart" of Yahweh (1 Sam. 13:14). The stories do not bother to conceal his weaknesses—there is no tinge of hagiography in them—and this is the point. When he gets too big, he does not dissemble or try to exculpate himself. David sins, and weeps.

DAVID'S KINGSHIP

The irony is that this ideal king—ideal in the eyes of Dtr—restored, or began the restoration of, the structures of Canaanite kingship. He set up a standing army, a mercenary force (2 Samuel 8; 23).

He secured his own capital city, Jerusalem, as a fiefdom, which became the locus of centralized rule. He had a "house" built for himself, a "house" after the model of Canaanite kingship. His desire to build a "house" for Yahweh smacks of the Canaanite institution of the temple for the creator god, and can be seen as a way of legitimating his own assumption of the trappings of Canaanite monarchy. David, with his "house," must have appeared conspicuously a king. There must have been murmuring about the disparity between his house and the tent shrine for Yahweh that David had had brought to Zion. Yahweh after all was the true ruler of Israel, yet here was this upstart ensconced in a king's palace. The only brake on the acquisition of absolute power was the institution of prophecy and the traditional mistrust of centralized power prophecy gave voice to. By its ability to designate a king, and to depose a king (as Samuel had declared Saul deposed), prophecy could keep kings honest, subordinate to Yahweh and his *ṣedeq*. If, though, the dynastic principle was in effect, power would pass from father to son, and there would be no intervention by Yahweh's spokesman. The next thing you know, some sort of divine status would be attributed to the king. He would be a "son of God." That was part of the Canaanite ideology of kingship. Once these changes were in effect, Israel would have come full circle, back to unbridled, absolute, cosmically legitimated centralized rule.

THE DYNASTIC ORACLE

These political and theological dangers Israelite tradition averted by a masterpiece of revisionist interpretation, the Dynastic Oracle of 2 Samuel 7. David's move to build a house for Yahweh's "sitting" (dwelling and enthronement) was rebuffed, and made the occasion for a reminder that *mišpāṭ* was Yahweh's:

> 5 You would build me a house for my "sitting"?
> 6 I have not "sat" in a house
> since the day I caused the Sons of Israel to go up from Egypt
> to this day. . . .
> 8 I am the one who took you from the shepherd's lean-to,
> from following the flock,
> for you to be leader
> over my people, over Israel.
>
> (2 Sam. 7:5–6a, 8)

The initiative lay with Yahweh, and continued to do so. Hence, rather than let David build a house for him, Yahweh would make him a house (v. 11). He would establish a dynasty, raising up David's seed, to whom kingly rule would belong for ever. "I will establish the throne of his kingship forever" (v. 13). Further: David's descendants would indeed be "sons of God," not in the sense in which members of the heavenly court and presumably also Canaanite kings were "sons of God/god(s)," but in an accommodated sense. "I will be to him a father, he will be to me a son" (v. 14a). In this statement of adoptive sonship, we have an assertion of the priority of Yahweh's *mišpāṭ* over the claims of the Davidic kings, and as well an echo of the language of treaties: the vassal was "son" to the "father" suzerain.[13]

The oracle of Nathan can be seen as a way of tempering, or relativizing, the structures of Davidic monarchy. David was Yahweh's son by covenant, adoptively, by Yahweh's own say-so. David's line would rule for ever, but that was Yahweh's choice, and besides, if they went against his commandments, Yahweh would chastise them (v. 14b), as "a father chastises the son in whom he is well pleased" (Prov. 3:12). Yet of course all this can be taken in two ways. Whatever was said to account for or explain away the promises made to David, in fact the dynastic principle was established, and an extraordinary status for the Davidic king. His word could have the force of Yahweh's word, his authority unquestioned and unquestionable, by Yahweh's own say-so.

PSALM 89

In Psalm 89 we have the same duality. There the promise to David is put firmly into the context of Yahweh's kingship:

> 5Let the heavens praise your wonders, Yahweh,
> yes your faithfulness in the assembly of the Holy Ones. . . .
> 9It is you who rule the raging of Sea;
> when its waves rise it is you who still them. . . .
> 11Yours are the heavens, yes yours earth,
> the world and what fills it you founded. . . .
> 14*Ṣedeq* and *mišpāṭ* are the dais of your throne,
> *ḥesed* and fidelity go before you.
>
> (Ps. 89:5, 9, 11, 14)

The imagery is that of cosmic lordship and "creation." Yahweh is the warrior god who defeats Sea and "crushes Rahab like a carcass" (v. 10); he is acclaimed by the divine council as the one who has the say, and has set up ("founded") all that is; he is enthroned upon a dais which consists of "justice and judgment." These age-old images serve to establish a context for the oracle to David. Yahweh is the true ruler. Kingship belongs to him. David's kingship is subordinate and derivative.

In fact, however, all this imagery of cosmic lordship has the effect of putting Davidic kingship in a new light, a rather baroque light at that. David's seed will be king because of the decree of the ruler of all. The Davidic dynasty will last for ever; it is of a piece with creation itself:

> 36His seed for ever shall be,
> his throne like the sun before me.
> 37Like the moon it shall be established for ever;
> it shall stand firm as long as the skies.
> (Ps. 89:36–37)

Not only that—the Davidic king has a share in Yahweh's creative power:

> 25I will set his hand over Sea,
> over River his right hand.
> (Ps. 89:25)

The cosmic *mišpāṭ* embodied in the language of victory over Sea is here attributed to the seed of David. He too will "rule the raging of Sea"!

In sum, Yahweh's divine kingship is the source and the validation of the Davidic dynasty's kingship, so that its kingly rule is limited. It is not self-validating. It is conditioned by Yahweh's *mišpāṭ*. The Davidic king is not a "son of God" except insofar as Yahweh says to him, "My son are you" (Ps. 2:7); only then can he say, "My father are you" (Ps. 89:26). As "son" he is subordinate. But all this works the other way, too. The Davidic king's power may be limited and derivative, but his position as "son"[14] is privileged. His power is derivative but because it derives from Yahweh it shares in the cosmic nature of Yahweh's kingship. The rule of David's dynasty is everlasting only because Yahweh's rule is everlasting; but it is everlasting.

SOLOMON

Small wonder, then, that with David's son Solomon royal rule took on absolutist features. The seemingly laudatory account of his reign in 1 Kings 4 and 10 echoes Samuel's warning in 1 Samuel 8. The king relied on "horse and chariot." The flowering of "wisdom" in Solomon's court reflects the growth of a royal bureaucracy, the king's "servants." (Officials have to be trained, so royal schools are needed, and schools are the locus of "wisdom.") The many treaties Solomon entered into, and the many dynastic marriages that were part of the treaty package (1 Kings 11:1–8), show that with Solomon Israel was becoming a nation-state "like all the nations round about." A high price had to be paid for making Israel a world power, however, and as always the people paid it. The bureaucracy and army were supported by the produce and labor of the people. Instead of the "tribal" system of *mišpāṭ*—families, clans, tribes—a centralized system of administration was imposed to exact the fruits of the people's toil (1 Kings 4:7–19).

And the House of Yahweh was built. The Temple of the cosmic Lord represented a return to the Canaanite symbol system of cosmic lordship: the House on the holy mountain, the place of the warrior god's enthronement, the source of *mišpāṭ*, central in the life of the people, their assurance of divine protection. The Deuteronomic theology makes all the proper distinctions—Yahweh is not said himself to dwell there, he makes his Name to dwell there; the House in itself is not a guarantee of divine favor; and so on—but for all practical purposes the House on Zion was the keystone of Solomonic power. Israel's experience of worshiping Yahweh was bound up with a recognition of the prerogatives of the House of David. Their sense of themselves as a people was shaped, from Solomon's time on, by the ideology of Yahweh's double choice, the choice of David's seed and the choice of Zion as his holy mountain.[15]

BACKLASH

Yet older traditions, and the consensus or sense of *ṣedeq* they embodied, survived. There was a feeling that Solomon was going too far. People obey only because they feel that *mišpāṭ* is being exercised according to *ṣedeq*. If they perceive a contradiction or tension they become rebellious. Enough is enough. The same sense of Yahweh's sovereignty that the Solomonic ideology appealed to as validation of Solomonic rule undercut that rule. By exercising absolute rule Solomon put his successors in danger of losing the people's allegiance. All those treaties and wives, all the "horse and chariot" and apparatus of royal power were storing up a day of reckoning. The older and more authentic sense of *ṣedeq* finds expression in a number of stories in 1 Kings. In one, Solomon is told

> Since . . . you have not kept my covenant and my statutes, which I commanded you, I will surely tear the kingship away from you and will give it to your servant. (1 Kings 11:11)

Yahweh "raises up" adversaries to Solomon (1 Kings 11:14, 23; cf. 11:26–40), leaders through whom the restiveness and discontent of the people—and, more importantly, the people's sense of *ṣedeq*—were given political expression.

The most telling incident, of course, is the story of how the Northern tribes broke away from the House of David. On what was to be the day of his enthronement, Solomon's hapless son Rehoboam finds himself confronted with a demand:

> Your father made our yoke hard:
> you, now, ease off from your father's hard service[16]
> and from his heavy yoke which he placed upon us,
> and we will serve you.
>
> (1 Kings 12:4)

Rehoboam's counselors offer conflicting advice. The older ones advise him to accede to the people's demands; the younger ones, his contemporaries, urge him to take a different line:

> My father laid upon you a heavy yoke:
> I will add to your yoke.
> My father chastised you with whips:
> I will chastise you with scorpions.
>
> (1 Kings 12:11)

Rehoboam chooses to follow the hard-liners' counsel, and the people refuse to accept him and his *mišpāṭ*. Then there were two kingdoms.

The older counselors were basing their advice on the same sense of *ṣedeq* that inspired the people's demand for Rehoboam to lighten their yoke and back off from the "hard service" Solomon's centralized rule imposed. It may be, of course, that they were being Machiavellian: promise them anything. Even so, however, their advice reveals a sense that the people's discontent was justified. The older counselors remembered, or knew of, a time before Solomon, and the way things were then. Their advice represented a recognition that the older ways were more authentic forms of Israelite existence than the innovations of Solomonic *mišpāṭ*. It is the viewpoint that informs the story of Samuel's warning in 1 Samuel 8. Memory is subversive.

Taking its origin from that conservative consensus, by way of backlash against the ideology of Davidic kingship fostered by Solomon, the Northern Kingdom, Israel, preserved an authentic sense of *ṣedeq* in limiting the power of kings and, especially, in resisting the tendency to establish dynastic rule. The dynastic principle never really took hold in the North. The sense both that human monarchic *mišpāṭ* was to be severely restricted and that dynasty—the automatic succession to power of the king's son—contradicted Yahweh's say in the matter of who should in the short run rule is seen in the story we have just sketched, as it is also in the story (Judges 8) of Gideon's rejection of the people's offer of dynastic rule:

> "Rule over us,
> you and your son and your son's son,
> for you have saved us from the hand of Midian."
> And Gideon said to them,
> "I will not rule over you,
> and my son will not rule over you.
> Yahweh rules over you."
>
> (Judges 8:22–23)

IDEAL KINGSHIP

In fairness to the Davidic traditions of kingship, two things should be said. One is that, in our sources read as a whole, election of David and of his house is always understood by reference to David himself. He is, as we saw above, the "man after Yahweh's own heart," who humbles himself before Yahweh, who does not save himself by his own hand, who lets Yahweh "judge." He is chosen to carry out Yahweh's purpose, and he does so. The other thing to say is that the representation of the Davidic king depicts him in terms of certain ideals, and those are authentically Israelite. The central position of kingship in the life of the people is continuous with the structure of the Canaanite political economy, but the king's task, or mission, is to establish "justice and judgment":

> Not by the seeing of his eyes shall he judge,
> and not by the hearing of his ears shall he decide.
> He shall judge by *ṣedeq* the needy,
> and decide by equity for the oppressed of the land.
> (Isa. 11:3–4)

The Davidic king "judges" the poor: exercises *mišpāṭ* on their behalf, to protect and vindicate them. Similarly, Jeremiah reproves the son of the good king Josiah:

> 15Are you a king—you—
> because you compete in cedar?
> Your father—did he not eat and drink
> and do *mišpāṭ* and *ṣ*ᵉ*dāqāh*?
> Then there was good,[17] with him.
> 16He adjudicated the adjudication[18]
> of the oppressed and poor:
> then there was good.
> Is this not knowing me?
> (Jer. 22:15–16)

As these quotations from Isaiah and Jeremiah indicate, it was the prophets who were the principal spokespersons of authentic *ṣedeq*. They kept alive and gave voice to the conviction that "Yahweh rules over you" (Judges 8:23). In so doing they came into direct conflict with the established ways of doing things and with the accepted understanding of royal power, "the *mišpāṭ* of the king" (1 Sam. 8:9, 11).

PROPHETIC REPROOF: IMPERIALISM

1. A series of stories at the end of 1 Kings (chaps. 18—22) is useful to show the ways in which this conflict of consensus played itself out. Ahab was the very model of a modern king. Israel under Ahab was

possessed of all the apparatus of a nation-state: bureaucracy and army. Ahab was allied with various Canaanite city-states. That is why Ahab was married to the daughter of the king of Sidon, Jezebel. In the stories in 1 Kings 18—22 we can see the traditions of Israel in tension with the demands of running a modern nation-state. In Old Israel war was Holy War. In an up-to-date nation, such as Ahab wanted Israel to be, war is an instrument of territorial expansion and commercial aggrandizement. The change can be seen in the story in 1 Kings 20. War with Israel is provoked by the Syrian king, Ben-hadad. In response to Ben-hadad's aggression, a prophet proclaims Holy War, and gives Ahab marching orders (20:13–14, 22, 28). Ahab is victorious, and is then approached by emissaries of the defeated Ben-hadad, who plead for the Syrian king's life. Ahab says, "Is he still alive? He is my brother" (v. 32). The emissaries quickly reply, "Ben-hadad is your brother" (v. 33). Both parties are using a declarative formula ("My brother is he") and the technical term for a treaty partner, "brother." Ahab is entering into an arrangement. The enemy king's life is the *quid*; what the *quo* is comes clear when the Syrian king meets with Ahab:

> 34The cities which my father took from your father I will restore, and you shall put bazaars for yourself in Damascus, as my father put (them) in Samaria. (1 Kings 20:34)

Ben-hadad's life will be spared in exchange for trade concessions and territory. The king of Israel began by fighting Holy War; he ends up making a deal.

One of the "sons of the prophets"[19] then acts out a playlet that gets Ahab to pronounce judgment against himself (vv. 35–42). The prophet tells Ahab,

> 42Thus says Yahweh:
> "Because you let go from (your) hand
> the man of my *ḥērem*,
> your *nepeš* shall be for his *nepeš*
> and your people for his people."
> (1 Kings 20:42)

The king of Syria had been defeated by Yahweh's power, and was "doomed to destruction" by him—he was "the man of my *ḥērem*." In swapping his life for trade and territory, however, Ahab violated the law of *ḥērem*. He transformed the nature of war in Israel, in his effort to make Israel an expansionist, imperialistic nation-state, and so he incurred the judgment of Yahweh, pronounced by the prophet.

PROPHETIC REPROOF: INJUSTICE

2. Ahab's imperialistic pretensions had domestic effects as well, as the story of Naboth's vineyard shows (1 Kings 21). To provision the army royal lands had to be amassed and a royal agribusiness had to be carried on. Yet the system of landholding characteristic of Israel, by which land was equitably distributed among families and clans and was in principle inalienable, provided an obstacle to the smooth functioning of such a "military-agricultural complex." From the viewpoint of the royal household the decentralized system of land tenure must have seemed a hopelessly irrational archaism. This conflict—between the social arrangements of Old Israel and the innovations required by modern "rationalization" of the social system—is concretized in the story of Naboth's vineyard. Naboth represents the Israelite yeoman, faithful to the old ways. He refuses the royal offer of a fair price or a swap in exchange for his property because he has no choice in the matter: "Yahweh forbid that I should give you the *naḥ^a^lāh* of my fathers." The *naḥ^a^lāh* (usually translated "inheritance") was the Israelite's share in the land and so his share in Israelite peoplehood. To alienate the *naḥ^a^lāh* was to give up one's identity as belonging to Israel, "God's *naḥ^a^lāh*" (2 Sam. 14:16). What Ahab saw as a tidy and reasonable transaction amounted, in Naboth's eyes, and in fact, to nothing less than betrayal of, and rebellion against, the *mišpāṭ* of Yahweh.

Ahab seems to realize this. He is at an impasse. There is no way he can tamper with the old traditions of Israel, and so he goes home "vexed and sullen" (21:4, RSV), having had his nose rubbed in the fact that monarchic power in Israel is limited and there is nothing he can do about it. Jezebel, however, being the daughter of a Canaanite king, is incredulous. For her, the impasse over Naboth's vineyard is not a matter of land but simply a question of limitations on royal power. To Jezebel, there are no such limits. She rails at Ahab, "Are you king over Israel or not?" (v. 7). Literally, her question is, "Do you

ɔver Israel?": for Jezebel it is kingship itself
' she understands the uses of power. To make
reak eggs. She contrives a judicial murder and
out of the way (vv. 8–14). Jezebel's managerial skills
beyond question.

> When Ahab heard that Naboth was dead
> Ahab arose to go down
> to the vineyard of Naboth the Jezreelite,
> to take possession of it.
>
> (1 Kings 21:16)

Again, the prophet comes forward to assert Yahweh's *mišpāṭ*:

> 17 The word of Yahweh came to Elijah the Tishbite:
> 18 "Arise, go down to meet Ahab, Israel's king in Samaria.
> Behold, he is in the vineyard of Naboth
> where he has gone down to take possession of it.
> 19 "Speak to him:
> 'Thus says Yahweh:
> "Have you killed
> and have you also taken possession?"'
> "Speak to him:
> 'Thus says Yahweh:
> "In the place where the dogs licked Naboth's blood
> the dogs will lick your blood, too:
> yours."'"
>
> (1 Kings 21:17–19)

We should note the interrelationship of all these elements. Ahab wants to be king the way that the kings of the nations are kings; he wants Israel to be a nation-state like all the nations round about. He therefore becomes a participant in the power-politics game of treaties and alliances; that is why Jezebel is his queen. He builds up the military apparatus of Israel, with "horse and chariot," in order to have political credibility in his neighbors' eyes. To supply the army and to feed his "servants" at "the king's table" he has to acquire land and work it, in an exercise of centralized royal power that runs counter to the normative traditions of Israel. And he legitimates this form of kingship by the vision of kingship regnant among the nations, a vision whose spokesperson is the Canaanite princess Jezebel. And why is Jezebel there, having the say about things? Why, because

Ahab is a participant in the power-politics game of treaties and alliances. And so it goes.

Israel remembered Jezebel not only because of Naboth but from her patronage of the cult of the Canaanite god Baal. The comic account, in 1 Kings 18, of the contest between Elijah, the prophet of Yahweh, and the prophets of Baal, reflects the crisis of that age. The treatment of the putative god Baal in that story is as rude as the treatment of his prophets is sanguinary. In taking on the Baalist functionaries Elijah is taking on the state in all its majesty. It all comes down to a simple question: who is god, Yahweh or Baal? Elijah was the spokesman of the *ṣedeq* and *mišpāṭ* of Yahweh.

THE "WORD" OF YAHWEH

In exercising his office, the prophet did not hesitate to claim for his "word" the authority of Yahweh's "word." "Thus says Yahweh: . . ." He is "sent" as representative of the covenant lord. The familiar account of how Isaiah got to be a prophet is clear on this point:

> I heard the voice of the Lord saying
> "Whom shall I send,
> and who will go for us?"
> And I said,
> "Here I am:
> send me!"
>
> (Isa. 6:8)

Not only is the prophet sent as a messenger, he knows the divine decree through and through. The reason is that he knows its legislative history. He stands in the divine council, and listens to its deliberations. The prophet Micaiah ben Imlah tells the king of Israel:

> 19I saw Yahweh sitting upon his throne,
> and all the host of heaven standing beside him,
> on his right and on his left.
> 20And Yahweh said, "Who will fool Ahab,
> so he will go up and fall at Ramoth Gilead?"
> And this one said so,
> and this one said such,
> 21and a spirit stood before Yahweh and said,
> "I will fool him."

> [22]And Yahweh said to him, "How?"
> And he said, "I will go forth
> and become a spirit of deceit
> in the mouth of all his prophets."
> And he said, "Fool him:
> yes, you will be able.
> Go forth, and do so."
>
> (1 Kings 22:19–22)

This is a cabinet meeting. The enthroned one, presiding, proposes the problem and invites counsel. The members of the council offer suggestions, until one comes up with a plan. Yahweh approves the plan, and commissions its author to carry it out. Micaiah has heard all this, and so the word he speaks is authentic.

It is precisely this ignorance of the authentic and authoritative word of Yahweh that makes false prophets false prophets. They presume to speak in the name of Yahweh, but

> [16b]the vision of their own hearts they speak,
> not from the mouth of Yahweh. . . .
> [18]For who has stood in the council[20] of Yahweh,
> and seen, and heard his word?
> Who has paid attention to his word, and heard? . . .
> [21]I did not send the prophets but they ran,[21]
> I did not speak to them, but they prophesied.
> [22]If they had stood in my council,
> they would make my people hear my words
> and turn from their evil way
> and from the evil of their deeds.
>
> (Jer. 23:16b, 18, 21–22)

This language is richly suggestive. It bespeaks authenticity and authoritativeness, as I have said, because it claims for the prophet an insider's knowledge of the divine purpose. He does not speak on his own, as if the *mišpāṭ* to which he gives utterance came from him, as if he himself had the say. He has been given familiarity with what Yahweh, as covenant lord of Israel, has in mind. He knows what the members of the divine council have proposed: Yahweh takes into account all the constituencies these "sons of god" know and speak for. The prophet knows that Yahweh weighs all these considerations and factors in forming his decree. As Yahweh has the final say, his counselors have made their contribution to his decree. As he presides, "god over all the gods," so his purpose takes precedence over, but subsumes and reconciles and integrates, all the purposes with which these heavenly beings are associated. Thus, the word the prophet speaks is not naively idealistic or impractical, but is in touch with what is most real. Those who would oppose Yahweh's decree, therefore, are out of touch with reality. Only the fool sets himself against Yahweh's *mišpāṭ* and his *ṣedeq*. Short-term gains and pragmatic "success" ultimately spell folly, and bring about doom for the people. This the prophets proclaimed, in season and out.[22] Since folly so abounded, so did the prophets' invocation of covenant curses. If you go down this path, it will lead to disaster: turn back.[23]

The same perspective informs the meditation on what it is to be Israel that we call the Book of Deuteronomy.

CHAPTER 7

Deuteronomy and the Deuteronomistic History

It would be useful at this point to draw together what we have already seen: to summarize the major themes that have emerged in our survey of the biblical tradition. "Thematizing," however, runs the risk of fostering a distancing, analytic way of thinking, as if a series of propositions could do justice to what after all was the lived experience of ancient Israel, and as if the convictions and choices of people then made no claims on us now.

So while we do well to aim at clarity, it should not be at the expense of imaginative involvement with Israel of old. We should allow our Now to become their Then—to share, as it were, a Today with them. A story would have this effect. As we saw in chapter 1, a story brings us into itself, into its world. Yet a story could also contain didactic elements. How would we combine a story's imaginative "identification-with" and didactic clarity? We could write a story in which the Israelites—and therefore we, sharing their Today—are being told some home truths. What they are told, for our purposes, would have to focus on their life as Israel, their identity as the people which accepts the *mišpāṭ* and *ṣedeq* of Yahweh. But, again, to avoid a series of propositions what they—we—are told should be in the second person: "you." And, again, what they and we are told should make a claim on us, putting our selfhood and the choices we make into the light of Yahweh's *ṣedeq* and *mišpāṭ*. Perhaps, then, what we need is a story in which Moses addresses the people, and therefore us, about how they are to live; what Yahweh desires for them; what covenant fidelity entails; what kinds of choices they are to make and to avoid; and what the consequences of those choices, for good or for ill, will be. We could use the covenant categories of blessing and curse to talk about those consequences.

This story of instruction and exhortation about peoplehood and choices that I have been sketching is, of course, the Book of Deuteronomy.

DEUTERONOMY

In Deuteronomy Moses is addressing the Israelites. They are about to cross the Jordan River and enter the land of Canaan. Moses himself is at the end of his days. He goes back over all that has happened to them—the exodus, wandering in the wilderness, battles against the kings on the east side of Jordan, the making of the covenant at the mountain of God—and instructs them about how they are to live in the land. The setting of his discourse is important: it is that privileged moment when they have not yet committed any irretrievable mistakes, and there is no reason they should not make a success of their life in the land.

Deuteronomy was written to give its readers a sense of what might have been, and what yet could be, in their life as a people. That is, people living, say, in the seventh century would have their minds taken back to a time before grievous mistakes had been made, to a time when things were different from what they are now. They would listen eagerly to Moses' discourse for clues to how they should live, always with the poignant sense that if only their ancestors had followed Moses' advice things now would be different. (The feeling people would get from the book was probably very much like the feeling we get when we read George Washington's warnings against entanglements in foreign alliances, or, for that matter, when we recall President Eisenhower's farewell address about the "military-industrial complex.") They would get a sense of how far they had wandered from the way Moses lays out for his audience. Especially, they would take warning from Moses' insistence on the consequences, in the real world, of their choices as a people.

So Moses' discourse is meant for the people who were to read, or hear, the book. They were to put themselves in the place of that first generation of Israelites, and with the superior knowledge of hindsight listen to Moses' instruction, and feel both compunction (because things Now are so different from what they might have been and should have been) and promise (because they would get a sense of what Yahweh had in mind for them as a people, and still has in mind: blessing). They would feel both salutary fear and renewing hope.

THE BOOK OF THE COVENANT

Deuteronomy is a book about what it is to be Israel. It is not a book about obedience to God's will, or the proper form of religious behavior, or punishment and reward. It is a book about "covenant": the way in which the political entity Israel is to understand itself and act, qua political entity. It is trying to get Israel, as a political entity, to do certain things and not to do other things.

1. What things? It would be easy to go through the book and pull out specific dos and don'ts: no treaties with the Canaanites, no worship of Canaanite gods, no intermarriage with the Canaanites, and myriad other prohibitions and commands. But it seems to me that all those specifics are secondary. The real point of Deuteronomy is contained in the recurring imperatives found in the first eleven chapters, which lead in to the specific "laws" of chapters 12 through 26. "Remember." "Do not forget." "Take heed" (or "watch"). "Hear." "Set your heart to . . ." These verbs all have to do with a mind-set or form of intentionality. Be focused on this, not on that. Let these things occupy the forefront of your consciousness. Hence the insistence on experience. "Your eyes saw." "Remember." "Learn." In effect: Be a people who keep these things in mind. Deuteronomy is a book whose purpose is to inculcate a certain form of self-understanding, to forge a consciousness.

2. What is the content of this consciousness? On what should Israel be focused? Correspondingly, what is the content of the false consciousness Israel is being warned against? Again, there is a series of verbs. "Love." "Serve." "Know." "Go after." "Hear" (or "obey"). "Fear." "Cleave." We recall that all these terms belong to the vocabulary of ancient Near Eastern politics.[1] They refer to allegiance. A city-state would "know" and "serve" its king; a vassal would "fear"

and "love" his overlord. Israel is to understand itself as a political entity which gives allegiance and shows loyalty and pays homage—which accepts and lives by *mišpāṭ*—a certain way.

3. To whom is Israel to give allegiance? What is the object of all these verbs? There are two objects, for all practical purposes. One (a) is Yahweh. The other (b) is the gods of the nations. Israel is to be a people focused on loving/knowing/serving/fearing/going after/hearing Yahweh, not one whose self-understanding is bound up with allegiance to other gods.

Yet "Yahweh" is not an empty category. In Deuteronomy he is the one "who brought forth" from slavery, because he "loved" Israel, and "chose" Israel, and "swore" to give them the land, and "keeps his oath" by "giving" them the land and the good things of the land, for he is the "passionate god" *('ēl qannā')*,[2] "a consuming fire" (4:24).

The "other gods," too, are specifically conceived, associated with certain attitudes, notably with "forgetting," and—most of all—with attributing possession of the land to one's own power and merit. But of this more below.

4a. "Loving" Yahweh will result in "life," and possession of the land, and "length of days in the land," and, in a word, "good."[3] Their "good" will be to "eat and be satisfied."[4] This is Blessing.

4b. Going after other gods will result in "death," and "evil," "destruction" and being "scattered" from the land, being "left few in number." This is Curse.

5. All this is presented against the background of the nations: "what the nations will say," how Israel will look "in the eyes of all the nations," "among all the nations round about."

6. And, as the consciousness of Israel is to be formed by reference to "what your eyes have seen," so Israel is to pass on to children and children's children all the "judgments" of Yahweh, so that they too may have the same sense of themselves as the authentic Israel, and may also enjoy "length of days in the land." What Moses tells Israel is set against the background of the nations and of generations yet to come.

Schematically, the structure of Deuteronomic thought can be presented as follows:

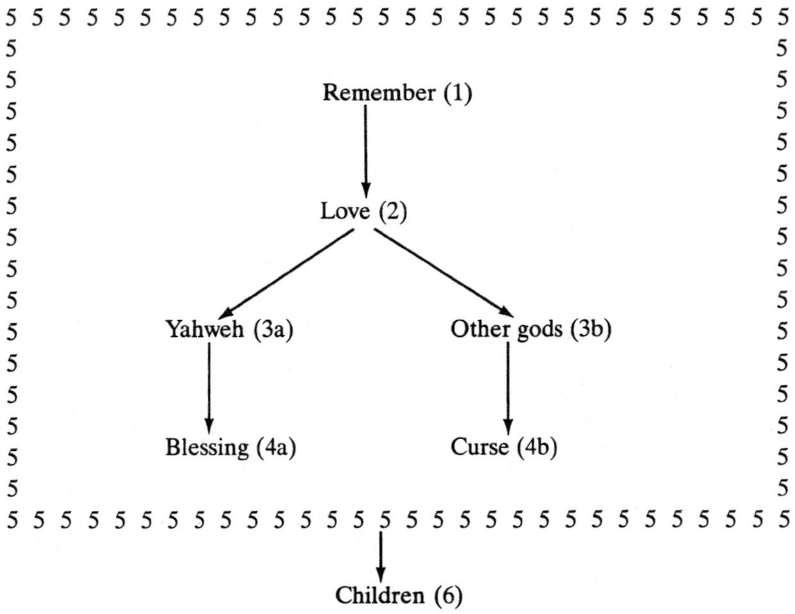

(1) Remember, do not forget, watch, learn, set your heart to
(2) Love, fear, go after, know, serve, hear/obey
(3a) Yahweh, who brought forth, loves, chose, swore, gives land
(3b) Other gods
(4a) Blessing: life, good, the land, length of days, "satiety"
(4b) Curse: death, evil, destruction
(5) The nations
(6) Teach, make your children know: length of days in the land

"VINEYARDS YOU DID NOT PLANT"

What is the "false consciousness" which results in going after other gods?[5] It is to focus on one's own efforts and deserts, and to understand oneself in terms of effort and deserving: as achiever. Several passages make this clear. In chapter 6, Israel is warned, when Yahweh brings them into the land—

> great and good cities you did not build,
> [11]houses full of every good which you did not fill,
> wells dug which you did not dig,
> vineyards and olive groves you did not plant—

> and you eat and are satisfied:
> 12watch yourself,
> lest you forget Yahweh,
> who brought you forth from the land of Egypt,
> from the house of slaves.
>
> (6:10–12)

The "good things" of the land are not the result of Israel's effort:

> Cities you did not build,
> houses you did not fill with good things,
> wells you did not dig,
> vineyards and olive groves you did not plant.

Two other passages in Deuteronomy shed light on this one. In them, "houses" and "vineyards" occur as part of a litany of good things standing for the central goods of life, the means and substance of human existence. One passage is found in the law of Holy War, in a list of those who are to be excused from fighting: anyone who has "built a new house and not dedicated it,"[6] anyone who has "planted a vineyard and not harvested it,"[7] anyone who has "married a wife and not taken her" (Deut. 20:5–7). In each case, the reason the man is to be sent home is "lest he die in war and another man dedicate it," or "lest another man harvest it," or "lest another man take her." The implication is, it would be a horrible thing if another were to enjoy the fruits of one's efforts: the natural consequence of work or intention would be frustrated. One's effort would be rendered futile. This is why the same triad—house, vineyard, wife—recurs in the list of curses in Deuteronomy 28 (v. 30). The Israelites are told that if they go after other gods,

> A wife you will betroth: another man will have her.
> A house you will build: you will not dwell in it.
> A vineyard you will plant: you will not harvest it.

Effort is to result in its payoff. If this natural order of things is frustrated, that is a curse, the "curse of futility," as Delbert Hillers has termed it.[8] This much is clear.

Clear also is that Israel is the "other" who will take over the good things of the land. The misfortune of the occupants of the land is not what is stressed, however, so much as the absence of effort: cities you did not build, wells you did not dig, vineyards you did not plant.

These good things are not achievement but gift. Israel is to keep this in mind. To think otherwise is to "forget Yahweh," the one who brought them forth from slavery and gave them the land.

"MY POWER AND THE STRENGTH OF MY HAND"

The point could be made more clearly if our passage in chapter 6 explicitly said, You will take possession of the land and its good things, but these goods you did not work for or achieve, so do not think that it is your doing that got them for you: do not forget Yahweh. As it is, all chapter 6 says is, You will enjoy good things you did not work for: do not forget Yahweh. For that missing step—do not think that it is your doing that got you these goods—we have to go to the expansion of chapter 6 we find in chapter 8:

> 11 Watch yourself,
> lest you forget Yahweh, your god, . . .
> 12 lest,
> (when) you eat and are satisfied,
> and build good houses and dwell in them,
> 13 and your herds and flocks multiply,
> and silver and gold multiply for you,
> and everything you have multiplies,
> 14 your heart be lifted up,
> and you forget Yahweh, your god,
> the one who brought you forth from the land of Egypt,
> from the house of slaves, . . .
> 17 and you say in your heart,
> "My power and the strength of my hand
> have made for me this wealth."[9]
> 18 Remember Yahweh, your god,
> for it is he who gives you power to make wealth,
> in order to cause his covenant to stand,
> which he swore to your fathers,
> as on this day.
>
> (8:11–14, 17–18)

By this long deployment of texts I have been trying to clarify what Deuteronomy 6 and 8 are saying. To attribute to one's own efforts or strength the good things of the land is to forget Yahweh. Authentic Israelite consciousness understands those good things as gift, not as something earned by one's power or the strength of one's hand. Authentic Israelite consciousness does not center on one's own effort but on Yahweh as giver of good things.

ENTITLEMENT

Neither are these goods something deserved:

7 Not because you are greater than all the peoples
did Yahweh embrace you and choose you,
for you are littlest of all the peoples:
8 but because Yahweh loved you
and because he keeps his oath he swore to your fathers
Yahweh brought you forth
with a strong hand,
and he freed you from the house of slaves,
from the hand of Pharaoh king of Egypt.

(7:7–8)

Again, the statement of Yahweh's purpose, the reminder that he is the one who frees from slavery. Israel has no special quality that deserves his favor. Israel only exists as a people because of that liberation.

Just as Israel is not to attribute its freedom or peoplehood to its "greatness," so the victory over the city-states of Canaan should not be attributed to its "justice" *(ṣ^{e}dāqāh):*

4 Do not say in your heart,
when Yahweh, your god, thrusts them out before you,
"It is because of my *ṣ^{e}dāqāh*
that Yahweh caused me to come in
to take possession of this land"—
it is because of the wickedness of these nations
that Yahweh is dispossessing them before you.
5 Not because of your *ṣ^{e}dāqāh* and uprightness of heart
are you coming to take possession of their land
but because of the wickedness of these nations
Yahweh, your god, is dispossessing them before you,
and in order to cause the word to stand
which Yahweh swore to your fathers,
to Abraham, to Isaac, and to Jacob.
6 Know that it is not because of your *ṣ^{e}dāqāh*
that Yahweh, your god, is giving you this good land
to take possession of:
for you are a hard-necked people.

(9:4–6)

The threefold repetition drives the point home: not because of your justice. . . . It is not that you are in the right, but that the nations are in the wrong. (The implication is that, as we shall see below, the same fate will befall Israel if they, like the nations before them, begin to practice *riš'āh,* "wickedness.")

The form of self-understanding and of action that Deuteronomy seems at pains to warn Israel away from, then, focuses on effort and deserts. This way of seeing oneself and reality understands the "good things" as something achieved, and as something deserved. It tells me to say, "My power and the strength of my hand are the reason for my success." It tells me to say, "I have all this because I am in the right." It uses the category of entitlement. I am entitled to all this because I worked hard for it. I am entitled to this because I am the one who is in the right.

A POLITICAL THEOLOGY

Deuteronomic thought on this point is obviously crucial for the question this book is treating, so I would like to go into it at some length. Deuteronomy is usually taken to inculcate certain attitudes, and to impart a spirituality; and so it does. I think that the caution of 8:17—"Do not say in your heart, 'My power and the strength of my hand have made for me this wealth' "—is central to this theological teaching. But what readers very often miss is that this is a political theology. It is Israel, as a political entity, a people, that is being given a spirituality. Deuteronomy is a meditation on peoplehood and politics. The warning of 8:17 is at the heart of the book's vision of political life. To explain this connection between selfhood and politics will take some doing.

If we anachronistically used philosophical categories like "spirit" and "matter," we could understand Deuteronomic thought as warning Israel against being caught up in the pursuit of material goods. That is simply wrong. The presupposition of these cautions is that the good things of the land are, precisely, good. They represent Yahweh's purpose for Israel. He swore to your fathers to give them this land. He embraced and chose you, to do and give you good. Far from denigrating these good things, Deuteronomy is at pains to tell Israel how to hold on to them, and to warn against the kinds of choices that will lose them for ever.

To try to clarify this matter of choice, though, I would like to commit some anachronisms myself, by introducing certain terms. One term is "intention"; another is "the Good"; a third is "embodiment" or symbolism. These labels can be helpful in answering questions raised by the passages we have just surveyed. What is the connection between effort and deserving: between focusing our selfhood on achievement and focusing our selfhood on being in the right? Why is attributing success to our own power or our own "righteousness" tantamount to going after other gods?

GOOD IN ITSELF, GOOD FOR ME

When I "intend" a good—set my heart on it and try to achieve it—I see it as embodying the Good. That uppercase "G" is meant to indicate that the specific good I aim at fits in with the vision of what my world tells me is seemly, desirable, valuable, important. It is not a good by my idiosyncratic say-so. It is "validated," as a good, by the consensus shared by all right-minded, morally sensitive persons. Anybody worth taking seriously would take this seriously. It is a good *in se,* in itself.

Besides being a good *in se,* what I set my heart on to achieve is a good for me. There is a fit between it and me. When we buy something to wear, we think, "It's me!"; and we hope that our friends will tell us, "It's you!" Just so, what I intend as a good is, in some sense, Me. It embodies who I am and what I am all about.

There is, then, a double embodiment. Because the good I intend is good in itself and good for me, it embodies the Good, and it embodies me. And so it links the Good and me. In intending it, therefore, I am making a double choice. I am choosing the specific good I intend, and I am choosing to be such and such a person.

Other people are important to my choice. I expect them to applaud or approve of—or "validate"—the good I intend. By their approval they validate me as chooser: as identified with what, in itself, is good.

And they validate me as identified, through that specific good, with the Good.

Choices

This is the structure of choice. Among the many choices I make, there are some that have more weight than others. Some goods are surrounded with a kind of aura. They have overwhelming importance. In my choice of them my very selfhood is at stake. Those fundamental choices express who I am, and they shape who I am. The specific good I intend can tell me, and others, who I am, at the core of my selfhood. These special goods are special, also, because they express my conviction about what is important and valuable, at the core of reality. They can become identified with Good itself.

These are the interesting choices, the ones in which my entire sense of myself and of reality are involved. I invest my whole selfhood in them. I desire those special goods with all my heart. They preoccupy me, pushing out other interests and concerns. They shape the way I spend my time and the way I deal with other people. My whole life is organized around them, like iron filings around a magnet. They are the "agenda" I live by. I talk about them a lot. I might even be a bit touchy about them. They are Me, and you better approve. If you don't approve it shows you lack discernment, or you're envious, or— well, I would defend my choice. I would vindicate myself and the Good.

Ṣedeq and Nāqām. If here we bring in some of the biblical terms we have been using we could put things this way. The choice of the good I intend is in conformity with *ṣedeq.* In identifying with it and achieving it, I make myself *ṣaddiq,* "righteous," "in the right." Those who disapprove of or are indifferent to me and the good I choose are outside the circle of *ṣedeq.* They are "wicked." So I want to see *nāqām* effected, to vindicate both me and what is right.

Idolatry. We could use the language of "idolatry." Because the good I set my heart on embodies or symbolizes the Good, and because it embodies or symbolizes Me, it can be called an *eidōlon,* "image." Because it shapes my perceptions and choices, and determines my sense of what is real and important, and altogether determines my life, it has a hold on me. I "worship" it: think about it, revere it, orient myself by it, am centered on it. It is in a real sense the object of *latria,* "worship." I worship an image, of myself and of the Good as I identify myself with the Good. I am an idolator.

Mišpāṭ. We could apply our term *mišpāṭ* to all this. In identifying myself with a good, and that good with the Good, I have the say about reality. I am exercising *mišpāṭ.* In striving to attain it, also, I am exercising *mišpāṭ.* In a real sense, I am creating myself, and am shaping reality in accordance with what I have determined reality will be. My whole sense of myself is bound up with this exercise of *mišpāṭ.* As idolator I am determined by my idol: it has infinite power over me. But, paradoxically, what is at stake is my sense of myself as having *mišpāṭ.* Because I try to have the ultimate say about myself, and about reality, I am the prisoner of the idol that promises to give me that power. I am powerless before it.

What if the good I intend is not simply egoistic but is unambiguously good? Suppose I set my heart on carrying out the works of mercy—feeding the hungry, say. Feeding the hungry is a good-in-itself, and to choose to be someone who feeds the hungry is good-for-me. Everybody would assent to that. But my choice could be idolatrous. I could so identify with that good that I corrupt it. I could make the good work of feeding the hungry the source of my very selfhood. It could become the be-all and end-all of my life. Then it would have turned into an absolute, making me incapable of seeing value in other human goods. Poetry and music and sports are a waste of time. People who indulge in such trivial pursuits are themselves trivial. If I am identified, at the core of my selfhood, with this good work, I see myself as "just," or "righteous": the *ṣedeq* of feeding the hungry makes me *ṣaddīq.* Because I am *ṣaddīq* I have the right to judge or dismiss those who are not. I have standing because of my "righteousness."

It is possible, analogously, to absolutize—to place at the core of my selfhood—wrongs done to me. Then I take my sense of myself from my feeling that I did nothing to deserve the wrongs I have suffered, and from the malice, or indifference, of others. I am in the right (since I did nothing to deserve what I have suffered), and my victimizers are in the wrong—and so is everybody who does not treat with the proper seriousness the gross injustice visited upon me. I am a victim, and demand that everyone else condole with me: my innocence entitles me to that much at least. My sufferings give me identity. They make me somebody, and give me standing. In many ways, this form of idolatry is the most gratifying of all.

Effort and Earning

What is central in the idolatrous form of self-understanding is the need to feel certain that the good I intend is really mine. If I want others to endorse my choice and my achievement of the good, and so to validate me as identified with it, I have to feel that I am entitled to their recognition. This is where effort comes in. It is intolerable that others would say, he did that by dumb luck. Luck, or the kindness of strangers, has nothing to do with my achievement. It was Me, my power and the strength of my own hand, that won me this success. I am entitled to recognition for it: it is a matter of fairness. Ultimately, it comes down to certain qualities in me: ability, diligence, "the right stuff." It was my righteousness that won me this success. I earned it, by effort and, ultimately, "righteousness." This "earning" mentality is immensely threatened by gratuity. It cannot tolerate anything like the prospect that there really is such a thing as a free lunch. It uses a rigorous calculus of debit and credit, of loss and gain. It stringently divides things between "mine" and "thine." It insists on the proportion between effort and its payoff. Everything has to compute.

Gratuity. Gratuity, then, is the enemy of this form of self-understanding. It simply bypasses a sense of earning and proportion and entitlement and deserving, as being beside the point. Gratuity can take a couple of different forms. One is playfulness. If you go about some project or activity in a spirit of playfulness, there is no further agenda at stake. You can invest vast amounts of effort and be wholly caught up in it, but all that matters is the love of it. Even if you are not that good a pianist, practice *The Well-Tempered Clavier* and its marvels will begin to disclose themselves to you. You will fall in love with it. It will be hard work but it will be a joy.

Another form of gratuity is, of course, love. But I have already indicated this. In talking about playfulness I found myself talking about love: love of music, love of J. S. Bach. To be caught up in the liberating joy of working at something, free of the self-regarding compulsion to prove oneself, shapes us in a certain way. It makes us capable of delight, appreciation, being surprised by joy. It enables us to let go of "mine" and "thine." It opens us up to others as they are in themselves, not as we need them to be.

DEUTERONOMY'S VISION

And this is what Deuteronomy holds up as the norm of what Israel is to be. Its vision of Israel is put in terms of warning against idolatry, but that warning has as its other face a promise of what we can be. Do not set your heart on what is not really central or primary or absolute: live in the real world. Do not be proving yourself—your righteousness, the power of your hand—by your attainments: you live in a world where things come as gift. Do not be calculating and grasping: you have nothing to prove. Do not anxiously strive for the fulfillment of your agenda: you can take delight in things for their own sake. Do not try to have everything "compute" ("I don't want any surprises"): be free enough to be open to surprise. Do not take everything as earned: you can be capable of saying Thanks.

These are attractive human qualities. The person who embodies the self-understanding Deuteronomy preaches is one capable of openness to the other, of listening, appreciation, graciousness, delight, reverence, trust, surprise, thanksgiving. Such a person is free of anxiety, the compulsion to prove himself or herself by constant effort and by always being in the right. Deuteronomy presents these qualities—this form of selfhood—as indispensable to "long life in the land." Once Bread is relativized (8:3), it comes as a byproduct. Take the land and the good things of the land as gift, not as object of anxious effort and jealous entitlement: they will be there for you. A political entity founded on concern for the other will be characterized by justice, equity, and abundance. Seek first the *mišpāṭ* of Yahweh, and his *ṣedeq,* and all these things will be added. These Deuteronomic qualities are essential if Israel is to "make it" as a people.

YAHWEH

But these qualities and the self-understanding they flow from are the human side of a theological reality. It is the counterpart of the way Yahweh is. He loved you and embraced you and swore to Abraham, Isaac, and Jacob. He led you through the wilderness and cared for you and gave you bread from heaven. He is the *'ēl qannā'*, the passionate god, and what he is passionate about is being gracious and generous. He cares about the other, as other, and wants you to be capable of the same openness to the other. That is the burden of all his "judgments." Accept his *mišpāṭ* and allow him to have the say, and you will have "good." Be free of the need to have and carry out your own *mišpāṭ*. That compulsion only subjects you to the power of the other gods. They would have you absolutize Bread, and security, and earning your salvation by your own power and your own righteousness. They teach you to see and deal with others only in so far as they figure in to your agenda, to take advantage of them in order to secure Bread or security. Their *mišpāṭ* is illusory, telling you that horse and chariot is the means to security and to long life in the land. They countenance injustice and the power politics of the nations. Have nothing to do with them, or with Canaanite ways, or with the ways of the nations round about. Follow the judgments and statutes of Yahweh, the god who brought you forth from slavery. This is life and blessing and good. Choose life, that you may live.

Yahweh, the "passionate god," cares passionately about these things, but he cares passionately also about *riš'āh*, "wickedness." This is clear from the passage we saw above, Deut. 9:4–5. The wickedness of the nations is what lost them the land. And in what did this wickedness consist? Why, in precisely the injustice and oppression and adventurism Israel is being warned against. The nations followed the *mišpāṭ* of their gods, who teach one to say, "My power and the strength of my hand got me this success," and to understand success—the be-all and end-all of human existence, the one necessary thing—as Bread. For that reason, they lost what they so absolutely set their hearts on.

BLESSING AND CURSE

The contrast is seen clearly in the blessings and curses at the end of the Book of Deuteronomy (28:15–68). There, the consequences of the two forms of peoplehood are spelled out. Life and death, blessing and curse. These are consequences, not punishments. "Punishment," to my ear at least, has the connotation of something extrinsic to an offense: a spanking, say, or being denied certain ordinary privileges. What the curses describe is sober political reality: invasion by a foreign enemy, siege, famine, breakdown of public order, epidemic disease, conquest, slavery, and exile. Reliance on horse and chariot, and entering into treaties and alliances, in order to guarantee security, entails domestic upset and the manipulation, not to say oppression, of the powerless, but it also involves Israel in playing the Great Powers game. This leaves Israel open to the demands of the Great Powers, with their contending claims. Israel thus becomes vulnerable to demands, owing to its foreign entanglements, and to the sanctions—*nāqām*—the Great Powers exact when their will is defied. Israel becomes vulnerable to invasion and conquest. Thus, Deuteronomy shows the connection between systemic contradictions in Israel's life as a people—negation of its fundamental identity as the people of Yahweh, through calculating manipulation of the poor and foreign adventurism—and the consequences of those contradictions: invasion and defeat.

THE HISTORICAL CONTEXT

This Deuteronomic understanding of what it is to be Israel, and of the consequences of fidelity and infidelity to their covenant Lord, is not the fruit of a dispassionate political analysis. It comes out of the anguish of having seen half the people Israel defeated and taken off into exile by Assyria, in the late eighth century B.C. It aims at getting the rest of the people, who survived that disaster—the kingdom of Judah—to turn from the same disastrous course, before it is too late. That accounts for the hortatory tone of the book. Choose life, that you may live. The Israel to whom Moses' words are addressed, in the seventh century, was involved in the same ruinous policies that had made the doom of the Northern Kingdom inevitable. They chose to stand outside the circle of Yahweh's *ṣedeq*. Deuteronomy wants to bring them inside the circle, in every aspect of national life and above all by freeing themselves from the claims of the gods of the nations in their worship and in their choices. The words of Moses are trying to get them to turn back to Yahweh.

THE DEUTERONOMISTIC HISTORY

This Deuteronomic political theology informs the account of Israel's history that we find in the books that follow Deuteronomy: Joshua, Judges, Samuel, and Kings. In Deuteronomy through 2 Kings we have Israel's story from Moses to the exile, from the thirteenth to the sixth centuries B.C. Because the ideas and themes that determine the presentation of this history come from the same school of thought that gave us Deuteronomy, these books taken together are called the Deuteronomistic History.[10] ("Dtr" is the abbreviation used for both the Deuteronomistic History and its author.)

Of course, not every part of every one of these books (Joshua—Kings) comes from the pen of Dtr. There are old poems, annals, census and boundary lists, genealogies, and narratives. Sometimes the narratives have already been gathered together into a collection or cycle of stories (e.g., the stories about Elijah and Elisha, or the so-called Court Narrative in 2 Samuel). These Dtr weaves together with linking passages, introductions, bracketing comments, and the like. We recognize the hand of Dtr in the vocabulary and literary style so characteristic of Deuteronomy, as well as in the ideas. For example, originally unconnected stories about the "Judges" of early Israel are linked together in the Book of Judges by an introduction (Judges 2:11–23) that tries to fit them into a pattern. The pattern goes like this: Israel's infidelity would lead to their being oppressed (for X years); Israel would groan, Yahweh would raise up Judges or saviors, and Israel would have rest (for Y years); then the whole process would start over. The stories of early Israel that had survived thus were made to exemplify the theories of the Deuteronomic school, the political theology sketched above.

Three aspects of Dtr deserve attention here: the picture of the "conquest" of Canaan presented in the Book of Joshua; the Books of Kings; and Dtr's view of Yahweh's part in the history of Israel.

THE BOOK OF JOSHUA

The Book of Joshua, as we have it, must be dated to the time when Dtr was composed, towards the end of the seventh century B.C.[11] It is important to understand the book in this historical context. There is the same distance in time between the Book of Joshua and the events it purports to narrate as there would be between a work written nowadays and the time of Richard II. Israel's taking possession of the land becomes the occasion for the writer to express some convictions about Israel and what Israel is to be, and to get that point of view across to the reader. The "conquest" is a metaphor for Israel's relation to the land and to the nations. The book presents the "conquest" as a rapid process. Yahweh gives victory that is entire, unambiguous, and consistent. Yahweh goes forth to battle as the Divine Warrior, and the enemy is thrown into panic; the theology of Holy War—rely on Yahweh, he wars for you—is strongly insisted on. The "conquest" is carried out by "all-Israel," not the individual tribes. The people work together; they are not seeking private or merely regional success. Joshua is presented as successor of Moses, and the "conquest" is clearly a continuation of the liberation from Egypt. At the end, the land belongs to Israel and Israel only: the nations are driven out or destroyed. The land is divided up in an orderly way, by divine authority, and in the covenant ceremony at Shechem the people become Yahweh's people-in-the-land, settling down to live happily ever after. Yet there is a cautionary note in the story of Achan (chap. 7). Achan violates the law of *ḥērem,* and Israel loses to the enemy; when Achan is discovered and cut off from his people, Israel wins. In the context of later Israel, the story's meaning is unmistakable. War is not to be fought for gain or profit. If war becomes a means for people to get rich, Yahweh will not be with Israel: they will lose.[12] Getting and, by implication, holding on to the land depends on fidelity to and reliance on Yahweh, as it also depends on Israel's being one people, united in common allegiance to Yahweh. And the nations, the Canaanites, come to represent all that would keep Israel from being the people of Yahweh. Have nothing to do with them. Ruthlessly cut them off from before you. Do not marry with them or make treaties with them or worship their gods.

The Book of Joshua, then, is not interested in imparting information about the taking of the land in the thirteenth or twelfth century. Its purpose is to teach a moral lesson to seventh-century Israel. Extermination of the "seven nations"—making them *ḥērem,* "dooming them to destruction"—is a metaphor for eradicating from Israelite life the values and ways of doing things of the Canaanite kingdoms. Only if that total separation from the ways of Canaan is effected will Israel be able to avoid losing the land Yahweh has given them. In the aftermath of the Assyrian invasion and defeat of the Northern Kingdom, that lesson would have special point.

THE BOOKS OF KINGS

Throughout Dtr, the Deuteronomistic Historian is at pains to show how unconditional fidelity to the covenant Lord is crucial in Israel's existence, and how ruin is the consequence of infidelity, but this is especially so in Kings. As we saw above, Solomon's infidelity to Yahweh precipitated the division of the kingdom:

> 9And Yahweh was angry with Solomon,
> for his heart had turned away from Yahweh, the god of Israel, . . .
> 11And Yahweh said to Solomon:
> "Because it has been this way with you,
> that you have not kept my covenant and my statutes,
> which I commanded you,
> I am going to tear the kingship away from you
> and give it to your servant.
> 12Only, I will not do it in your days,
> for the sake of David, your father:
> from your son's hand I will tear it away.
> 13Indeed, the entire kingship I will not tear away:
> one tribe I will give to your son,
> for the sake of David, my servant,
> and for the sake of Jerusalem, which I have chosen."
> (1 Kings 11:9,11–13)

Hard-headed political theory would find this analysis beside the point. It seems to be the kind of thinking we hear from TV preachers (the gypsy-moth invasion is retribution for the repeal of blue laws). We would prefer to look to more immediate causality than the divine anger. Yet I think that Dtr's analysis is right on target. Consider. Solomon's policies aroused opposition. His policies—a buildup of horse and chariot, an edifice of alliances and treaties, the forced labor and expropriation necessary to sustain his imperialism—offended the Israelite sense of *ṣedeq*. That sense was rooted in the vision of Israel as a people formed out of the experience of oppression and liberation, the people which accepted the *mišpāṭ* of the god who brings forth from slavery, and which knew in its heart that unlimited royal power represented rebellion against that *mišpāṭ*. Hence, Solomon's adversaries were inspired in their political opposition by their allegiance to the normative traditions of Israel, and ultimately by their allegiance to Yahweh. Yahweh raised up adversaries to Solomon (1 Kings 11:14, 23). Just so, the prophet who designated Jeroboam as king and legitimated the start of a new kingdom acted in the conviction that he was sent to proclaim the *mišpāṭ* of Yahweh. The breakaway kingdom had the effect of vindicating authentic Israelite *ṣedeq*. The motive force, then, in the dynamics of Israelite political life was the *ṣedeq* and *mišpāṭ* of Yahweh. This shaped people's sense of themselves as Israelites and so their reaction to royal policies, and moved them to action.

In 2 Kings 17, Dtr gives an analysis of the dynamics leading to the fall of the North: it came about

> because the Sons of Israel sinned against Yahweh, their god, the one who had caused them to go up from the land of Egypt, from under the hand of Pharaoh, king of Egypt: they feared other gods. 8They walked according to the statutes of the nations which Yahweh had dispossessed before them. . . .
> 11bThey did wicked things, causing Yahweh to be anguished,
> 12and served the idols of which Yahweh had said to them, "Do not do this."
> 13Yahweh warned Israel and Judah, by the hand of all his prophets, every seer, saying, "Turn from your evil ways and keep my commandments, my statutes, according to all the instruction which I commanded your fathers and which I sent to you by the hand of my servants, the prophets." 14They would not listen, but . . . 15. . . they went after emptiness and they became empty, and after the nations which surrounded them, like whom Yahweh commanded them not to act. . . . 18Yahweh was very angry with Israel, and caused them to turn away from his face: none remained except the tribe of Judah, by itself. (2 Kings 17:7–8, 11b–14a, 15b, 18)

As we saw a chapter ago, it was indeed the policies of the kings that brought about doom, and those policies were at heart choices of other gods: absolutizing Bread and security. It was as simple as that. The stance that people took toward Yahweh and toward his claims on them determined their life as a people; their choices, and the consequences of their choices. In focusing in on this, Dtr deserves high marks for political analysis.

THE PASSIONATE GOD

Yet, in Dtr, Yahweh is represented as more than just the point of reference for people's perceptions and choices. He is active, "raising up" Judges and adversaries, selling Israel into the hand of the oppressor, sending "his servants," the prophets, to proclaim his "word" of *mišpāṭ*. He is not remote or inert. He is an actor in the political life of Israel. He is involved, warning, pleading, anguishing, remonstrating. The involvement of Yahweh is presented as a real working, not simply letting things play out according to an immanent logic. He reacts to events, and brings about events.

So Dtr understands Israel's history according to the Deuteronomic categories of choice and consequences, and aims at getting people to change before it is too late. But Dtr also sees an active involvement of Yahweh, vindicating his *ṣedeq* and his *mišpāṭ*. To Deuteronomic ways of thinking, the destruction of the Southern Kingdom at the hands of the Babylonians would have seemed one more—one last?—instance of his involvement in the life of his people, and would have raised agonizing questions. How could he give up on Israel? Was it really, finally, too late? Were things irretrievable?

CHAPTER 8

Exile and Apocalyptic

Dtr was not designed to explain the exile. Why were the people of Judah besieged and taken into exile by the Babylonians? In its original form, Dtr aims at explaining the dynamics that led to the fall of the North to the Assyrians in 721 B.C., not the fall of Judah in 587.[1] It was trying to avert just such a disaster, as I tried to show in the previous chapter, by exhorting Judah to be faithful to Yahweh's *mišpāṭ* and by warning against the consequences of infidelity. But writings take on different meanings in different historical contexts. Read against the background of the exile, Deuteronomy and Dtr might well seem to be saying, It was all your fault, in "I told you so" fashion. This could sit poorly with those lamenting the loss of their homeland. Dtr thinks macrocosmically, and people who have suffered a loss tend to think more particularly. They might search their consciences and find that, as far as they were concerned, they were not at fault. They might feel that they were in the right, and be puzzled at what had happened to them. If they believed, as they almost certainly did, that the exile represented an act of Yahweh's *mišpāṭ*, they could question its justice. Is Yahweh's *mišpāṭ* just? Can it claim *ṣedeq?* The agonized question, full of rage and bewilderment, was asked. We know that it was asked, because it is the question at the heart of the Book of Job.

THE BOOK OF JOB

Part of the fascination of that book is its seeming universality—its timelessness and lack of connection to any specific historical context. Job is not an Israelite. He lives in the mythic land to the east, where wisdom flourishes and deep discussions are the accepted thing. There are no historical references or topical allusions. The questions it treats, in story and dialogue form, are perennial questions: judgment and justice. Yet I think we have to read the book in the light of just the sort of anguished questioning sketched in the previous paragraph: the challenge to Yahweh's *mišpāṭ* that the exile would have precipitated. Far from being perennial or universal, Job is a tract for the times, and the times are the times of exile.[2] At the very least, the Book of Job would read with a special poignancy in the sixth century B.C. It would be natural to take as one's own the story of a man suffering heavy blows and shaking his fist at his Creator. Writings take on meaning in the context in which they are read.

Job knows himself to be in the right. He has done nothing to deserve what he has suffered. Yet he proclaims the hopelessness of his plight: how can he win his case? God is his accuser and judge and jury:

> 15Though I am in the right I cannot answer:
> for my *mišpāṭ* I must ask mercy.
> 16If I called him [to trial] and he answered me
> I would not believe that he gave ear to my voice. . . .
> 20Though I am in the right my mouth would put me in the wrong;[3]
> Integrity is mine—he would make me twisted. . . .
> 22. . . It is all one: therefore I say,
> [both] the person of integrity and the wicked he destroys.
> (9:15–16, 20, 22)

> 2I will say to God, Do not put me in the wrong,[4]
> make me know why you have contended with me.
> (10:2)

Job's friends have no doubts about who is in the right. It is not Job. They have come to "comfort" or "console" Job (2:11). Their task is *naḥ^{a}māh,* "consolation." The root *nḥm* means to change the way one thinks or feels or acts: his friends want to change Job's outlook. Most often people are clumsy at this ("In a hundred years . . ."), unless they come with an objective piece of news ("The war is over!"), and Job's comforters have only conventional bromides to offer. Curiously, the root *nḥm* in some contexts takes on the meaning—or at least is translated—"repent," as in the old translation of Ps. 110:4, "The

Lord has sworn and he will not repent," or Jonah 2:9. Job's friends' self-appointed task is as much to get him to repent as to console him. It is all one. In any case, one of the first things out of Job's self-incriminating mouth is a testy

> [8]Would that my request might come true
> and that God would give me my desire:
> [9]that God would be pleased to crush me,
> that he would let loose his hand and cut me off!
> [10]This would be my consolation [my *naḥ*ᵉ*māh*].
> (6:8–10a)

The consolatory bromides Job's friends offer, though, sound suspiciously like the conventional wisdom Israelites would assent to. Yahweh is just, and his judgment is right. If bad things happen they are deserved. Bad things don't happen to good people. The wicked man is cut off: if you happen to be cut off, it shows you're wicked. And so on. They are applying to Job's case a calculus of right and wrong, merit and culpability. The one unquestionable given is that God is always in the right. Hence, Job must be in the wrong.

This Job vigorously rejects. He is not in the wrong, God is. He does not deserve what has happened to him. In his case, bad things have happened to good people. Hence, God's *mišpāṭ* is not fair. *Ṣedeq* is not on God's side.

The one point in the argument that Job cedes to his consolers—and that the reader, identifying imaginatively with Job, is tricked into granting as well—is that matter of calculus. Merit, deserts, entitlement. Job uses the categories of deserving and not deserving, in his railing about justice and judgment, just as much as his three friends do in their artless attempts at theodicy. And it is this that the voice from the whirlwind seizes on at the end of the book, the "answer" to Job. Are you so sure of the way you see things that you can call God to account? Do you have things so thoroughly figured out? Who (in effect) do you think you are?

Job goes silent. It is presumptuous to try to figure out the way God runs things. Mortals cannot read his purposes. God operates by a different calculus than the tidy equations we set up. Who has been his counselor?

JOB AND "DEUTERONOMIC" THOUGHT

The connections with Deuteronomy and Dtr are plain. On the one hand, Deuteronomic thought could easily be read—make that misread—as presenting a calculus of deed and retribution, whether reward or punishment. (It is still misread that way, as I tried to show above.) Worse, this pseudo-Deuteronomic theodicy can be turned around, from saying, "If you're bad bad things will happen to you," to concluding, "Bad things have happened to you so you must be bad." That wealth and long life were seen as reward, and the illation made that rich and long-lived people were therefore good people, is clear from the wisdom literature, so it is not surprising that popular thinking would read Deuteronomy in this way. It is precisely this folk wisdom that the Book of Job is attacking. (Ironically, of course, the strong Deuteronomic insistence on not attributing success to one's own merits runs directly counter to this "works-righteousness" mindset.)

THE CREATOR GOD

On the other hand, there is a deeper issue at stake. The cloud of unknowing that chastens Job calls into radical question our ability to figure out what God is up to. But the Deuteronomistic corpus has as its purpose, at least in part, to insist on precisely that: the divine purpose is plain, and Yahweh is passionately involved in the life of Israel as a people. He does not acquit the guilty, but those who put their trust in him will not be confounded. This is at the heart of the dynamics of history so choose accordingly. In the view of the author of Job, this is presumptuous. The god who speaks from the whirlwind, challenging Job to declare how he can be so sure of things, is the Creator God:

> 4Where were you when I laid the foundations of earth?
> Tell me, if you know understanding.
> 5Who set up its measurements—for you know!
> Or who stretched the line upon it? . . .
> 8Or who shut in Sea with doors
> when it burst forth from the womb,
> 9when I made cloud its garment
> and thick darkness its swaddling band,

10and prescribed my statute for it
and set bars and doors,
11and said, "Up to here shall you come, no farther,
and here shall your proud waves be stayed"?
(38:4–5, 8–11)

Here we recognize the old language of cosmic lordship, "creation." Yahweh is the one who set things up the way they are, fashioning the structure of reality, subduing Sea. If Job cannot understand the intricacies of the universe, if he must stand silent before its vastness and the cunning workmanship that gave it shape, how can he know what Yahweh is up to in the murkiness and ambiguity of human existence? Only the "Creator God" can be known (and that only in awe and silence), not the god who acts in history.

If Job can be read, in the context of the exile, as a rebuttal of popular versions of Deuteronomic (or pseudo-Deuteronomic) thinking, and as an attack on even asking the question *why,* the portion of the Book of Isaiah we call Second Isaiah (chaps. 40—55 and 34—35) can be read as an answer to Job.[5]

SECOND ISAIAH

The setting of Second Isaiah is the exile, and its purpose is "consolation" or "comfort." The book begins with a dialogue in the heavenly court. Yahweh gives a command to the divine council, to "comfort" his people: to bring them *naḥᵃmāh.* They are to "cry" or "call"—the technical term for what a messenger does: really, "proclaim"—and what they are to proclaim is that the servitude of Jerusalem is over. Thus, the *naḥᵃmāh* these divine messengers bring does not consist of the bromides of Job's comforters: these messengers have hard news. The commission is carried out by a voice proclaiming the beginning of return to Zion. The "way" of Yahweh is to be prepared in the wilderness, leading from Babylon to Jerusalem. Mount Zion herself is to lift up her voice as a "herald of good tidings": to stand on tiptoe and announce the news to the cities of Judah. The "good news" is that Yahweh comes, on his processional way, leading his people back home, to his holy mountain. This "good news" is expressed, in 35:4, this way:

> Be strong, fear not!
> Behold, your god with vindication comes,
> with divine recompense he comes to save you.

The motif of the warrior god marching to his holy mountain, the place of his enthronement, goes back to earliest Israel and, of course, to pre-Israelite tradition. This is the Creator God, the one who subdues Sea and establishes what is. He is the god who has cosmic *mišpāṭ*. As if to make the point unmistakable, Second Isaiah asks a series of questions that sound like the voice from the whirlwind in Job:

> 12 Who has measured Waters in the hollow of his hand
> and the heavens delimited with a span,
> enclosed the dust of the earth in a measure
> and weighed mountains in scales,
> hills in a balance?
> 13 Who has delimited the spirit of Yahweh,
> who as his counselor instructed him? . . .
> 17 All the nations are as if not, before him,
> as nothingness and the void are they reckoned.
> (40:12–13, 17)

Yahweh is creator. Who can presume to say what he can and cannot do? Why should the nations, of all things, be an obstacle to his working? They are like a drop from a bucket (40:15). This has been known from the beginning: why don't you understand (40:21)? Yahweh is enthroned above the circle of the earth (40:22); he brings princes to nought, makes rulers as nothing (40:23). The Book of Job argued that the Creator's ways are incomprehensible, and so we should not presume to try and figure out what he is up to. Second Isaiah turns the argument around. The Creator's ways are incomprehensible, and so we should not presume to limit what he can and cannot do. He has *mišpāṭ;* the nations are no problem.

The Divine Warrior imagery used in the opening of Second Isaiah (Yahweh "coming" on his processional way to the holy mountain) implies Yahweh's cosmic *mišpāṭ*. The old language of creation and divine kingship serves as introduction to the verses about his incomprehensibility, and about the folly of thinking his *mišpāṭ* somehow fails before the power of the nations, of "kings and judges" (40:23). Thus, the Jobian use of creation imagery is outflanked. But the imagery does something more. It recalls the exodus. The image of the Way—Yahweh marching to his holy mountain, bringing his people in his train—echoes that originative event. Throughout these chapters recurs a dialectic, between the "former things" and "new things"[6] The former things are a clue to the new things, so there is continuity, but the new things are beyond imagining. They are new. The days of old are a type of what is to be, but what Yahweh is now about to bring off will be simply astonishing. What are the "former things"? They are creation and exodus. The new thing is the return from exile to Zion. The god who subdued Sea, and who made a way for those he redeemed from slavery, will now make a way for his own to pass from exile. His mighty arm will do this:

> 9Awake, awake, clothe yourself with strength,
> O arm of Yahweh!
> Awake as in former days,
> generations of eternity!
> 10Was it not you that dried up Sea,
> Waters of the Great Deep,
> making the Depths of Sea a way
> for the redeemed to cross?
> 11[So] the ransomed of Yahweh will return
> and come to Zion with exultation. . . .
> (51:9–11)

The Creator God dried up Sea in primordial times. The Redeemer God made the Depths of Sea a way, from Egypt to freedom. So now, he will make a way in the wilderness, and his people will "come" to Zion, led by the god who "comes with vindication."

Starting with the opening command to the divine council, then, this "good news" of "consolation" to Israel unfolds, together with many other and immensely rich themes (too many and too rich, alas, to treat here), throughout Isaiah 40—55. It is all foreshadowed in the address to desolate and despairing Israel:

> 27Why do you say, O Jacob,
> and speak, O Israel:
> "My way is hidden from Yahweh,
> from my god my *mišpāṭ* passes away"?[7]

28 Do you not know,
have you not heard?
The god of eternity is Yahweh,
creator of the ends of earth.
He does not weary, he does not falter,
nothing is hidden to his understanding.
29 He gives to the weary power,
and for those with no might he multiplies strength.
(40:27–29)

The Jobian lament, that Yahweh has disregarded *mišpāṭ*, springs from the anguish of an exiled people. It is not enough to proclaim the "good news" of return from exile. The reasons for the disaster have to be given, and so they are, as part of the "consolation" the poet offers. Part of the reason was Judah's infidelity:

21 Yahweh was pleased, for the sake of his *ṣedeq*,
to magnify his *tôrāh* and make it great.
22 But this is a people despoiled and plundered,
trapped in holes, all of them,
in prison houses hidden.
They have become a prey, with none to deliver,
a spoil, with none to say, Restore. . . .
24 Who gave Jacob up for plunder,
Israel to the despoiler?
Was it not Yahweh, the one we sinned against,
in whose ways they were unwilling to walk,
whose *tôrāh* they would not hear?
(42:21–22, 24)

This and other passages[8] echo conventional prophetic views. Yahweh gave his people over to destruction because they rejected his *mišpāṭ*, and so they reaped the bitter fruit of their infidelity. They experienced in their lives and their bodies the logic of that rejection. They knew his *mišpāṭ* in the disaster that overtook them. They are blind and deaf, imprisoned, helpless, cast off, weary, "deeply despised, abhorred by the nations" (49:7, RSV). But those nations themselves will reap the fruit of their actions. They will be made to drink the cup of Yahweh's wrath which Jerusalem had been made to drink (51:17–23). Yahweh will bring "a bird of prey from the east" to requite the Babylonians for their mercilessness (46:8—47:15).

THE SERVANT

Besides this vision of vindication for Israel and retribution for Israel's plunderers, there is another theme. Israel is Yahweh's servant, and Yahweh has a purpose for him. The redemption he has in store will affect not only Israel but the nations as well. Kings and princes will be astonished. The nations will marvel at Israel's restoration, as they marveled at Israel's affliction. Israel, his servant, will cause Yahweh's *mišpāṭ* and *ṣedeq* to go forth to the nations. The restoration will not be a private happiness for Israel alone; it will show the nations that there is "none other":

> 6I give you as a light to the nations,
> to be my salvation to the ends of the earth.
> 7Thus says Yahweh, Israel's redeemer, his Holy One,
> to one despised of *nepeš*, abhorred by the nations,
> a servant of rulers:
> "Kings shall see and arise;
> princes, and they will prostrate themselves,
> for the sake of Yahweh, the Faithful One,
> the Holy One of Israel, who has chosen you."
> (49:6b–7)[9]

If this is Yahweh's purpose for Israel his servant, it is focused in the mysterious figure, who is and is not Israel, of the final Servant Song, 52:13—53:12. The man afflicted and despised and rejected as a transgressor is looked on with amazement both by kings and by the people, and his vindication astonishes both parties. His suffering is healing for the people. Though he was reckoned as outside the "circle" of *ṣedeq*, he will bring the many within that circle: this seems to be the core of the very difficult verse 53:11.

The puzzling figure of the Suffering Servant, taken in the context of the entirety of Second Isaiah, confirms the audacious insight of these chapters. Yahweh brings unimagined and unimaginable good even out of injustice and oppression and affliction. Where sin abounds, there his *ṣedeq* and compassion more abound.

"ESCHATOLOGY"

As we saw above,[10] the office of prophet was symbiotic with the institution of kingship. With the end of monarchy in Israel, in the exile, prophecy properly so called came to an end. The writings of Second Isaiah and, from the early days of the restoration, the oracles of Haggai and Zechariah represent a last hurrah for prophecy, and mark the beginning of something new. In the postexilic period the forms of prophecy continued to be used, but in new ways, corresponding to the new political situation. Israel was part of the Persian Empire; the former kingdom of Judah was now the province of Yehud. The governors of the Persian king allowed a certain autonomy to the people of Yehud, the *Yᵉhūdīm,* and they could carry on their way of life according to the covenant traditions, but they were not constituted as a political entity in their own right. They were scattered, with a large and by now well-established Jewish community in Mesopotamia, and, at the other end of the Persian Empire, communities in Egypt and of course in Palestine. Their identity no longer derived from a life shared in a single land, under the rule of a king or even "Judges." In a sense Jews now had dual citizenship, but their membership in the "Sons of Israel" was a shadow citizenship. To the extent that its claims conflicted with Persian *mišpāṭ,* Jews would find themselves (to be anachronistic) *ʿapiru* in the eyes of the empire. Satraps and spies would look suspiciously at anything that might burgeon into a movement of national liberation or weaken the control of the Persian king. Talk of restoring monarchy, say, would be construed as subversive. And, really, it must have been hard for Jews to know what the future held. The only clues they had as to what their future as a people might be were in the "former things," the days of old. Yahweh's purpose could be known in the stories and traditions about nationhood and Judges and kings and prophets, but how that purpose might be realized in the changed political situation, and in the Diaspora, was shadowy. And it had to be kept shadowy, lest the authorities take alarm. The Jewish sense of peoplehood, as Israel, could be talked about only with the utmost circumspection. This accounts for a characteristic feature of postexilic Jewish writings, their seeming timelessness. Someday, in time to come, "at the end of days":[11] visions of a future are hedged about with expressions like these. The desire for an imminent restoration of full peoplehood, and even the expectation of it, may have been there, but it does not find expression except, as it were, between the lines.

Scholars use certain terms to describe these characteristics of postexilic thought. The backward look to olden times as a clue to what the future held—a reminder both of Yahweh's purpose and of what it is to be Israel—and the looking forward to the restoration of those features of Israelite life are referred to by the term "typology." As there was an old covenant, so there will be a new covenant. So, also, there will be a new David, a new Moses, a new gathering to Yahweh's holy mountain, Zion. The old is a "type" of the new. And the apparent "timelessness" of the postexilic writings, and the political hopes they embody, is referred to by the term "eschatology." The covenant will be renewed, and the everlasting kingship of the house of David restored, "at the end *(eschaton)* of days."[12]

"APOCALYPTIC"

So matters remained, through the two hundred years of Persian domination of the Near East and into the period of Greek rule. Some things differed, of course: the Jews in Babylon, in Egypt, and in Palestine found themselves ruled by various successors of Alexander the Great, at various times. During the third century B.C. the Ptolemaic dynasty in Egypt controlled Palestine, so there was free interchange between Jerusalem and Alexandria (as the traditions about the origins of the Septuagint indicate). After the Seleucid dynasty took over control of Palestine, at the beginning of the second century, that connection changed. In any case, Greek culture assaulted Jewish identity.[13] Where the Persians had taken a live-and-let-live attitude Greeks showed a proselytizing zeal. They had a *mission civilisatrice* to the natives. Greek culture, diet, religion, political institutions, urban design, ways of thinking were imposed on the benighted barbarians of the East. As with the Raj, or Indochina, or a score of other colonialist situations in modern times, the result was a polyglot pastiche, and a spiritual crisis for the culture so assaulted.

In the Book of Daniel, and other writings of the early second century B.C., we can hear the echoes of this assault. Very likely dating from the Ptolemaic period, certain stories later incorporated into Daniel tried to put into proper perspective the changes and challenges Jews were being subjected to. Once upon a time, for example, a young Jew was brought to the court of the king of Babylon and found himself beset by troubles of every sort. He was pressured to adopt the diet and manner of the Babylonian court, but resisted and—miraculously—was preserved in health and life. Various enemies tried to bring about his downfall, but they fell into the trap they themselves had set. And so on. The message is clear, to Jews wanting to be faithful to their ancestral ways but confused and scared by the incredible pressures of the dominant culture: be faithful, Yahweh will sustain you.

Why the Babylonian court? The stories we read in the first part of the Book of Daniel are set hundreds of years before the times they actually reflect, and in a distant country. As with the "eschatological" character of writings from the Persian period on, so in these stories there is a distancing from the current situation. The plight of the young Jew in the Babylonian exile is emblematic of the problems Jews under Greek rule faced. If interrogated about these tracts their authors could say, "Oh, this is just a bunch of stories about long ago—just harmless antiquarianism."

The approach is that of underground literature *(samizdat)*: a story about Ivan the Terrible has uncanny resemblances to what happened under Stalin. Or people in Nazi-occupied Paris put on *Antigone*: the conflict between conscience and the tyrant's decrees resonates in the minds of everyone in the audience—everyone except the occupying authorities. The oppressor tends to miss the point. Or rather, the oppressor senses that there is a point, but is at a loss about exactly what it is. The oppressor has to be suspicious about everything, therefore, since he is—by definition—unable to put himself in the place of the oppressed and so cannot fathom what is being said. Unable to discern what is and is not a challenge to his legitimacy and power, he sees subversion everywhere. Solzhenitsyn: for a country to have a great author is like having another government. The capacity to tell and hear stories—to enter imaginatively into another world—is the Archimedean point from which worlds are moved. The oppressor is an outsider to the circle of storyteller and audience, clinging to his own world of control and security, fearful of facing what his imagination might encounter.

Another literary ploy that develops in the period of Greek domination is the "testament." That is as good a term as any for the genre. Some great figure of the remote past, Moses for example, tells what is to befall Israel. He moves through the centuries from his own time to the time of the writer, laying out all that is to happen: the Judges, the kings, the divided monarchy, the fall of the North, the Babylonian exile, the Persian Empire, until he reaches the period of current events. It is all foreknown. Yahweh has a purpose, and is at work. He does not improvise. He is not blind-sided by events. Tyrants may rage and nations trample his sanctuary, the wicked may seem to prosper and the just to be helpless, but Yahweh knows what he is doing. He saves, in his own time and in his own way. Those who put their trust in him will not be confounded. So do not cast your lot with the wicked. Hold on. Be faithful.

Besides the testament, there is the dream. Again, an account of a dream is innocuous: it was only a dream. I saw something like a beast, and then. . . . The dream, of course, reflects what is happening in people's lives, but it also refracts the elements of their lives, so that they can be recognized only by those in the know. The outsider—the oppressor—hears only bizarre imagery and senseless shifts of scene. The meaning of the dream is hidden, for the oppressor, behind a veil. But its meaning is plain to those who are suffering. As a matter of fact, the dream unveils the meaning of what people are going through. It puts into proper perspective the chaotic violence they know in their daily lives, by showing what will happen to the persecutor: by recalling Yahweh's purpose, and his *mišpāṭ*. We shall look at an example of this dream genre below, but now note that the usual term for the kinds of writing we have been surveying is "apocalyptic." Greek *apo-kalypsis* is "un-veiling" (Latin *re-velatio*). It unmasks the pretensions of the oppressor and pulls the veil of anguish and despair away from the minds of the oppressed.

These literary forms—the synoptic survey of Israelite and Jewish history, the exhortation by the great figure of the past, the apocalyptic dream—served to strengthen the resolve of Jews pushed and pulled by their pagan rulers. They took on special importance during the reign of the Seleucid king Antiochus IV, at the beginning of the second quarter of the second century B.C. The Greeks tried to coerce Jews in Palestine to adopt Greek ways and to worship Greek gods.

Antiochus must have been puzzled to find his modernizing and civilizing efforts resisted by the Jews. There was an enlightened minority of Jews who went along with the authorities—contemporary writings call them, simply, "the wicked"—but mostly Antiochus had to force his reforms on the people. This is the setting for the activity of the Maccabees, in 167 B.C., who turned Jewish opposition into open revolt. Not everyone minded to resist Antiochus's persecution went along with the Maccabees. Other groups, called by the collective sobriquet *ḥ*^a^*sīdīm,* "faithful ones," or "pious ones," refused to take up arms and save themselves by their own hand. It is their viewpoint—that of the middle way between the armed activism of the Maccabees and the collaborationism of the "wicked"—that informs the Book of Daniel.

DANIEL 7

In chapter 7 of Daniel, there is a dream. Not only does the dream have the effect of distancing the events it reflects, the dream itself is distanced in time: Daniel is writing down what he saw four centuries before any of the events happen. The imagery would seem bizarre to a non-Jew, but for those in the know it is full of resonances. There is Sea, stirred up. There are beasts from the Sea. The first looks suspiciously like a Babylonian bas-relief, the winged lion, and the others can easily be understood to represent the empires that succeeded the Babylonians. The fourth and last beast could well be the Greek Empire of Alexander and his successors. At least, the beast has ten horns, and there were ten rulers; but it's only a dream. This beast devoured and smashed and trampled. Suddenly among the ten horns another horn erupted, displacing three others. This is Antiochus, the persecutor. We recall the imagery of the "horn" in Israelite tradition ("his horn shall be exalted"), and how it metonymously stands for puissance and power. Only, this last horn is "little." It has eyes and a mouth, and its mouth "talks big" (7:8). So much for Antiochus.

In a few strokes of the cartoonist's pen, the cavalcade of world history is limned and the despot caught to the life—and dismissed. It is not Sea itself—the chaotic force opposed to Yahweh's rule—but merely beasts from the Sea that appear. They are the second team. And Antiochus is not a beast: he is an excrescence on the beast, popping out from amidst the other horns, and as a matter of fact he is "a little horn," talking big.

All this is only prelude to the big scene. We are in the heavenly court. Thrones are placed. The "Ancient of Days"—the primordial one, the one from of old—is enthroned, surrounded by fire and by myriads, the Holy Ones, his ministers, his court. A tribunal is in session; books are opened. Suddenly the only sound is that of the little horn talking big, mindlessly chattering away, spectacularly unaware of what is to befall him. In midsentence the beast is slain and its body destroyed by burning.

We should note here the conception of the heavenly court and of Yahweh's *mišpāṭ* reflected in this dream. The solemn session of the heavenly tribunal is in striking contrast to the cabinet meeting described by Micaiah ben Imlah in 1 Kings 22, where Yahweh seeks the counsel of his court, and after some give and take arrives at a decree.[14] In Daniel, the divine judgment is contained in the books: it is from of old. The difference in conception reflects the different situation of the writer. He is trying to assure people that the doom of the oppressor is ineluctable, foreordained from eternity. Yahweh is not improvising. The only one who does not know this is the tyrant himself. Destruction will overtake him unawares.

There is one more element in the dream. Anomalously, in this scene of the heavenly court, there appears a human figure. More accurately, it is "someone who looked like a human being."[15] What is *he* doing there? He "comes" with the clouds of heaven. Is the word "come" used in the sense of a triumphal procession, as it so often is? The cloud imagery suggests that this is so. This is the old language of theophany and exaltation, applied now to the person who looks like a man who has made his triumphal appearance in the heavenly court. For he is presented before the Ancient of Days, and is given "authority and splendor and kingship," which is everlasting and indestructible.

Theories abound about the identity of this humanlike figure. The language is reminiscent of the Dynastic Oracle (the everlasting kingship), and we recall that the Davidic king was similarly exalted, being enthroned at Yahweh's right hand (Ps. 110:1) while his enemies are trodden under foot. It may simply be the Jewish people corporately conceived,[16] or their guardian angel.[17] It is hard to identify everybody in a dream. Maybe it is all these figures, wrapped up in one.

The central point is that not only will the persecutor be overthrown by Yahweh's *mišpāṭ*: Israel itself will be restored as a political entity, with "authority and splendor and kingship." The dream encourages the oppressed to be faithful in their resistance, and to be trusting of Yahweh, whose judgments are certain. And it holds out to them a vision of a future in which once again they will be a people. Not a shadow people, not a people by sufferance of foreign rulers, or living out their identity in the interstices of dual citizenship: they will be the people—the political entity—Yahweh long ago purposed to form, and which Yahweh again and again redeems (buys back) from the hand of the oppressor, at a great price.

CHAPTER 9

The New Testament

The dissociation of "Old Testament" and "New Testament" is one of the oldest Christian heresies. I want to show the continuity of all that we have seen so far with the proclamation of the "good news" of Jesus, and to show how that continuity is dialectical. I follow the chronological order of the development of NT tradition, by examining the expectations which determined the way Jesus' person and activity were understood, and the reversal or transformation of those expectations; the early Christian and, especially, Pauline understanding of Jesus; and the narrative theology of the Synoptic Gospels.

EXPECTATIONS AND FULFILLMENT

A Palestinian Jew living under the Pax Romana, in the reign of Augustus or Tiberius, might imagine the future in a variety of ways. The apocalyptic vision of Daniel 7 might serve: in the beast from the Sea one could recognize the current embodiment of the force arrayed against Yahweh and his people, the Roman Empire. Yahweh would crush the occupying power and restore "authority, splendor, and kingship" to his people. Or Yahweh might raise up an anointed one, from the House of David, in whom the still-outstanding promise of everlasting kingship would be realized. Or Yahweh might raise up a "savior," like Gideon, who would lead Israel in Holy War against the nations (read: Romans) and while he was at it deal with the "wicked," the unfaithful Jews who collaborated with the Romans in imposing crushing burdens on the poor. Or he might raise up a prophet to declare such a Holy War and to recall the people to covenant fidelity.

In all these scenarios of a future, Yahweh's *mišpāṭ* was central. Yahweh would "judge." For the wicked and for the nations, his "judgment" would mean a bloodbath. They would drink the cup of divine wrath, writhe in anguish as they beheld the Day of *mišpāṭ* dawning, panic and flee before the "coming" of the warrior god and his heavenly hosts, with cloud and fire and earthquake. They would experience Yahweh's *nāqām* as vengeance, being "doomed to destruction": *ḥērem*. They would know the curses of the covenant. Those who stood outside the circle of Yahweh's *ṣedeq* would know its power, as they suffered the fate ordained for the wicked.

For the just, though, Yahweh's *mišpāṭ* would be good news. They would be "consoled" by his vindication. Yahweh's "coming," on his Day, would mean "salvation" from the hand of the oppressor, and they would be led with exultation to his holy mountain, there to enjoy the abundance of his kingship, the feast of celebration, the blessings of the covenant. For the just, Yahweh's *mišpāṭ* meant redemption, peoplehood, salvation, vindication, the beginning of the new age, fullness of life.

The double expectation—of vengeance for the wicked and the nations, of vindication for the just—was all one. There were those within the circle of *ṣedeq* and there were those outside it. To those who looked for the Day of Yahweh, the retribution to be visited upon the wicked and upon the nations was indispensable to the full vindication of the just and of *ṣedeq*. The curse and the blessing went hand in hand.

JESUS

It is against this background of expectation, flowing from the sense of *ṣedeq* and the belief in Yahweh's *mišpāṭ* found in the Scriptures, that Jesus is to be understood. In his own time, people seem to have applied to him these terms and images and motifs, and looked to him as the realization of their desires. "We were hoping he would be the one who would redeem Israel." They thought he might inaugurate the Day of Yahweh, and effect *ḥērem* on the nations and the wicked; as a savior, perhaps even as a *nāzīr*,[1] he might lead them in Holy War. He would be the new David, the anointed of the Lord, enthroned in Jerusalem. And so on.

After the time of Jesus, too, the early church used words derived from the Scriptures to talk about who he was and what his life meant for the world. They named him "anointed one" and "savior" and "redeemer," and a host of other terms. They saw him as, in some sense, that "one like a son of man" on whom "authority, splendor, and kingship" were bestowed. He was the just one vindicated by God, the servant of Yahweh. He was, like the Davidic king, the one who called Yahweh "My father," whom Yahweh called "My son," and who was—like the Davidic king—exalted, enthroned at Yahweh's right hand. They saw his death as instituting a "new covenant" (as in Jer. 31:31). Using prophetic language, they "proclaimed" the story of Jesus as "good news."

"Fulfillment"

Early Christian tradition, and the writings through which we have access to this tradition, spoke of "fulfillment." By their use of this term I think people meant something at once simple and complex. It is simple because they felt that the expectations aroused by Scripture[2] were realized in Jesus: that in and through him the *mišpāṭ* of Yahweh became a reality. He is the one spoken of by the prophets and the Law. If you want to understand Jesus, that language of "fulfillment" suggests, look to the Scriptures. There you will see what and who he is.

It is complex, however, because a dialectic is at work. Scripture reveals who and what Jesus is, but at the same time he reveals what Scripture was really saying. He redefines the very terms used to talk about him, and causes us to read Scripture with new eyes. Jesus is to be seen in the context, and in the terms, of expectations derived from Scripture, but himself transforms those expectations. The dialectic worked along these lines. The followers of Jesus, in the early church, instinctively applied to him the expectations and vocabulary of Israelite and Jewish tradition. When they found those expectations eluded or confounded, however, they went back to Scripture, in their puzzlement, and read it with new eyes. Familiar passages, known by heart, suddenly took on new meaning. The words came alive. I imagine their reaction as being something like, "But I never knew before. I never dreamed. . . ." Zeffirelli captures this moment of realization in his film *Jesus of Nazareth,* in the Good Friday sequence where Nicodemus rounds a corner and beholds the three crosses on the hill of execution. He falters in anguish, and then, as tears stream down his cheeks, the words of Isaiah come unbidden to his lips:

> Surely he hath borne our griefs, and carried our sorrows:
> yet we did esteem him stricken,
> smitten of God, and afflicted.
> But he was wounded for our transgressions,
> he was bruised for our iniquities:
> the chastisement of our peace was upon him;
> and with his stripes we are healed.
>
> (Isa. 53:4–5, KJV)

Some moment like that, I fancy, lies behind the NT language of "fulfillment." "Now I know what those words meant. Now their meaning is made clear. I never knew before. Of course!"

Justice and Judgment

At the heart of this early Christian understanding of Jesus is the question that lies at the heart of Israelite tradition, the question of *ṣedeq* and *mišpāṭ*. The redefinition of the terms of the tradition centered there. It was not (as is so often said) that the Scriptures envisioned a "political messiah" and Jesus corrected that view, or that the kingdom of God was taken to be this-worldly and Jesus proclaimed an otherworldly, spiritual kingdom, or that Jews expected a transformation of human existence ("a new creation") on this earth and Jesus displaced that expectation to life after death. Those views seem to me to proceed from a misunderstanding of the dialectic between Israelite tradition and Christian self-understanding, largely because they depend on the importation of certain categories from another thought-world. The "new" understanding of Kingdom and Messiah and New Creation does not come from an abandonment of political concerns. At its heart is the old, very political question of *ṣedeq* and *mišpāṭ*.

What caused this sea change in the understanding of Scripture—of *ṣedeq* and *mišpāṭ*, of *nāqām* and Yahweh's kingship—was the manner of Jesus' death. The crucifixion of Jesus was an execution. He died a criminal, a malefactor, an evildoer. The evangelists are at pains to show the authorities plotting and, finally, shouting for his death. The authorities saw Jesus as standing outside the circle of *ṣedeq,* and therefore subject to *nāqām.* The wicked man has to be placarded as guilty. Obloquy and scorn are to be poured on his head. He is to feel the hot anger of divine wrath. He is accursed of God. Jesus had to drink the cup of divine wrath. Justice required it.

"A Curse of God"

One phrase in a passage in Deuteronomy (21:22–23) turns up in a number of different streams of early Christian tradition: "a curse of God is every one hanged upon a tree."[3] It seems anomalous and even shocking that Jesus would be called "a curse of God," but the echoes of the Deuteronomic passage are unmistakable. Jesus was hanged upon a tree.[4] It is as if Christian faith rejoiced in the picture of Jesus cast out from the circle of *ṣedeq;* alienated from God, a malefactor, lawless, reckoned with the wicked: "accursed of God." The relationship between the crucifixion and the resurrection is usually put in terms of a contrast: "Jesus died, but was raised; he was humiliated but then exalted; he was condemned by men but vindicated by God; he was delivered over into the hands of wicked men but delivered from the power of death." That contrast between suffering and vindication, death and new life, shame and glory is indeed central to the paschal mystery, but early tradition seems to want to see both parts of the contrast together, as a unity, not dissociated. It was precisely the one cursed of God whom God exalted. "Let all the house of Israel know that God has made both Lord and Messiah this Jesus whom you crucified" (Acts 2:36). Why does Christian faith exult in that? Something in the experience of early Christians corresponded to that sense of being outside the circle of *ṣedeq* and, precisely there, knowing the living God, and so coming to a new, freeing understanding of Yahweh and his justice.

EARLY TRADITION, AND PAUL

I want to trace this theme in Paul and in the Synoptic tradition, to show that, throughout early Christian experience and tradition, the cross—the symbol of execution—embodied a new understanding of *ṣedeq* and *mišpāṭ*, and that this new understanding is central to Christian faith. It is reflected in the earliest writings we have, and in the preliterary remains embedded in those writings. The Pauline letters present an entire structure of christological thought and a well-formed christological vocabulary, not as something being worked out but as something presupposed, already given, in place. The vocabulary is derived from the exaltation language associated with the Davidic king, from the "good news" of Second Isaiah, and from the covenantal and prophetic language of "justice and judgment." And, in this doctrine about Jesus as exalted Lord, the cross is central. "Announcing to you the mystery of God, . . . I did not judge that I knew anything among you except Jesus Christ—and him crucified" (1 Cor. 2:1–2). God's purpose is now revealed, in the criminal's death and in God's vindication of him. The one condemned as a malefactor, reckoned among the wicked, God, by raising him from the dead, exalted. The one accursed of God was made judge, having "authority."

I think to understand why this is so emphasized, and what might have been the experience that found expression in this exultant doctrine of the cross, we do well to go into the matter of the Principalities and Powers.

PRINCIPALITIES AND POWERS

The Principalities and Powers are central to the vision of life and reality, and to the understanding of Jesus and what God effected in and through him, that we find in the Pauline writings. Paul is writing to people to whom these, to us, shadowy figures of Hellenistic cosmology were vivid realities, and he continually puts them into the context of the cross, and vice versa. The Principalities and Powers are sometimes dismissed as merely part of the intellectual "furniture" of Hellenism, having no real theological or christological importance. I think they are not separable from the structure of Pauline thought or even of Christian faith. The pre-Pauline hymn cited in Phil. 2:6–11[5] suggests that from the earliest days the Principalities and Powers were a reference point for understanding the execution and exaltation of Jesus. They provide the "cosmic" context for the lordship of Jesus, and so are integral to NT Christology.

The Principalities and Powers are best seen against the OT background of the "divine council." We saw in chapter 2 that in the world view of the ancient Near East—including Israel—people had a sense that a multiplicity of divine beings (the "sons of god," the "Holy Ones") were at work in reality. Different goods and ends and purposes make different claims on us. Some seem to make absolute claims on us. They are surrounded by a kind of aura, and obsessively determine how we see things and how we choose to live. They determine how we choose to live, most of all, by determining our range of choices to a narrow few. Other possibilities than those given do not even occur to us. We see ourselves and others entirely in their light. Thus, for example, we might envision ourselves primarily as Americans and see everybody else as "non-Americans"—or, if they share our citizenship but in our judgment do not live up to its demands, as "un-American." Or we might radically define ourselves as male or female: our sexual identity might become the whole story about us. Or social status and corresponding roles and expectations and tasks might take over our lives and tell us who and what, at the core of our selfhood, we are. Actually, for twentieth-century Americans, underlying nationality or sexual identity or social status, there is a more basic sense of what we are. As I suggested in chapter 1, we moderns, as children of the Enlightenment and of liberalism, tend to be determined by the self-evidently absolute good of "control": we think of ourselves as controller, shaper, capable of mastery and domination. In any case, whatever the hierarchy in which they are arranged, these kinds of goods and purposes and ends, absolutized and hence defining of us, are a given for us; they constitute our world and us. They are embodied in, and exercise their power through, societal institutions and structures: economics, politics, culture, race, religion, ethnic affiliation, familial roles and expectations—the various ways in which "citizenship" in various groups is defined and lived out. Children pick this up early, as their playground exchanges show. "I'm Irish, what are you?" "You can't do that, you're a girl." "My daddy knows the president." The conversation of their elders is as revealing as the boastful playground prattle of children, though. "Who does he think he is?" "What do women want, anyway?" "Don't get mad, get even." "Those people seem to want the world on a silver platter."

"You can't fight city hall." "Do they expect a free lunch?" "There are winners, and there are losers." Our sense of ourselves and the world and—for this is what it comes down to—*ṣedeq* is determined by all these structures, these societal givens. Because these structures—of thought, politics, economics, social roles, sexual identity, membership in a political entity, status in society, standing in the human and cosmic scheme of things—correspond to our deepest and most definitive sense of ourselves, commanding our imaginations and thoughts and hopes and feelings, keeping us awake at night or allowing us to sleep the sleep of the just, they have power over us: they are absolutes. We keep them at the forefront of our consciousness, deep in our hearts. They have divine status. Indeed, they seek to be equal to God.[6]

The Hellenistic world view captured the absoluteness of these goods and ends and purposes, these structures and societal givens, and the deterministic power they have over us, by speaking of them as forces, in part blind and impersonal, in part animated by purpose and consciousness. They are the Principalities and Powers, the "rulers" *(archontes)* of the age or world *(aiōn)* in which we live. Their sway is immutable. It is as unthinkable to live free of their determinism as it would be to change the eternal order of the starry skies—not surprisingly, for the Powers are identified with the stars themselves. The notion survives, trivially, in the astrology columns we find on the comic pages, but its pedigree goes back to the Babylonians.

The Powers govern our destinies and every aspect of our lives, then. They determine our past and have the say about our future. They tell our story. If we try to defy their power we acknowledge it. I am as much determined by my culturally mediated identity as a male when I define myself, mirror-image fashion, over against *machismo* as when I go along with it. In negating ethnic identity I pay homage to it: its categories define my choices. So I seem to be caught. I can go along with the Principalities and Powers or I can try to rebel against them. In either case, they determine my life.

Breaking Their Power

What would it be like to live free of their determinism? Suppose the roles and structures and categories the Principalities and Powers absolutize were to lose their absolute character. Suppose the Powers lost their power. They would become genial guardians of the order of things, a kind of advisory panel rather than the grim politburo they pretend to be. We would take our bearings by them but would no longer be their puppets. The goods and ends and purposes they are associated with would continue to be important—perhaps even centrally important in the short run—but no longer obsessively so. They would lose their aura.

But how would we thus demote the Principalities and Powers from their primacy in our lives and in reality? Conformity and rebelliousness alike merely strengthen their hold over us. Put it in terms of *ṣedeq*. If the Principalities and Powers have the say about what is right, just, fair, seemly, worthwhile, and even thinkable—about what is *ṣedeq*—how would we get beyond the sense of *ṣedeq* they impart to some other sense of *ṣedeq?* If the "justice" they impose on us is illusory, how would we expose it for what it is? How could we discover, and come to live by, the justice of God?

The answer is surprising. It is surprising to us and it was surprising to them (1 Cor. 2:8; Eph. 3:9–10). The answer is seen in the cross. The way to shake loose of the determinism of the Principalities and Powers is not going against them, or getting around them, but, so to speak, letting them do their worst. Let them do their worst and you will show them up for what they are. Let them rage and have their head and enforce their will and assert their absolute claims, and the true limits, the pitiable emptiness, of their supposed absoluteness will appear for all to see. They will be discredited. Confounded, they will find themselves a laughingstock, like the tyrant jeered at in the old taunt song of Isaiah 14. They will have to accept their proper place in the scheme of things, and acknowledge that the *ṣedeq* they represent is not *ṣedeq* itself. It is not the whole story but is only part—and a subordinate part—of the story.

The cross embodies this process of submission and powerlessness. According to the *ṣedeq* of the authorities Jesus was outside the circle. He was a malefactor. That sense of *ṣedeq* was absolute and so mandated his death. Those who had him executed thought they were upholding the justice of God. In bringing about Jesus' arrest and death, they were acting under the compulsion of a profound sense of what was right, as that sense was shaped by and embodied in the Law. And Jesus submitted to the Law. He allowed the absolute claim of the Law, and the sense of justice that gave the Law its power, to do its worst. Death was the enforcer. Jesus was marked as a sinner deserving of death. He did not resist or rebel or cling to what he was entitled to, but was obedient, even to death: even to the death of a criminal, "a cross-death." And so God marked him as his own, exalting him, giving him a name above every name. The one outside the circle of *ṣedeq* proved to be, in reality, the one who showed what God's *ṣedeq* is. And the Powers woke up to what *ṣedeq* is. They had to do homage to the obedient one over whom they had thought they triumphed. Their power was broken by his powerlessness. The emptiness of their claim to define and enforce *ṣedeq* was demonstrated by his embracing of "unrighteousness."

Jesus went beyond "being in the right," and so broke the power of the Principalities and Powers. But what, in this light, is *ṣedeq?* What was the positive *ṣedeq* Jesus embraced in his embracing of "unrighteousness"? If the crucifixion of Jesus redefined *ṣedeq,* what does *ṣedeq* turn out to be?

GALATIANS

The relatively short letter to the Galatians is useful to answer this question, especially since Paul's polemic purpose in writing to the Galatians allows the new understanding of *ṣedeq* to be brought out in sharp, even shocking, relief. The Galatians, though they are not Jews, have taken up the observance of the Jewish Law. Paul is writing to reprove them for this, and to get them to abandon their "infatuation"[7] with the Law. They have switched from the true gospel to another gospel, he tells them, and in effect have abandoned "the One who called you in Christ's grace." They have fallen out of the realm of grace. "Grace" (Greek *charis*) is only one of a dozen terms that make up a dense and immensely rich complex of thought in this letter. Let us try to sort out these elements.

Justification

Central to the letter is the question of "justification": being "justified." The verb as such does not appear in the Greek translation of the

Scriptures, but it must be understood in the light of Israelite and Jewish convictions about *ṣedeq*. To that extent its meaning comprises two aspects. There is the subjective aspect: to be "justified" is to be made "righteous." This is what people usually understand Paul to be talking about, as if he is concerned with moral dispositions and choices and self-understanding. This ties in with traditional religious concerns, about holiness and "salvation." How can we be made to be, and know that we are, "good people"? How can we "get right" with God? To some extent, this is part of the meaning of "justification": being in the right, having *ṣedeq* on one's side, standing within the circle of *ṣedeq*. My mention of that "circle," though, reminds us of the covenantal and prophetic contrast between those within it (the "just") and those outside it (the "wicked"), and also suggests that there is more to "justification" than merely private, moral dispositions. *Ṣedeq* is something that defines a community as well as a person (not that the two can be treated separately). Israel was the people, the political entity, that accepted the *ṣedeq* of Yahweh: that acceptance was what made them a people. And Yahweh's *ṣedeq* had to do with an entire way of life: the way people dealt with one another, in politics and economics and work, the whole network of relationships that constitutes the life of a people. Yahweh's "justice" was to be the measure and the animating principle of Israelite life, both day to day and in the overarching institutions and structures that defined day-to-day existence. It would ensure that equity and compassion characterized the way people got along with one another. As we saw above,[8] it can be understood to mandate "going beyond" one's own interest, to the neighbor, the person in need: to the other precisely as other. That "justice" would result in abundance, "satiety," peace. Where Yahweh's *ṣedeq* is established, people do not get exploited or go hungry. Where his "justice" prevails—within that circle—the covenant blessings and the feast of the kingdom can be experienced as reality. Blessing, Life, Good: these are Yahweh's purpose for his people.

So the question of "being justified" is not simply a matter of "righteousness." It is a question about how Yahweh's purpose can be made a reality. How can justice be established? How can his kingdom, or kingship, prevail?

Law and Its Works

It seems the Galatians were not asking precisely these questions. They seem to have asked, instead, a somewhat different question: how do we get inside the circle of *ṣedeq*? How do we "get right" with God? The answer the Galatians came to give to that question was, on the face of it, not so silly. The way to get inside the circle, they said, was the way Scripture spells out. Follow the "judgments" of Yahweh. Obey his covenant. Accept his *Tôrāh* (instruction, "Law"), and do the works of Torah. Justification comes from Torah.

This option of the Galatian Christians Paul considers a betrayal of the good news he proclaimed, and a rejection of God's call and God's *charis,* "grace" or "graciousness." To show them why that is so, he takes up the terms of Torah itself. The covenant promises Blessing and Life. Infidelity to the covenant guarantees Curse and Death. Very well, Paul says, let us go into all that and see how Blessing and Life can be gotten.

Paul weaves together a series of scriptural texts to show that, on its own terms, Torah spells Death and Curse, not Life and Blessing and justification. The one who does the works of Torah "will have life by them" (Lev. 18:5), but "accursed is everyone who does not abide by all the things written in the book of the Torah, by doing them" (Deut. 27:26). So failure to do all the works of Torah ensures that one will not have life but will be under a curse. Before God no one is justified by Torah. Scripture itself says "the just one has life by faith": in this quotation (from Hab. 2:4), Paul finds three of the terms he is working with. What makes one "just" is faith. And that faith gives life as well. Torah, therefore, is unavailing. Only faith gives justice and life and blessing.

Earning and Grace

Here it would be possible to speculate about what lies behind Paul's thinking. He is convinced, it seems, that there is no one who actually does all the works of the Torah. If God enters into judgment with us, there is no one who can claim to be in the right (cf. Ps. 143:2, quoted in Gal. 2:16). And what stance would Paul have us take toward Torah? Is he implying that since it is unavailing for justice we should disregard it, or oppose it: that we should be quit of its claims upon us, as a dead letter? Torah has a compelling power over us. It shapes our sense of right and wrong, our sense of ourselves and of reality. It exacts retribution for nonobservance: the "curse." It is in effect one of those Principalities and Powers that claim to have the ultimate say about us and our lives, to be the whole story about us. What would it be like to live by a different vision of *ṣedeq* than the one Torah imparts and commands? What would it be like to live not for and by Torah but for and by God? It would mean living according to a vision of God as the one who does things for us, not one who commands us to do things for him.

That vision would center on *charis,* graciousness and generosity, not on "works." It would reject effort and entitlement, "earning," as both needless and impossible. Impossible, because, if it comes down to an audit of merit, no one is just before him. Needless, because it is God who establishes his justice, not us, and because God is not an auditor. A vision of God as moved by *charis* would ignore the tidy categories of just and unjust, at least to the extent of imagining God "going beyond" the circle, to those outside it. It would therefore take seriously our incapacity to do all the works of Torah and to effect our justification, and it would consider that incapacity to be good news. It would lead us to admit gladly that we are sinners, outside the circle of *ṣedeq*, subject to God's *nāqām*; we would be glad to admit this because we would see God as eager to heal our wound and respond to our need: he is gracious. It would imagine that the *mišpāṭ* of Yahweh is that of a father—generous as a father is, and in Yahweh's case all-powerful to effect our good, as the good of children he loves with all his heart. It would be happy to confess need and sinfulness and injustice, because it would have a sense that Yahweh's *nāqām* is vindication of *his* justice, and his justice is "going beyond" considerations of merit and earning and deserts, to the other as other. If *that* justice is going to be vindicated, then that is good news. The only person who does not need to be the object of vindication and deliverance, and to be brought within that circle of *ṣedeq,* is the person who is already there inside. If we have the sense we are there, inside the circle, that can be dangerous, because the chances are that we are not. To be anxious to be within the circle can lead us to deny that we are not there yet, and can lead us to try to get there by our own efforts (the "works of the Law"). It can make us treat God as one who, like us, uses a calculus of effort and deserving, and as one who bestows a seal of approval for what we do. It can make us say, my power and the strength of my hand have done this for me. It can make us focus on our moral achievement as the center and source of our selfhood, and treat God as one irrelevant to our project of justifying ourselves, except perhaps as an obstacle. We can have the agreeable feeling that we are all right, and feel good about ourselves, but if God uses the same calculus we do we can never trust him not to find a debit we missed or an omitted entry. We will be edgy about him. Who knows how this exacting critic will rate our performance? His justice is stringent, and if he is like us, calculating debits and credits, he will make no allowances. No slip will be allowed, or forgiven. On the other hand, if God does allow slips, and is gracious, he is unfair. He is arbitrary, unpredictable. We don't know where we stand. He renders all our effort futile and deprives us of the just reward of our labors. He changes the rules of the game. We can't be sure of our footing. He is our enemy, if he is gracious. Fair is fair, and he doesn't play by our rules.

To imagine God as infinitely gracious, therefore, destroys our tidy sense of right and wrong, winning and losing, justice and injustice. Alternatively, it could cause us to feel immense relief: he is not like us, grasping and calculating, rigorous in evaluating effort and achievement, strict in reckoning what we deserve and what we are entitled to. He is not a respecter of persons. He is eager to fill us with good and life and blessing, irrespective of what we deserve. If I feel that I deserve little or nothing, I will be relieved. He is eager to show himself a father, dealing with a child full of need. Or a father willing to pay any price to make up for the debts I have incurred. He will be a father anguished at how easy I find it to be destructive, to myself and others, suffering from the unhappiness I choose as my life.

Faith and Works

This radical vision of God's *charis* is at odds with Torah, to the extent that Torah is made a matter of earning and works. To accept this way of imagining God, and to act on it, is called faith *(pistis)*. It will mean that I will lack any sense that I have standing in God's eyes.

It will mean that I will give up trying to earn such standing, by my performance of Torah works. And that will put me in a funny position. Believing in and putting my confidence in God's *charis,* not Torah works and not my performance of them, I will be "lawless," a sinner, no better than a heathen or a publican—so far as Torah is concerned. And Torah—as one of the Principalities and Powers—will exact its retribution. It will be enraged, and enrage good people against me, and they will feel they are doing God's will in making me feel the consequences of my rejection of Torah. Torah will put me under a curse, just as someone who accepts Torah and lets it define him but fails to do all that is written in it is under a curse. I will be indistinguishable, in the eyes of Torah, from any sinner—I refuse to allow it to have the final say about me and about reality. Torah will see me as lawless, one of the unjust, and under a curse.

This is why Paul says that Jesus became a curse, for our sakes. Jesus was under Torah and subject to the retribution it exacts. He was reckoned among the wicked, and put to death as a criminal. The cross was the instrument of this retribution. The cross symbolizes, for Paul, Jesus' identification with those outside the circle of *ṣedeq,* those under a curse. Paul applies to Jesus the saying of Deut. 21:23, "Accursed is everyone hanged upon a tree." He experienced in his body the full power of Torah, becoming a "curse." To people who repose their hopes in justifying themselves by their performance of Torah works and by what they earn, the cross is a "scandal," a stumbling block. It makes no sense.

On that Friday Jesus was hanged upon a tree, his followers must have anguished over that "scandal": the one they knew as the just man had been condemned and executed as a malefactor. It made no sense. And to their anguished question the experience of the risen Jesus came as the answer. God raised him from the dead. He was vindicated, as God's own. He was delivered from the power of death. He was exalted, enthroned, made both Lord and Messiah, this Jesus who was crucified. Like the servant in Second Isaiah, the one reckoned among the wicked and smitten by God was the just man who would "justify the many." Everything was turned upside down.

Jesus was obedient even to a cross-death, the death of a criminal. The one who did not know sin God made to be sin, for our sake (2

Cor. 5:21). This is the core of NT proclamation: the scandal of the cross, and the vindication of the crucified one. God has given Jesus a name which is above every name. What the Galatians are choosing to reject is the scandal. They are thereby rejecting God's *charis*. To reject the cross and seek to be justified by Torah works is to reject the vision of God as Father, who goes beyond deserving and earning and dissolves, in his love, the neat but demonic categories of just and unjust, and so dissolves the power of sin those categories serve. And it is to reject the Spirit, by which we know God as gracious: by which we know God, or rather are known (Gal. 4:9), and grasp God, or rather are grasped (Phil. 3:12). It is to reject that being conformed to Christ which makes us willing to bear one another's burdens, generously and graciously. It is to reject God's *ṣedeq,* which enables us to love even those who have no claim on our love and to see in our enemy one loved by God even as we are loved. It is to live by "the flesh," grasping and calculating and self-absorbed, insensitive to others and unfree within ourselves. It is to try to find life by our own efforts, and that is death.

Galatians 2:15–21. All this we find in Gal. 2:15–21 (RSV). The passage continues the address Paul made in his confrontation with Peter (2:14).

> 15We ourselves, who are Jews by birth and not Gentile sinners, 16yet who know that a man is not justified by works of the law but through faith in Jesus Christ, even we have believed in Christ Jesus, in order to be justified by faith in Christ, and not by works of the law, because by works of the law shall no one be justified. 17But if, in our endeavor to be justified in Christ, we ourselves were found to be sinners, is Christ then an agent of sin? Certainly not! 18But if I build up again those things which I tore down, then I prove myself a transgressor. 19For I through the law died to the law, that I might live to God. 20I have been crucified with Christ; it is no longer I who live, but Christ who lives in me; and the life I now live in the flesh I live by faith in the Son of God, who loved me and gave himself for me. 21I do not nullify the grace of God; for if justification were through the law, then Christ died to no purpose.

Roughly paraphrased, it goes like this. We are not justified by Torah works but through Christ faith, and so I have torn down the whole structure of Torah and justification by Torah. If I build up again what

I tore down I prove myself a transgressor: I allow Torah to have power over me, and define me, and condemn me. So far as Torah is concerned, I am dead: it has no claim on me, any more than it would have on a dead man; and by Torah's own way of reckoning things I have earned what it guarantees to those who do not keep it—death. But I died to Torah so that I might live to God. I am as much a malefactor as Christ: suffering the penalty of Torah, accursed, crucified together with him: "I am co-crucified with Christ." But I have life. It is not *my* life but the life which Christ has: he lives in me. That is the life that counts. And the other kind of life, my human existence, I live in faith, the faith of the Son of God who loved me and delivered himself up for my sake. "Delivered himself up": the echo of Jesus' cross-death sounds in the use of this term from earliest Christian tradition.

The Proclamation of the Cross. Faith is the ability to imagine a God of *charis,* God as Father, and the willingness to believe in and act on that vision. It comes from hearing the proclamation of Jesus the crucified one, who did not separate himself from sinners but identified with them, even to the point of suffering the fate that by rights is theirs; the proclamation that this one, who chose to "go beyond" what passes for justice, is God's own; the proclamation that that gift of trust and of loving is available to us, so that we can know God as Father, as Jesus did. The proclamation plants a seed. What if my anxiety to get right with God gets in the way of knowing him and loving my neighbor? What if God really does identify with me so totally that he would give up his only Son for my sake? What if he does not condemn but rather seeks to heal me and to fill me with his gifts? What if the way to life is through that apparently death-dealing choice, to let go of entitlement and instead let myself be given gifts? What if my relationship with God is not in spite of my sinfulness and need but precisely in and because of it? What if God's justice is established, and his kingship and its blessings made a reality in our lives, precisely through such an identification with the wicked, so that I could love my enemy?

What the proclamation of the good news leads us to, then, is the startling possibility that this is the way things are, and the choice to try that possibility out, and so to know that this is indeed the way things are.

SUMMARY

Paul has a vision of God's purpose and his ways of achieving that purpose. His purpose is to free us from the deadly determinisms of the Principalities and Powers, so that we can live according to God's *ṣedeq*. Where God's *ṣedeq* is established—where "justification" is effected—there are no children with bellies swollen with hunger, no people bowed under crushing burdens of injustice; there is no exploitation or lethal enmity. There is Blessing, Life, Good. And what is God's way of effecting this "justification"—of bringing all within his circle of *ṣedeq?* His way is *charis:* generous, gracious identification with those in need, with those outside the circle. His *ṣedeq* means going-beyond, to those who do not live by his *mišpāṭ,* so that he bears our burdens and shares our anguish. His way is not to be a respecter of persons but to love his enemies. This going-beyond and identification-with is seen in the cross: the man who was God's own, the Son, paid the price exacted by our murderous, grasping sense of justice. Becoming a curse, being made sin, Jesus revealed the justice of God. The Galatian option represents a fundamental misunderstanding of what God is up to. Their efforts, through the works of Torah, to "get right" with God mean a rejection of his purposes and his ways—a rejection of his *ṣedeq*.

THE SYNOPTIC TRADITION

In the Synoptic tradition we find the same redefinition of justice and judgment as appears in Paul's writings, but with a difference: the Gospel writers use narrative. Narrative allows the redefinition to unfold in the reader's imaginative experience. We are led to enter in to the story. Seeing Jesus through the eyes of the disciples, and of the crowds, we are brought along a path that leads from initial expectation through incomprehension to fulfillment in the very reversal of those expectations.

So the expectations are central in this dialectic process. These the Synoptic Gospels set up at the very beginning of the story. Jesus' appearance, and the start of his ministry, are set against the background of Israel's tradition. Matthew and Luke, in different ways, take their time in recapitulating that tradition in their opening chapters, up to and including the proclamation of John the Baptist, and Mark simply uses the figure of John to provide a context for the appearance of Jesus. Let me show what I mean by sketching the opening scenes of Mark's Gospel.

MARK

The very term "gospel"—"good news"—recalls the complex of motifs found in the opening verses of Second Isaiah.[9] John the Baptist is a mouthpiece for Mark to present, in a few strokes, those motifs. His is the voice of the proclaimer: Prepare the way. We expect to hear mention of "consolation" *(naḥ^a^māh)* to a people in exile, and of the "good news" that the Lord is "coming." And so it is. John proclaims "a baptism of *metanoia* for the taking away of sins" (Mark 1:4). *Metanoia* is usually translated "repentance," but in context it clearly echoes the *naḥ^a^māh* of the beginning of Second Isaiah.[10] The baptism John proclaims and effects takes away sin. People who undergo it enter into the waters of ordeal and judgment, admitting their sinfulness, their need to be forgiven, and asking to be "put in the right" by being brought through the waters.[11] This baptismal confession of sin is both an admission that one stands outside the circle of *ṣedeq,* and an appeal to Yahweh as Judge, as the one who will establish *ṣedeq* on the Day of his "coming," to put one inside that circle before the Day of vindication. It is a rite preparatory to Yahweh's *naḥ^a^māh,* his "consolation," by admitting one's need for it. Thus, the subjective counterpart of Yahweh's consolation is "repentance." Into this scene Jesus "comes" (1:9) and takes his place among those confessing their sinfulness, to be baptized. The voice from heaven then identifies him as both Son and Servant, by addressing to him the words spoken to the Davidic king—"You are my son" (Ps. 2:7)—and to the servant of Yahweh in Second Isaiah—"My beloved, in whom I am well pleased" (Isa. 42:1).

This is the setting, then, in Mark for the "coming" of Jesus: expectation of God's imminent *mišpāṭ* and the establishment of his justice. In anticipation of that Day, people are taking stock of where they stand, and if they find themselves outside the circle of *ṣedeq* they admit their need for forgiveness: to have their sins "taken away." Mark finishes setting the scene by referring to John's being "delivered up" (1:14). The word *(paradidonai)* is that used in early Christian tradition for the fate that overtook Jesus, and John is shown to be doubly a forerunner of Jesus, first as proclaimer and then as one arrested by the authorities.

When, in this context, Jesus does "come," his message is electric:

> 14After John was delivered up,
> came Jesus into Galilee,
> proclaiming the good news of God
> 15and saying,
> Fulfilled is the *kairos,*
> and near is the kingdom of God:
> repent *(metanoeite)* and put faith in the good news.
> (1:14–15)

Jesus proclaims "the good news of God" (again, the term from Second Isaiah). He says that the *kairos* is near: the appointed hour, the moment of opportunity, when the time is ripe. He says, "*Metanoeite,* and put faith in the good news." *Metanoeite:* change your thinking to take account of what is happening, wake up to the reality that the good news proclaims. In effect, receive the consolation of Yahweh.

Thus are expectations created, and a context given for what Jesus is about to do, or what is to be done through him. In the stories about Jesus, and the sayings of Jesus, that Mark has collected and edited, we can follow a process of rising excitement and gradual disappointment. At the start of Jesus' proclamation people are "astonished" and "amazed" at the "authority" of his words and the "authority" with which he rebukes evil spirits, and even takes away sins. It is the "authority"[12] conferred on the "son of man" figure of the vision narrated in Daniel 7, only now exercised not in the heavenly court but "on earth" (1:23–27; 2:10). But there is an ominous drumbeat in the background. People are taking counsel together against him. Jerusalem, in the person of the authorities, shadows the scene (3:22). More and more, things fail to go according to people's expectations. Jesus offends the "just" by sharing table fellowship with harlots and tax collectors. The people he chooses to eat and drink with are those outside the circle of *ṣedeq,* who surely have no share in Yahweh's kingship, no place at the feast of the kingdom. Again and again Jesus violates the Sabbath law. He scandalizes the good people.

PARABLES[13]

The parables we read in Matthew and in Luke are especially helpful to give us a sense of Jesus' proclamation. These stories open up the imagination of their hearer to new possibilities; they put things in a new light by drawing us imaginatively into a new world. Many of them answer the question about Yahweh's *mišpāṭ*. How does God rule the world? Where is the evidence that he is involved in any way whatever? When can we expect to see his *mišpāṭ?* And the answer comes in images and in stories. God's *mišpāṭ* is like a seed: a seed is planted and it grows; you do not see it growing, you cannot track its growth, but it yields a miraculous harvest. God's *mišpāṭ* is hidden, but efficacious.

Or, God rules the world like this. Once there was a king who gave a feast, and invited certain people. When he saw that the banquet hall was still not full, he sent his servants to invite just anybody. That king wanted everybody to enjoy his feast; he wanted his banquet hall full.

Or, God rules the world like this. Once there was a father whose son demanded to be given what was his, and left home. He went from bad to worse, squandering his life, until he was in want, and came to himself and resolved to go back to his father. He practiced a little speech: "Father, I have sinned against God and before you. I am not worthy to be called your son. Treat me as one of your hirelings." And the father, seeing his son still a long way off, ran to meet him, and would not let him get his speech out, but embraced him and threw a party for him: for the son had been dead but now was alive, was lost but now was found.

Or, this is what God's *mišpāṭ* is like. The owner of a vineyard hired some workers, and agreed on a just wage with them. Later on in the day, he hired others; and throughout the day he added still other workers to the crew. When it came time for the workers to be paid, the owner of the vineyard started with those who were last hired, who had worked only an hour or two—and gave them the full day's wage!

We could multiply examples. The point is clear, though. The good news Jesus proclaims through his parables is that in his exercise of *mišpāṭ* God is generous and gracious. He is eager to bring everyone into the feast, to share in his kingship and participate in its blessings. His *mišpāṭ* extends to everyone, and will fill us all with abundance. He is constantly working, laboring, searching out new ways to fill us with joy.

If I thought of myself as one who had no hope of sharing in God's kingship, or if I thought that the exercise of his *mišpāṭ* would surely mean my condemnation, because I know myself to be outside the circle of his *ṣedeq,* these stories would come as good news indeed. If I were conscious of having made myself God's enemy, or of being deeply in debt to him, or of having no merit to claim before him, I would want to believe that his *mišpāṭ* really was like what the king or the father or the vineyard owner did. It might be hard for me to believe it: it would seem too good to be true. But wouldn't it be consoling? The seed would thus be planted, and I would come to see the world and myself in a new way.

But if I were conscious of standing squarely within the circle of God's *ṣedeq,* of never transgressing one of his commandments, of knowing and loving and obeying him, these stories would scandalize me. The king and the father and the owner, as one man, lack even the most elementary sense of justice. They do not treat people as they deserve. Fairness is simply dismissed. People who work all day are treated the same as those who work only an hour. Wastrels are embraced, and clothed in fine garments, and given a party. Riffraff are allowed at the king's table. This is supposed to be good news?

The parables as we have them reflect this reaction. The wastrel son's older brother ("Never have I transgressed your commandment") refuses to come in to the feast. Those who worked all day and bore the heat of the sun complain bitterly. Those who were originally invited to the banquet refuse the invitation. And people took counsel against Jesus.

By his baptism, and his table fellowship with sinners, and the proclamation that God's *ṣedeq* is not based on earning and deserving but on need Jesus was himself a parable of grace.[14] He did not distance himself from sinners but identified with them. He thereby frustrated people's expectation that the wicked would get what was coming to them, and that the just would be vindicated. He seemed to deny divine justice. So he himself became an object of *nāqām*. He had to be shown to be outside the circle of justice, and made to suffer the fate the wicked deserve. After all, he identified so totally with sinners it was only fair that he share their lot, and be made to drink the cup of wrath that is theirs to drink. Justice is justice, and must be upheld.

So he was executed.

THE PASCHAL MYSTERY

The accounts of Jesus' execution labor to put it into proper perspective. He is the poor man unjustly condemned, the suffering servant by whose stripes we are healed, the faithful one who cries out to God, Why have you forsaken me? He is despoiled and broken, a worm and no man. He is the just one against whom the wicked plot: He trusted in God, let God deliver him if he delight in him. But these scriptural allusions are made only in the light of resurrection faith, by which people came to see what God had been up to. The sense of justice and fairness and right that had caused Jesus to be executed appeared, now, to be the ways of man; they were not God's ways. In raising Jesus to new life, God had indeed vindicated the just man, according to the assurances Scripture gives. But the just man so vindicated was one who identified with sinners and took a place, with them, outside the circle of righteousness. He did not cling to what was rightfully his. He drank the cup of wrath. He accepted being made *ḥērem,* curse, sin. In accrediting Jesus as his own, God revealed what his idea of *nāqām* is. It is upholding and vindicating *ṣedeq;* but his *ṣedeq* is compassion, "going beyond" to those in need, identifying with them so totally that he will pay the price our "justice" exacts. In proclaiming Jesus his Son, God showed what kind of Father he is.

NT faith claims to fulfill the expectations set up by Israelite tradition, with a twist. There is justice and judgment and vindication. There is the new creation. Yahweh's kingship is exercised and his word proclaimed. The sanctuary, the seat of his enthronement, is the community of those who believe, a building of living stones. He gathers a people, who accept his *mišpāṭ* and his *ṣedeq:* "the Israel of

God" (Gal. 6:16, RSV). His rule, proclaimed and embodied in Jesus, breaks the idols of injustice and oppression, the Principalities and Powers. His Spirit, the Spirit of Jesus, "consoles." He is at work where the need is greatest, outside the circle of *ṣedeq,* where sin abounds.[15] He is present and known in our reluctance to be trusting or to believe or to love. Our readiness to judge, to dismiss, to resent, to entertain murderous rage is a denial of his *charis* and a rejection of his Spirit: that is where God is to be found. We worship the idols of effort and entitlement—we say to the works of our hands, "My God!"—and think we have standing to condemn our neighbor. Those are the moments when God is closest. We have only to be where we are: in need, full of anxiety, full of unlove, full of "unrighteousness" in our very quest for "righteousness." We seek to play God in our own lives and the lives of others, and arrogate *mišpāṭ* to ourselves: God then becomes our enemy, the enemy of our selfhood. That is when we can know that God's *ṣedeq* is not ours: he loves his enemies, and calls them to his feast, and bids them sup with him.

To put this in other words: Yahweh is the god of *ʿapiru.*

CHAPTER 10

Summary and Conclusions

SUMMARY

The following is a brief, necessarily partial summary of the principal points developed in the preceding chapters.

1. A political entity is held together by a common vision (consensus) centering on what is right and good *(ṣedeq)*, and by adherence to a certain governance *(mišpāṭ)*, which makes that consensus a reality in people's communal life.

2. *Mišpāṭ* derives its legitimacy, and therefore authority, from people's sense of *ṣedeq*. *Mišpāṭ* without *ṣedeq* is, in the long run, unsustainable. *Ṣedeq* without *mišpāṭ* is inefficacious.

3. Israel was the political entity formed from the oppressed and marginated of Egypt and Canaan (thirteenth-eleventh centuries B.C.). What formed them as a people was adherence to the *ṣedeq* of Yahweh, the god who hears the cry of the oppressed and saves them from the hand of the oppressor. Their adherence to his *ṣedeq* meant a renunciation of the oppressive *mišpāṭ* of the Canaanite kings and of the *ṣedeq* which legitimated it, and at the same time meant a renunciation of the gods associated with that *ṣedeq*. It meant "withdrawal" from the established, "legitimate" order of Canaan: Israel was an *ʿapiru* people, outside the "circle" of legitimacy. Yahweh was the god of the *ʿapiru*.

4. The *ṣedeq* of the nations focused on "Bread": security, fertility, survival. This absolutizing of "Bread" entailed centralization of power, exploitation, reliance on "horse and chariot."

5. Yahweh's *ṣedeq*—and therefore the consensus that made Israel

Israel—focused on "justice": compassion for those in need, refusal to take advantage of others, a determination to "go beyond." It led to a "tribal" form of governance: decentralized and egalitarian. Central to Israel's existence as a people was trust: they were to be free of the nations' obsession with "Bread" and security; they were not to rely on "horse and chariot."

6. The "Divine Warrior" imagery used in Israelite tradition asserted Yahweh's cosmic *mišpāṭ*. He was god above all other gods, and his *ṣedeq* superseded any other. The one who has the final say about reality is the god who frees from oppression. Further, the language of covenant was used because what was in question was Israel's constitution as a political entity, a people; political language was therefore indispensable. The Israelites were to "love," "know," "serve" Yahweh, and rely on him alone. If Israel attempted to secure salvation by their own hand, it amounted to rebellion against Yahweh as covenant lord, and denial of Israel's foundational identity. It put them outside the circle of his *ṣedeq*.

7. Those who lived according to Yahweh's *ṣedeq* and covenantal *mišpāṭ* (within the "circle" of *ṣedeq*) were the "just." Those who rebelled against Yahweh's *ṣedeq* were the "wicked." The "wicked" were, so to speak, *ʿapiru* vis-à-vis Yahweh.

8. Yahweh's *mišpāṭ* as cosmic lord and as covenant lord of Israel took the form of saving his people, in Holy War, from the hand of the kings of Canaan, exercising *nāqām* against them: vengeance for his "haters," vindication for those who loved him.

9. *Mišpāṭ* in Early Israel resided with Yahweh. It was not focused in any one figure. The authority of those who exercised Yahweh's *mišpāṭ*—the "Judges"—was derivative, provisional, and temporary. The tradition emphasizes that the ideal Judge was one who had no pretensions to save anyone. Innately weak, he would be "raised up," overtaken by the "spirit" of Yahweh.

10. The pretensions of monarchy to *ṣedeq* and *mišpāṭ* were restrained and relativized by the institution of prophecy, which gave voice to authentic Israelite *ṣedeq* in an authoritative "word" of *mišpāṭ*. The prophets' office was to reprove kings and people in the face of injustice, power politics, and the cultus of the gods who legitimated

these royal policies. In urging reliance on Yahweh alone, the prophets kept alive the old Holy War theology.

11. The teaching of Deuteronomy and Dtr is a political theology. It warned Israel against living by a false *ṣedeq*, one focused on Bread and centering on "earning" and entitlement. If Israel chooses to live by allegiance to Yahweh, the god who leads forth from slavery, the consequence of that choice will be Blessing and Life: abundance and equity will characterize their life as a people, and they will avoid the foreign adventurism that provokes defeat at the hands of an enemy. If Israel chooses to go after "other gods," living by their illusory *ṣedeq,* the consequences of that choice will be systemic contradictions entailing injustice and invasion: Curse and Death.

12. The postexilic writings continue to give voice to the claims of Yahweh's *mišpāṭ*: arguing against simplistic understandings of it and its *ṣedeq* (Job), proclaiming the consoling "good news" that it will bring about return from exile (Second Isaiah), asserting its efficacy by unveiling the meaning of the sufferings of persecution: the persecutor will be destroyed and Yahweh's people will be vindicated (Daniel).

13. Jesus, and NT faith, are to be understood in light of *ṣedeq, mišpāṭ,* and *nāqām*. Jesus died as one outside the circle of *ṣedeq,* suffering the curse the wicked deserve. Christian faith asserted that by vindicating Jesus Yahweh showed the nature of his *ṣedeq:* it is to "go beyond" justice, to those in need, outside the circle. He showed the nature of his *mišpāṭ:* it consists in identifying-with rather than separating-from; he "judges" the wicked by loving them. Yahweh therefore is the god of the *ʿapiru*. "Justice" is to be established—we are "justified"—by the God who loves his enemy. The same sort of love—the love of enemy—is the fruit of "faith" and the Spirit.

CONCLUSIONS

RELIGION AND POLITICS

The first thing to say is that, in as much as its focus is *mišpāṭ* and *ṣedeq*, the biblical tradition is irreducibly "political." This should not be dismaying, though nowadays people tend to dissociate "religion" and "politics." In the context of the ancient world, what moderns are pleased to call "religion" was political and politics was "religious"—or rather, something cosmically grounded and cosmically validated.

Our neat categorizations into "religion" and "politics," however, lead us to approach the biblical tradition with something else in mind. We tend to be interested in what it says about the relationship between God and "man." This neglects the historical facticity of that tradition: its rootedness in particular times and places. This is not to deny that it is applicable to us and our times. But that applicability is not simply analogous. It is a matter of direct continuities. To be an Israelite in Early Israel, say, was to be incorporated into a political entity: to become a sharer in the people that called itself the "Sons of Israel," adhering to Israel's sense of *ṣedeq* and to Yahweh's *mišpāṭ*. The first-century movement within Judaism that became the church understood itself as being in continuity with that formation ("the Israel of God," Gal. 6:16). Nothing has changed. Everyone who is a sharer in that people, whatever his or her nationality, sustains "dual citizenship" (cf. Phil. 3:20). If there is a conflict between the sense of *ṣedeq* that defines our membership in "the people of God" and the sense of *ṣedeq* that governs our national citizenship—if there is a "conflict of consensus"—it is clear which citizenship must supersede which. One's primary allegiance is to the *mišpāṭ* and *ṣedeq* of Yahweh.

THE JUSTICE OF GOD

The second thing to say, therefore, is that for people who identify with the "people of God" the *ṣedeq* of Yahweh is absolute. That relativizes every other good, purpose, form of self-understanding, and citizenship (both actual and metaphorical). It shatters our idols.

And in what does that *ṣedeq* consist? What does Yahweh consider to be good and just and right and seemly and important and worthwhile . . . ? Why, justice.

There are two sides to this coin. One is that justice is the "one necessary thing." The cry of the poor, the need of the other, the claim the powerless make on us is central and nonnegotiable. This is what Yahweh, the "passionate god," takes with absolute seriousness. He wants to feed the hungry and clothe the naked. He wants his banquet hall full. And he wants us to share the same passion. I might add that, in view of what we saw about the Deuteronomic theology, there is no question of hearing the cry only of the "deserving" poor. God is not a respecter of persons. He looks only to need.

The other side to the coin of justice, however, is unsettling. It is the tradition's emphasis on powerlessness. One knows the living God as one is either just or wicked. The just are those within his "circle," the wicked those without. But the just are the poor, the oppressed, the powerless. They are those who must rely entirely on him. They are unable to save themselves, so far gone in despair of their own resources that they cast all their care upon him. They are needful. They are the ones who cry out. They look to Yahweh for *nāqām.* In a real sense, they are the only ones who know the meaning of *nāqām:* they are so little able to exercise self-help that *nāqām* comes, when it comes, as something surprising (Luke 18:1–8). All they can do is cry out.

The tradition insists: God hears the cry of the poor. We know him, the living God, only in our powerlessness and needfulness.

SELF-JUSTIFICATION

How do we get ourselves to this point of despairing of our own resources? The answer is, we do not. We do not "get ourselves" anywhere. If we try to do that, we are the wicked: playing God, trying to "earn" our own salvation, relying on our own resources, exercising *mišpāṭ.* We invest ourselves in projects and works, displacing our needfulness onto the "works of our hands," and look to them for our salvation. "We say to the works of our hands, 'My God!' " We rely on horse and chariot, or the works of the Law. We become idolators.

We contrive idolatrous images of God as a stay against needfulness and as a guarantee of our own "righteousness." God is the teacher who will give us an A, the critic who gives us rave reviews. We make him the enemy who threatens our autonomy and so must be placated.

Others, too, get caught up in our idolatry, as allies or enemies. Our desperate need to earn a sense of amounting to something on our own brings us to grab them by the lapels and make them collaborators in our project of self-justification. We see them as we need them to be, not as they are in themselves. We become deaf to the need of our neighbor. We live by a *ṣedeq* of our own devising.

Worse. Our attempts to be "just" can in the short run pay off. We can feel good about ourselves. Then we feel that we have standing to judge others. They do not behave. They are wanting. They make unfair demands on us. They do not treat us as we deserve, or they treat unfairly people we identify with. They do terrible things. They do not live by *ṣedeq*. They are outside the circle we are so securely inside of. They deserve obloquy and Curse and *nāqām*.

The problem is that there *are* wicked people, and they do deserve *nāqām*. But for us to say this of any one person or any group of people is to "judge": to exercise *mišpāṭ*. It is to arrogate to ourselves a divine prerogative (" '*nāqām* is mine,' says the Lord"). And that is rebellion against Yahweh. This is the great irony of it all. To point the finger of accusation at those who violate the *ṣedeq* of Yahweh is to violate the *ṣedeq* of Yahweh.

For his *ṣedeq* means "going beyond." It means identification-with, not separation-from. His *nāqām* takes the form of unconditional fidelity. He loves his enemies.

So this is the paradox. To the extent that we try to play God, in our own lives and in the lives of others, we become enemies—"haters"—of God, rebels against his *ṣedeq* and *mišpāṭ*. Our desperate attempts to be autonomous and earn our own justification put us outside the circle of *ṣedeq*. And that means that we are really needy. We lack the capacity to trust and we lack the capacity to love. We are locked into the loneliness of demonic self-sufficiency. We can hear neither the cry of the oppressed (we are the oppressor) nor the assurance, Fear not, I am with you. We make God our enemy, and everyone else as well. We are full of need. Our attempts to have and exercise power make us utterly powerless.

That is when the good news might find a hearing in us, when we come to ourselves and realize our powerlessness to live out the good news of God. When we realize we are outside the circle, we cry out, and find out the truth of the assurance, I am with you: fear not. Seeing that our ordinary sense of ourselves and of life excludes any sense of that passionate God, and his involvement in our lives (except as enemy), we confess our need: Lord, be merciful to me a sinner.

Then, coming to terms with our powerlessness, we experience the living God, who in mercy shatters idols.

The biblical tradition is unanimous on this, then, that only in needfulness, powerlessness, and yes "unrighteousness" do we see the salvation of our God (Exod. 14:13–14). The only difference between the just and the wicked is that the just do not have the illusion that they are just. They know their need. In this, that they do not separate themselves from the wicked, they live by the *ṣedeq* of Yahweh.

STRATEGIES: WHAT AM I TO DO?

What does this all tell us we should do about famine or death squads or persecutions? What are we to say to victims of injustice? It would be consoling to them to tell them that Yahweh hears the cry of the oppressed, but what then? Shall we go on to say that he is not a respecter of persons, that he loves his enemies, and that they should too? We could tell them, correctly, that a day of wrath is stored up for those who prey on the widow and orphan, but then are we to turn around and say that the debt the wicked have accumulated has been paid, and it was the Just One who paid it?

I began this book with a vignette, that despairing couple in Detroit I saw from a bus window. The one thing I failed to see in that scene, or even consider, was what from the biblical viewpoint is central: that God is passionately involved in our lives. That though that might have been their last dime it was hardly their last hope. That where sin abounds there grace—*charis*—more abounds. That all they had to do was "cry out."

I fantasize a scene. I jump off the bus and tell them all that. They say, "How do you know?" I think, then have to say, "I don't. I am too preoccupied with playing God in my own life, and now in yours, to know any of that. I have never accepted my needfulness, either. You probably know more about these things than I do. Who do I think I am feeling compassion for you, so I can feel good about myself, so I can prove my theories about poverty and exploitation and powerlessness, projecting my own grievances onto you and having no real sense of what you—*you*—are going through. Using you to make a rhetorical point. I'm sorry." Then I put my hand over my mouth and get back on the bus.

So I have no strategies to recommend for dealing with injustice. But that in itself is a strategy. Do not think it is all up to you. Do not assume that your heart is in the right place. Do not assume you are inside the circle.

If we do not assume that we are inside the circle ("I thank you, God, that I am not as other men"), our approach to people will change. We will not be so ready to dismiss them or impugn their good faith. We will not think we have standing to judge them. I cannot guarantee that that will make a difference to them, but I do know that people act the way they are treated, and none of us is moved to change by being treated as a fool or a villain. If we cease our busy attempts to effect *nāqām* at least we will not get in the way of God's, and his is more efficacious than ours.

THE PRESENT AGE

I write at a time when Americans are "standing tall" again. We are standing up to the Russians, and the Cubans, and the Nicaraguans, and the Libyans. Self-congratulatory phrases fill the air, like "the free world," and "responsible nations," and "civilized people." Other nations and groups are depicted in lurid terms and people do not hesitate to think of them as simply, irredeemably evil. Gangs of youths beat up bums because "we work for a living and they're freeloaders." Crowds gathered for an execution exult when the lights dim inside the death house. Old people wither away in nursing "homes" unvisited, drugged. Earnest, good people argue that it is a human right—a matter of controlling one's own destiny—to end a pregnancy. Mentally deranged people, unable to care for themselves, are "mainstreamed" so budgets can be cut. Very many of my students grow catatonically anxious when class material does not directly and obviously lead to getting into law school or to getting a job: they are like Atlas, the weight of the world on their shoulders; they do not know joy.

In all this I detect something of the sense of *ṣedeq* that focuses on earning and merit and entitlement, and proving oneself by one's own works, and denying one's own need by projecting it onto others. I think I see at work a sense of power which is hard to reconcile with what the biblical tradition imparts.

What is that, finally? After all we have seen, I think we can draw some final conclusions.

WHAT IS POWER?

1. Power is a matter of *ṣedeq* and *mišpāṭ*. In a real sense, there is no such thing as "power." Rulers have power because people obey them, and people obey them either out of agreement with their policies, because they share the same *ṣedeq*, or out of fear (*ṣedeq* consisting in that case of "staying alive"). Change the *ṣedeq*: the rulers will not long continue to rule.

2. Our modern vision of *ṣedeq*, freedom-as-control, is a negation of the biblical tradition. It sets up a master-slave dialectic that can only result in struggle and cruel self-absorption. It makes us think in terms of winners and losers, and be terrified of being losers. It makes love impossible. There are no commitments, only bargains.

3. To the question about power, I think the biblical tradition answers, What do you think is *ṣedeq*? What do you think good and right and important? And it tells us: *ṣedeq* is "going beyond," to concern for the other. If you cannot do that, you are in great need. You are powerless. If that is so, then you are in a position to know what power is. You will know Yahweh's *mišpāṭ.*

And Yahweh's *mišpāṭ*? It is not "controlling." It is the constant, self-emptying, gracious, efficacious working of the passionate God, seen in the unconditional fidelity the prophets proclaimed, and in the cross: that compassionate, free choice of powerlessness that broke the stranglehold of the Principalities and Powers and empowered us to love and to bear one another's burdens.

To my mind much of what I have been trying to say is embodied in the figure of Hazel Motes, the protagonist of Flannery O'Connor's novel *Wise Blood* (New York: New American Library, 1983). The young rustic saw Jesus as a figure to be avoided, someone who would try to get him to "turn around and come off into the dark where he was not sure of his footing." What Hazel wanted was the security of his home town, "with his two eyes open, and his hands always handling the familiar thing, his feet on the known track, and his tongue not too loose" (p. 10). He fails. He cannot get control of his life, so he could be sure of his footing. In the preface to the 1962 edition of *Wise Blood,* O'Connor notes that many readers admired Hazel Motes for his integrity, trying to rid himself of the influence of Jesus. "For the author Hazel's integrity lies in his not being able to."

O'Connor continues: "Does one's integrity ever lie in what he is not able to do? I think that usually it does, for free will does not mean one will, but many wills conflicting in one man. Freedom cannot be conceived simply" (p. 2).

Notes

CHAPTER 1. INTRODUCTION: POWER, SELFHOOD, SOCIETY

1. See John Lyons, *Language and Linguistics: An Introduction* (Cambridge: Cambridge Univ. Press, 1981), 326–28, on "loan translation."

2. This understanding of *nāqām* owes much to the work of George Mendenhall: cf. chap. 3, n. 12.

3. Sigmund Freud, Letter to James J. Putnam, July 8, 1915, in *Letters of Sigmund Freud*, ed. Ernst L. Freud, trans. Tania Stern and James Stern (New York: Basic Books, 1960), 308.

4. Cf. Shirley Hazzard, *The Transit of Venus* (New York: Viking Press, 1980). Dora was "convinced that if she pressed on kind intentions hard enough they would disclose their limitation; and in this, time after time, had proved herself right" (p. 41). "He had seen how people grew cruel with telling themselves of their own compassion: nothing made you harder than that" (p. 160).

5. George Grant, *Technology and Empire* (Toronto: Anansi, 1969).

6. When I said earlier that power is at the heart of human selfhood, chances are that the reader understood this along the lines just sketched: to be human is to be in control. That is the way we have been shaped.

7. So destructive are the effects of this identification of being-human with being-male that I avoid use of "man" in its generic sense, except ironically (as above) and, of course, when translating literally from ancient texts.

CHAPTER 2. THE GODS OF CANAAN

1. The myths from Ugarit were published by A. Herdner as Texts 1–6 in her collection *Corpus des tablettes en cunéiformes alphabétiques* (Paris: Imprimerie Nationale, 1963), hereafter abbreviated *CTA*. The tablets are fragmentary, and their sequence is not certain, but scholars tend to agree on the broad outlines of the stories, partly on the basis of comparison with the plot

of the Mesopotamian myth *Enūma Eliš,* which it has been argued is a Babylonian borrowing and adaptation of the Canaanite story of the conflict between Baal and Yamm. See Thorkild Jacobsen, "The Battle Between Marduk and Tiamat," *JAOS* 88 (1968):104–8. The Ugaritic texts are treated at length in F. M. Cross, *Canaanite Myth and Hebrew Epic* (Cambridge: Harvard Univ. Press, 1973), 3–194 (hereafter abbreviated *CMHE*). A translation of *CTA* 1–6 is available in M. D. Coogan, *Stories from Ancient Canaan* (Philadelphia: Westminster Press, 1978), 86–115.

2. Meaning is the resultant of the interplay between discourse and what the reader or hearer brings to its understanding: experience, moral sense, predispositions, need, and so on. These determine what is attended to in the discourse, and the way it is understood. See Stanley Fish, *Self-Consuming Artifacts* (Berkeley and Los Angeles: Univ. of California Press, 1972). What makes something mythic is that the hearer's very selfhood becomes engaged in the story, and becomes in effect what the story is about. Nothing is mythic in itself but only dialectically so.

3. Thorkild Jacobsen's careful and sympathetic treatment of Mesopotamian stories is a model for this sort of attempt. See his *Toward the Image of Tammuz and Other Essays on Mesopotamian History and Culture,* ed. W. L. Moran (Cambridge: Harvard Univ. Press, 1970), esp. the title chapter, 73–103; and idem, *The Treasures of Darkness* (New Haven: Yale Univ. Press, 1976).

4. See Amos 4:1, and Cross's discussion in *CMHE,* 4–5 n. 6.

5. Cross, *CMHE,* 151–56. Aloysius Fitzgerald, F.S.C., "A Note on Psalm 29," *BASOR* 215 (October 1974), 61–63.

6. "Buffalo": literally, "son of buffaloes," i.e., member of the genus "buffalo." Cf. below, n. 9.

7. The words quoted come from a speech of Baal, in which he derides Mot:

> Let Mot call from his *nepeš,*
> let the Beloved grumble in his innards:
> I alone am the one who will be king over the gods,
> who will fatten gods and men,
> who will satiate the multitudes of earth.
>
> (*CTA* 4.7.47–52)

Baal is asserting his sole claim to be king and to do what a king does; but the implication is that Mot, in challenging Baal, would pretend to "fatten" and "satiate." In a sense, what Mot "calls" and "grumbles" is the very claim, "I alone am the one who will be king. . . . " On the term "satiate," "satiety," cf. below, chap. 5, n. 32.

8. Cf. Jer. 5:22; Ps. 89:9; Job 7:12; 38:8–11.

9. This "son of ________" idiom figures in several passages to be treated later, and we might note it now. A "son of man" is a member of the genus

"man," a human being. A "daughter of man/men" is a female human being. The usage is clear in the poetic parallelism of, for instance, Ps. 8:4, "What is man that you remember him, the son of man that you look after him?" Hence in Ps. 72:1, "God, give your judgment to a king, your justice to a son-of-king," the parallelism is synonymous; the psalm is not praying for two people, one a crown prince. The idiom has nothing to do with filiation or biological descent. I like to call it a "partitive" usage. As we shall see, the "Sons of Israel" are members of the group "Israel," whatever their descent.

10. The reading of *ʿdn,* and the understanding of the passage as the decree of El, I owe to Professor Frank Cross (private communication). Cf. also his *CMHE*, 148–49.

11. See the parallelism of "sit" *(yṯb)* and "judge" *(ṯpṭ)* in the text found in *Ugaritica V,* 2.1.2–3. Hebrew *yāšab* has the same nuance: see the discussion of the word in Norman K. Gottwald, *The Tribes of Yahweh: A Sociology of the Religion of Liberated Israel, 1250–1050* B.C.E. (Maryknoll, N.Y.: Orbis Books, 1979), 512–34.

12. I use "theme" in the sense explained by A. B. Lord in his account of oral tradition, *The Singer of Tales* (Cambridge: Harvard Univ. Press, 1960), 68–98, and used by Cross, *CMHE*, 112–20 especially. Lord uses the term to mean "the groups of ideas regularly used in telling a tale in the formulaic style of traditional song" (p. 68). For example, a story might consist of themes like Challenge, Preparation for Battle, Catalogue of Troops or Ships, Journey to Battle, Combat, Victory Celebration, each theme comprising various subthemes. Themes are, as it were, the building blocks of the story, which the singer of tales puts together to form the whole. By giving the bard the security of a firm outline and sequence of episodes, and a repertoire of descriptive and narrative details, they make it possible to improvise the story afresh each time, perhaps introducing themes from other stories.

13. Cf. Jer. 9:21 for a vestige in Israelite tradition of the same notion.

14. And in the *Enūma Eliš:* cf. Thorkild Jacobsen, "Primitive Democracy in Ancient Mesopotamia," in *Toward the Image of Tammuz,* 157–70; and his later study, "Early Political Development in Mesopotamia," in ibid., 132–56.

15. The same combination of tasks is seen in Job 36:31,

> for from [the clouds] he adjudicates peoples,
> gives food in abundance.

See Mitchell Dahood, "Some Rare Parallel Word Pairs in Job and in Ugaritic," in *The Word in the World* (Moriarty Festschrift), ed. R. J. Clifford and G. W. MacRae (Cambridge, Mass.: Weston College Press, 1973), 28–29.

16. And the converse is true: *because* Baal is king, this is what a king does. Myth not only reflects consciousness and social order, it shapes them.

17. Why this should be so is puzzling. Anat after all pleads for a house for Baal "like the gods' "; the assumption is that he is not yet like the seventy sons of Asherah. His divine status is the point, not, directly, his kingship.

(Does this imply that Baal is a parvenu among the gods?) Yet the house (of cedar!) does function as a symbol or emblem of kingship. See 2 Sam. 5:11–12, where after Hiram—a Canaanite king—built David a house of cedar "David knew that Yahweh had established him as king over Israel"; and 2 Sam. 7:7, where Yahweh through the prophet Nathan rejects David's offer to build a house for Israel's god: "Did I ever speak a word . . . saying, 'Why have you not built me a house of cedar?' "

18. See Gottwald, *Tribes of Yahweh,* 212–14, 391–98; G. E. Mendenhall, *The Tenth Generation* (Baltimore: Johns Hopkins Press, 1973), 21–25, 142–53; and idem, "The Hebrew Conquest of Palestine," *BA* 25 (1962) 66–87; reprinted in *The Biblical Archaeologist Reader 3* (abbreviated *BAR 3*), ed. E. F. Campbell and D. N. Freedman (Garden City, N.Y.: Doubleday Anchor Books, 1970) 100–201.

19. W. F. Albright, *Archaeology and the Religion of Israel* (Garden City, N.Y.: Doubleday Anchor Books, 1968), 192.

20. We might put it this way: El makes things to be; Baal makes things to be such and such.

21. Cf. below, chap. 6, under "Prophetic Reproof: Injustice."

CHAPTER 3. THE ORIGINS OF ISRAEL

1. See the texts assembled in Ivan Engnell, *Studies in Divine Kingship in the Ancient Near East* (Oxford: Basil Blackwell & Mott, 1967), esp. 80–81, 137, 153–54, 170.

2. See chap. 2, n. 9.

3. This historical reconstruction follows Mendenhall, "Hebrew Conquest," and *Tenth Generation;* and Gottwald, *Tribes of Yahweh.* My theoretical presuppositions differ markedly from Gottwald's, but any treatment of early Israel must be in conversation with his work.

4. The royal correspondence discovered at Tell El-Amarna in Egypt is our chief source of knowledge about fourteenth-century Canaan. The Amarna letters *(EA)* are here cited from the collection of M. Greenberg, *The Ḫab/piru,* AOS 39 (New Haven, Conn.: American Oriental Society, 1955). See E. F. Campbell, "The Amarna Letters and the Amarna Period," *BA* 23 (1960):2–22; reprinted in *BAR 3,* 54–75. The king of Byblos, Rib-Adda, in these letters speaks of "my cities" and "the king's cities" interchangeably; but he uses the latter designation to emphasize Pharaoh's stake in coming to his aid, as we shall see below.

5. "Race" and "ethnicity" are modern categories we should be most cautious in applying to ancient documents. See Mendenhall, *Tenth Generation,* 27–28, 144, 152–53, 188–89, 220–26; and idem, "Hebrew Conquest," in *BAR 3,* 117–19.

A Boston schoolteacher, Robert P. Largess, in 1976 objected to the "racial census" of his students a court-ordered desegregation plan required. He explained that this requirement forced "the myth of race" upon children innocent of it. Many of the students came from the Cape Verde Islands and other areas of Portuguese Africa. "These children make no distinctions between themselves or others on the basis of racial type and their older brothers and sisters are often married to people of other ethnic groups (or 'races' in the categories of the laws)." Largess adds that children of Dominican, Honduranian, and Trinidadian cultural backgrounds also lack racialist consciousness (*Washington Post,* Sept. 11, 1977, p. B5). This kind of "colorblind" consciousness may well have prevailed in the ancient Mediterranean world. At least we should avoid assuming that that world lived by the same racist myth we are burdened by. Absence of racialist consciousness in the ancient world of Greece and Rome is shown by Frank M. Snowden, *Blacks in Antiquity* (Cambridge: Harvard Univ. Press, 1970).

6. Cf. the discussion of ancient Near Eastern political vocabulary below, chap. 4, under "The Language of Politics." For now we note that a vassal is to "love" his overlord.

7. In fact, in the Amarna letters the term is written with the ideogram *SA.GAZ* or simply *GAZ,* but this is to be read *'apiru,* the way the sign *&* is read "and" or *viz.* is pronounced "namely" in English. Another spelling for *'apiru* in the ancient texts is *ḫabiru.*

8. The *'apiru* turn up in texts from Mesopotamia, Syria-Palestine, Anatolia, and Egypt, from the late third to the late second millennium B.C. It is clear that they were not an ethnic group. Since they served as mercenaries, Gottwald (*Tribes of Yahweh,* 401–6) thinks the term *'apiru* used in the Amarna letters denoted "circumscribed bands of armed 'outsiders' loosely related to the feudal system as auxiliaries or brigands" (p. 405); other uses—applications of the term to those who use these bands, and to anyone who threatens the established order—Gottwald sees as extended or metaphorical. Doubtless *'apiru* lived in "circumscribed bands" but what is essential to their identity as *'apiru* is their "outsider" status.

9. As mercenaries, of course, they did follow orders but their military service was not from loyalty due a sovereign; it was given on their terms. The point of being *GAZ/'apiru* was not owing allegiance.

10. "Hebrew Conquest," in *BAR 3,* 105–6.

11. "Conservative governments throughout [Central America] regard Nicaragua as a threat to regional security. Many Honduran commanders, in particular, see the existence of the Sandinista government as intolerable and believe it must be eradicated" (Christopher Dickey, *Washington Post,* May 5, 1981, p. 1).

12. This is Mendenhall's understanding of *nāqām;* see "The 'Vengeance' of Yahweh," in *Tenth Generation,* 69–104. His discussion of the root *nqm* in Scripture is most illuminating, but his views about extrabiblical occurrences of *nqm* need to be emended. See the study of Wayne Pitard, "Amarna *ekēmu*

and Hebrew *nāqām*," *Maarav* 3, no. 1 (January 1982): 5–25, and my comments on his views in my essay "Lordship of Yahweh, Lordship of Jesus" in *Above Every Name: The Lordship of Christ and Social Systems,* ed. T. E. Clarke, S.J. (New York: Paulist Press, 1980), 61 n. 20.

13. ". . . there are no provisions for the *hupšu* ['serfs'], and therefore they defect to the sons of Abdi-Ashirta," *EA* 118:22–26.

14. Gottwald, *Tribes of Yahweh*, 192–219, gives three models of the Israelite settlement: Conquest, Immigration, and Revolt.

15. Ibid., 489–97.

16. The "later *Yahwistic* union of tribes adopted that name [viz., Israel] because an earlier association of Canaanite underclasses had employed it and it was the single comprehensive term available with adequate historical associations to communicate the intent of Yahwistic Israel to be an egalitarian social order" (ibid., 495).

17. See Manfred Weippert, *The Settlement of the Israelite Tribes in Palestine* (London: SCM Press, 1971), 55–102; and the articles in *JSOT* 7 (1978)—A. J. Hauser, "Israel's Conquest of Palestine: A Peasants' Rebellion?" (pp. 2–19); T. L. Thompson, "Historical Notes on 'Israel's Conquest of Palestine: A Peasants' Rebellion?' " (pp. 20–27); G. E. Mendenhall, "Between Theology and Archaeology" (pp. 28–34); and N. K. Gottwald, "The Hypothesis of the Revolutionary Origins of Ancient Israel: A Response to Hauser and Thompson" (pp. 37–52). Weippert after a long philological study allows that the equation of *ʿapiru* and "Hebrew" is defensible, though he disagrees with Mendenhall's position.

18. Judges 5:4–5 (Ps. 68:7–8); Deut. 33:2–3; Ps. 68:17; Hab. 3:3–6. See Cross, *CMHE,* 100–103, for a study of these passages and the "ubiquitous motif of the march of Yahweh from the southern mountains (or from Egypt) with heavenly armies" (p. 100).

19. Recall 1 Kings 18:26–29.

20. This is a *reconstruction* of the kind of predicates that were applied to El, the "Creator of Creatures," as they might appear in epithets or, especially, cultic formulae. Cross (*CMHE,* 66–71) asks whether the name "Yahweh Sabaoth" might not have originated in an epithet of El, "He who creates the heavenly armies" (p. 71).

21. This accounts, I think, for the tone—both wheedling and bullying—of Anat's and Asherah's intercessions with El to secure the House for Baal: *CTA* 3.5.27–42; 4.4.40–46.

22. Cf. below, chap. 7, pp. 121–22.

23. Gottwald sees the social change wrought by Israel as a process of "retribalization" in conscious opposition to the centralized, feudal structures of Canaan (*Tribes of Yahweh,* 323–34), and provides a most helpful sociological study of the "tribe" as a social reality (pp. 294–301) and of early Israel—the tribes of Yahweh!—as a confederation of tribes (pp. 237–341).

24. In "Mesopotamia: The Good Life," in *Before Philosophy,* ed. H. Frankfort and H. A. Frankfort (Baltimore: Penguin Books, 1972), 218–23, and his own *Toward the Image of Tammuz,* 37–38.

25. See Cross, *CMHE,* 75 n. 120.

26. Gottwald, *Tribes of Yahweh,* 655–63.

27. Rather than quote the entire text here, let me just refer the reader to Exod. 15:1–18. In general I follow the treatment of the Song in Cross, *CMHE,* 121–37.

28. See chap. 2, n. 11. The "sitters" of Philistia and Canaan (vv. 14–15) are the enthroned.

29. Taking *qōdeš* as a collective: Cross, *CMHE,* 129 n. 61.

30. On the name Yahweh, see Cross, *CMHE,* 60–71, and n. 20 above. For the passage, see ibid., 127 nn. 50, 52, 53.

31. El in olden times had been a warrior himself, but, by the time of Baal's ascendancy in Canaan, his military prowess was only vestigial in the myths. See Patrick D. Miller, "El the Warrior," *HTR* 60 (1967): 411–31.

32. Cross, *CMHE,* 128–29 n. 59.

33. This detail admittedly comes from the Epic (JE) traditions, e.g., Exod. 13:21–22; 14:24.

34. In "Lordship of Yahweh, Lordship of Jesus," 37, 44, 60 n. 7, I suggest a pattern—descent, conflict, ascension—which combines what Cross (*CMHE,* 155–56) has distinguished as two patterns.

35. Or "ruling": see chap. 2 n. 11, and n. 28 above.

36. See the brief discussion of the word "salvation" in my "Lordship of Yahweh, Lordship of Jesus," 43, 62 n. 22.

37. The usual translation is "a jealous god," but that is misleading, I think. It can claim only the authority of long usage, arising from the LXX (and Latin) translation of *qannā'* with *zēlōtēs*. Latin *zelus* gives English "zeal" as well as "jealousy." The translation "zealous god" would be better than "jealous god."

If *'ēl* in the phrase *'ēl qannā'* is taken not as appellative ("a god") but as the proper name El, then *qannā'* is an epithet of El, as in "El Elyon" (Gen. 14:18–19, 22), "El Olam" (Gen. 21:33), and "El Shaddai" (Gen. 17:1; 28:3; 35:11; 43:14; 48:3; 49:25; Exod. 6:3). (But see Cross's discussion, *CMHE,* 46–60.) Yahweh is El, only "passionate."

CHAPTER 4. COVENANT

1. Gerhard von Rad, "The Problem of the Hexateuch," in *The Problem of the Hexateuch and Other Essays* (New York: McGraw-Hill, 1966), 1–78. Cf. José Porfirio Miranda, *Marx and the Bible* (Maryknoll, N.Y.: Orbis Books, 1974), 144–45: "If we keep in mind that the Sinaitic account (Exod. 19—Num. 10) is a much later narrative insertion, then the conclusion is unequivocal: Israel's adoption of laws [narrated in Exodus 18] was originally

connected with the libertarian (Exodic) tradition and the laws were adopted in order to do justice between a man and his neighbor." Thus Miranda sets up a strong opposition between exodus, on the one hand, and Sinai and covenant, on the other.

2. See Gottwald, *Tribes of Yahweh,* 88–114. There is a good reason why "Sinai" does not figure in the historical credos. The making or renewal of covenant, in the cult, was itself the context for the recital of "salvation history." The first instance of covenant making would therefore not need to be mentioned: what was important was the *present* instance of covenant making. A distant analogy: none of the old Christian creeds mentions Eucharist. That is because Eucharist is itself the setting for the gathering of the community and its profession of faith.

3. The storm theophany manifests the cosmic lord: see above, chap. 3, p. 49. On the trumpet blast, see below, chap. 5, n. 6.

4. The participle *hammôṣî',* "the one who brings forth," makes this even clearer. It is used in Exod. 6:7; Lev. 22:33 (P); Deut. 8:14; 13:6, 11; Judges 2:12 (Dtr).

5. See the discussion of the gods and the divine council above, chap. 2, under "The Divine Council," and cf. Psalm 82.

6. After the series of apodictic laws comes another series having to do with sabbath and feasts, in 23:10–19, and then a kind of coda about the taking of the land, in 23:20–33, but I omit consideration of these here.

7. The word comes from the Greek *deiknumi,* "to point." The term "apodictic" is used in logic to mean "demonstrative," having a "Q.E.D." quality, but I think of the James Montgomery Flagg illustration of Uncle Sam pointing at the viewer. Apodictic laws have that air about them. This means *you.*

8. See the story in Lev. 24:10–16.

9. Though it begins "If . . . ," presents a case, and tells how that case is to be dealt with, and so formally resembles the previous case laws, this verse (Exod. 23:4), together with the following verse, belongs with the apodictic laws. The case laws oblige to certain procedures or remedies for wrongdoing or damage done. Here there is no damage needing to be made good, and no wrongdoing. The law does not oblige you to handle a case in certain legal ways; it obliges you to be generous even to an enemy.

10. On the "redeemer" *(gō'ēl),* see Gottwald, *Tribes of Yahweh,* 262–67.

11. See Erhard Gerstenberger, *Wesen und Herkunft des "Apodiktischen Rechts"* (Neukirchen: Neukirchener Verlag, 1965).

12. And, given its "exemplary" function, much of the body of case law as well.

13. It is also given fresh point by being addressed to people who have just come out of oppression. Their existential situation provides a context for it.

14. Cross, *CMHE,* 267.

15. See W. L. Moran, "The Ancient Near Eastern Background of the Love of God in Deuteronomy," *CBQ* 25 (1963): 78–80. On the treaty usage of "know," cf. H. B. Huffmon, "The Treaty Background of Hebrew *yādaʿ*," *BASOR* 181 (1966): 31–37.

16. As leaders in war were said to "go out before" and "come [in, in victory] before" the people: cf. 1 Sam. 18:16.

17. "Obey" of course etymologically means "hear": Latin *ob-audire,* French *obéir.*

18. See Erhard Gerstenberger, "Covenant and Commandment," *JBL* 84 (1965): 38–51.

19. Moran, "Ancient Near Eastern Background of Love of God," 79: In "the terminology of international relations [found at Amarna] . . . ['love'] denotes the friendship between . . . rulers. . . . Like *ṭābūtu,* with which it is virtually synonymous, this friendship is the object of agreement and established by treaty." Akkadian *ṭābūtu* corresponds to Hebrew *ṭôb*: "goodness," "good." See W. L. Moran's article, "A Note on the Treaty Terminology of the Sefire Stelas," *JNES* 22 (1963): 173–76.

20. Cf. 1 Kings 20:32 ("brother"); 2 Kings 16:7 ("servant and son").

21. What would a specifically "religious" vocabulary be in the ancient Near East? Delbert Hillers's *Covenant: The History of a Biblical Idea* (Baltimore: Johns Hopkins Press, 1973) is most useful for understanding the relationship between Near Eastern treaty and biblical covenant.

22. Cf. chap. 1, n. 7.

23. I owe this reading to Marvin Chaney, in an unpublished study of Judges 5, "Philology, Textual Criticism, and Social Models in the 'Song of Deborah' " (paper given at the SBL, October 31, 1975).

24. *Ṣidqōt* is the construct plural of the word *ṣᵉdāqāh,* another form (for all practical purposes) of *ṣedeq*.

25. Gottwald, *Tribes of Yahweh,* 556–58.

26. See ibid., 521–25, for a historical reconstruction of the Gibeonite ruse narrated in Joshua 9.

27. Ibid., 526–27, 165–75.

28. Ibid., 108.

29. Cf. above, 54–55.

30. Exod. 3:12; Judges 6:17–22, 36–40.

CHAPTER 5. EARLY ISRAEL

1. Gottwald, *Tribes of Yahweh,* 358–75, argues that the seemingly canonical number twelve for the tribes of Israel was a matter of happenstance: when David became king there just happened to be twelve tribes in Israel, and the number was frozen there.

2. This is the reading of Patrick D. Miller, Jr., *The Divine Warrior in Early Israel* (Cambridge: Harvard Univ. Press, 1973), 123–28. In the phrase "the

nation of his enemies," "his" refers to the subject (understood) of the verb *yiqqōm,* which is most likely Yahweh. "Nation," *gōy,* is the proper term for the centralized, feudal nation-states from which the Israelites had been freed; but see Gottwald, *Tribes of Yahweh* 509–10.

3. "Power and strategy": cf. 2 Kings 18:20. Both the centrality of trust and the folly of seeking to save oneself—to achieve victory on one's own terms or by one's own resources—is the point of the story in Num. 14:39–45.

4. Either "inhabitants" or "enthroned ones": cf. chap. 2, n. 11. In light of the parallelism of Exod. 15:14–15, we should probably understand "sitters" here as "enthroned ones."

5. See chap. 4, n. 16.

6. Cf. Judges 7:19–22. The *tᵉrûʿāh,* "shout," seems an important part of theophany. It is associated with the storm phenomena, it is the battle cry, and it is the acclamation of the victor enthroned in his sanctuary. The sound of the trumpet was so familiar an element of theophany, as replicated in Holy War and in liturgical procession, that it finds its way into the account of Yahweh's descent on Mount Sinai (Exod. 19:16, 19). The story of the battle of Jericho (Joshua 6) presents warfare as liturgy: the processional of the warrior god is all that is required for victory.

7. Cf. Ps. 2:2, where the same parallelism of "kings" and "princes" (the rare word *rōzᵉnīm*) occurs, as they make common cause against Yahweh; and the concluding exhortation to them (v. 10), *haśkîlû hiwwāsᵉrû,* " 'wise up,' be warned."

8. Following Cross, *CMHE,* 100–01.

9. I follow Marvin Chaney's reading in the paper referred to in chap. 4, n. 23. "Kings" in v. 6 is attested in G. In v. 8, RSV translates "among forty thousand in Israel." The "thousand" represents the Hebrew *'elep,* which does indeed mean "thousand," but as G. E. Mendenhall suggested years ago the word also is a term for a social subdivision. "Forty *'eleps*" would equal one "tribe." See his "The Census Lists of Numbers 1 and 26," *JBL* 77 (1958: 52–66; and Gottwald, *Tribes of Yahweh,* 270–78.

10. So, "the gates of hell," in Matt. 16:18, means the power structure of the nether world, all the resources of Sheol.

Cross, *CMHE,* 122–23, takes Judges 5:8 in an entirely different way. He reads *'lym,* "chiefs" (literally "rams"), instead of MT *'lhym,* "gods," emends *'z lḥm* to *'zy l⟨q⟩ḥm,* and construes MT *šʿrym,* "gates," as *śʿrym,* "captains" (literally "bucks"). The lines then read

> They choose new leaders,
> Yea, they took for themselves captains.

Animal names, like "bucks," were used as titles for warriors or rulers. In Exod. 15:15, the "leaders of Moab" (RSV) are the "rams of Moab," and the "chiefs of Edom" are *'allūpê 'ĕdōm,* which suggests a play on words, *'allūpê/*

'alpê, "bulls." See the "Keret" epic (*CTA* 15.4.6–7), "seventy bulls, eighty gazelles," where lords and ladies are in question.

11. Note the double *inclusio:* the word "gates" links v. 8 and v. 11, and the phrase "people of Yahweh" links vv. 11 and 13; "people" is picked up with the catalogue of the tribes or tribal divisions of Israel, in vv. 14–18.

12. Still, there is rejoicing in the downfall of the enemy and in the shedding of his blood. This exultancy offends modern sensibilities, but some comments are in order.

First, we have to attend to the kind of experience that might lie behind this poetry, by attending, in our own world, to the experience of people who suffer injustice: people who have the fruits of their labor taken from them, or who are constant prey to violence; people who know the terror of the death squad, or of the midnight knock on the door. Study the faces of mothers carrying placards with photographs of their "disappeared" children (*desaparecidos*). Drive slowly along country roads lined with corpses. What do we feel? Anger, resentment, outrage, a desire to see the wrongs righted and the score settled.

This is the kind of feeling given voice in the exultancy of the Song of Deborah and in much of biblical poetry. We may deny that we ever feel anything like it, but in fact it is the emotional point of movies and television programs and novels we routinely allow ourselves to be caught up in. The Bad Guys (muggers, Nazis) get what is coming to them, and we do not blink. They are the Bad Guys. We identify with the Good Guys. The enemy are cardboard figures; they are not persons in their own right. To the extent that they are real, it is as embodiment of evil; so when violent justice is meted out we applaud. This is true of our reactions to the news as well. We hear of "body counts" and do not flinch. We deplore the "desensitization" such reactions evince, but it is important to recognize also that they evince a deeply rooted sense of justice. The conventions of movies tap and give expression to that sense of justice. We are, imaginatively, as capable of exulting in bloodshed as the poet of Judges 5. It is dangerous to deny it.

13. My colleague Jouette Bassler pointed out to me these social implications of Deborah's leadership role. See J. Cheryl Exum, " 'Mother in Israel': A Familiar Figure Reconsidered," in *Feminist Interpretation of the Bible*, ed. Letty M. Russell (Philadelphia: Westminster Press, 1985), 73–85, esp. 84–85.

14. See 1 Sam. 11:7, where Saul sends out parts of sacrificed oxen throughout Israel: the pieces speak eloquently of the covenant ritual of oath taking, which involved just such dissection. Judges 19:29 represents a variant of this practice.

15. The phrase *'ezrat Yahweh baggibbōrim* (Judges 5:23) means the process by which Yahweh "helps" in fighting the military elite of the Canaanite kings. "Meroz" is cursed by Yahweh's messenger or herald, in the heavenly

court, because "they did not come"—turn out for battle—for this *'ezrat Yahweh baggibbōrim*. *Yahweh* here is a subjective genitive.

16. "Clan" is *'elep,* as in Judges 5:8; see above, n. 9. "Father's house" is a technical term for a social unit, as Gottwald shows, *Tribes of Yahweh,* 285-92.

17. Ibid., 261.

18. Cf. chap. 6, under "Prophetic Reproof: Imperialism."

19. *Tribes of Yahweh,* 543–50. His hypothesis is "that behind the *ḥērem* lie selective expulsion and annihilation of kings and upper classes and the selective expropriation of resources such as metals—all with the aim of buttressing the egalitarian mechanisms of Israelite society and providing a solid, renewable support base for the peasant economy" (p. 550).

20. Cf. 1 Sam. 21:4–5; 2 Sam. 11:9–13(?).

21. Cf. Deut. 20:5–7.

22. Cf. the military prowess of the nazirite Samuel, 1 Sam. 7:13. The difficult opening of the Song of Deborah (Judges 5:2) can be construed to say, "When locks hung loose in Israel, / when a people acted generously." ("Acted generously": I am trying to render *hitnaddēb,* which means to make oneself *nādîb;* cf. below, 78.) Did those who "came, for Yahweh's help against the warriors" sport dreadlocks?

23. I translate MT mostly, but see P. Kyle McCarter, Jr., *I Samuel,* AB 8; (Garden City, N.Y.: Doubleday & Co., 1980), 67–71, for a reconstruction of the text.

24. "Horn": the image is of a powerful animal like a bull lifting its head in triumph; see n. 10 above. Cf. the fuller explanation of McCarter, *I Samuel,* 71–72.

25. Omitting MT *ky 'yn bltk:* cf. ibid., 68–69.

26. And cf. Num. 14:9. In American slang an enemy easy to defeat is a "piece of cake." The reverse of 1 Sam. 2:1 is seen in Ps. 35:21, as often in Scripture.

27. Cf. Exod. 2:25; Isa. 29:15; Pss. 33:13–15; 53:2; 94:7; etc.

28. That is, *'ēl dēʿôt,* which I have literally, and clumsily, translated "a god of knowings," uses the "treaty" sense of *ydʿ* mentioned in chap. 4 (n. 15 there). See Amos 3:2. Possibly *dēʿōt* should be emended to the singular, *daʿat.*

29. The unidiomatic "causes to" is my attempt to render the force of the Hebrew causative stem.

30. The motif of the "breaking of the weapons" is seen in Pss. 46:10; 76:4; and most familiarly in Isa. 2:4 (= Micah 4:3). See R. J. Clifford, S.J., *The Cosmic Mountain in Canaan and the Old Testament* (Cambridge: Harvard Univ. Press, 1972), 142–57.

31. Similar imagery is found in the story of David and Goliath. David dons, then takes off, the armor of Saul (1 Sam. 17:38–39).

32. "Satiated," "sated," "filled": there is no happy translation of Hebrew *śbʿ*. Its opposite is *ḥsr,* "to be in want," as in the familiar opening of Psalm 23, "Yahweh shepherds me, I shall not be in want."

33. Gottwald, *Tribes of Yahweh,* 538–40.

34. Gottwald has another view. "Israel seized hold of ('inherited') kingship by asserting a valid claim to the sovereign power that the 'throne' represented and Israel thereby preempted the former sphere of royal sovereignty as its own rightful jurisdiction under the tutelage of Yahweh" (ibid., 538).

35. "Straits" rather than the usual "pillars": see McCarter, *I Samuel,* 73. "These *(m^{e}ṣūqê 'ereṣ)* are the great rivers of the underworld. The tradition of the foundation of the world upon the waters is well known in the cosmogonic lore of Israel (Ps 24:2, etc.) and other ancient Near Eastern societies."

36. "Against them": MT *'lw* should probably be read *'ly,* the divine name Eli, "the Exalted One." Cf. ibid., 73.

37. Yahweh "crushes" *(yḥt)* those who contend with him (v. 10), as he "crushes" the warriors' bows (v. 4).

38. "Adjudicates" in v. 10 is an attempt to translate *yādîn* by a word other than "judge," which I reserve for *špṭ*. The root *dyn* connotes something less inclusive than *špṭ,* something more properly judicial.

39. McCarter (*I Samuel,* 72) speaks of "the catalog of reversals of fortune" in vv. 4 and 5, "the divine balancing out of human experience."

40. Note the theological presuppositions of the reading of the Song of Hannah as a paean to omnipotence. Yahweh's power is unspecific. It is enough that he is all-mighty. There is no content to his omnipotence except being omnipotent. It could be said that his power aims at putting the arrogant in their place, but that is tautological. George Grant's argument sketched in chap. 1 (pp. 11–12) seems to me to shed light on this matter.

41. I owe this suggestion to my student L. J. Rockey. See now Gottwald, *Tribes of Yahweh,* 537–38, who speaks (p. 537) of the barren-fecund contrast as that of "a well-fed and fertile upper class and of a depleted, infertile country folk."

42. I follow W. F. Albright's classic study of these difficult texts, "The Oracles of Balaam," *JBL* 63 (1944):207–33.

43. See above, chap. 4, pp. 61–62, 78.

44. Albright ("Oracles of Balaam," 215 n. 43) translates "royal majesty doth clothe him," reading MT *t^{e}rû'at* as *tôra'at,* " 'majesty' (lit. 'terror-producing'). . . . Cf. the parallel development and use of *puluḫtu, melammu,* etc., in Accadian." I follow Albright in reading *hbṭ* and *r'h* as passives. "Among them" is literally "in him" (viz., Israel).

45. See n. 6 above.

46. Note in Num. 24:7–8 the same sequence: mention of Yahweh's kingship over Israel, followed by a reference to the exodus.

47. Reading

dār^{e}kū kôk^{e}be-m ya'^{a}qōb,
w^{e}qāmū šibṭê-m yiśrā'ēl,

with enclitic *mem* in the construct chain; cf. Albright, "Oracles of Balaam," 219 nn. 82–84. "Tribes" *(šᵉbāṭīm)* is of course also "staffs," "scepters."

CHAPTER 6. KINGS AND PROPHETS

1. Gottwald, *Tribes of Yahweh,* 410–17.

2. This is the basis for the distinction—for what it is worth—between totalitarian and authoritarian regimes. The difference does not lie in the *mišpāṭ* exercised so much as in the claims that that *mišpāṭ* makes for its own legitimacy. What are today called "totalitarian" regimes are based on a vision of the human good that is exclusive and negating of all other goods. The *mišpāṭ* of "authoritarian" regimes is grounded in force, so that it is simply *mišpāṭ,* making no claims to legitimacy beyond its own, unambiguous givenness. In principle it allows the legitimacy and—in principle!—autonomy of other associations (unions, church) and the goods they represent, but jealously guards its own control against their claims. The distinction between "authoritarian" and "totalitarian" regimes is typological at best.

3. Miranda, *Marx and the Bible,* 38–39.

4. I mean "know" in a double sense. If Yahweh is other, we become aware of that otherness in the otherness of the neighbor: concretely we know Yahweh *in* the other. And "know" is a covenantal term, meaning "acknowledge," "recognize" as having a claim on us. (Cf. above, chap. 4 [see n. 15 there].) We "know" him as covenant lord by attending to the need of the other.

5. If the reconstruction of the "Proto-Israelite" movement in chap. 3 holds water, Israel took its origins from the experience of outlawry and insecurity. The god of those *ʿapiru* is the god of people who have let go of security: he is known precisely in their weakness and insecurity.

6. Cf. 1 Kings 12:3–14.

7. "Prophet," derived from the Greek *prophētēs,* is the standard translation of Hebrew *nābîʾ*. Despite its misleading connotation of "fore-telling" or "pre-dicting," *prophētēs* (and "prophet") should be taken to mean one who speaks "for": on behalf of, in place of. On continuities in the prophet's function from the pre-monarchic period into the time of monarchy, see James Ackerman, "Prophecy and Warfare in Early Israel: A Study of the Deborah-Barak Story," in *Essays in Honor of G. Ernest Wright,* ed. Edward F. Campbell and Robert G. Boling, *BASOR* 220/221 (Dec. 1975, Feb. 1976): 5–13.

8. Some of the other stories about Saul depict him as a judge like Gideon or one of the other charismatic leaders. "The spirit of God came mightily upon Saul" (1 Sam. 11:6, RSV), and he led the Israelites in Holy War. To that extent he was successful in holding off the Philistine threat. To that extent, also, nothing had changed, except, as it seems, the life tenure Saul enjoyed as leader. For a historical reconstruction of the kingship of Saul, see Joseph

Blenkinsopp, "The Quest of the Historical Saul," in *No Famine in the Land*, ed. James W. Flanagan and Anita Weisbrod Robinson (Missoula, Mont.: Scholars Press, 1975), 75–99.

9. Cf. 1 Sam. 15:11, literally "to cause my words to stand."

10. "Contend my contention": may Yahweh make my *rîb* (grievance) his own, and settle it himself. Cf. Prov. 23:11, cited above, chap. 4, p. 59.

11. See Mendenhall, *Tenth Generation*, 83–84.

12. Jon Levenson, "1 Samuel 25 as Literature and as History," *CBQ* 40 (1978): 11–28, esp. 19: "Abigail assures David that the vengeance of YHWH will visit Nabal if only David restrains himself from usurping the divine prerogative, . . ."

13. Cf. 2 Kings 16:7.

14. Note that nowhere is the Davidic king called "son of God" or "son of Yahweh." Instead Yahweh says, "I will be a father to him and he will be a son to me" (2 Sam. 7:14), or says to him, "My son are you" (Ps. 2:7), as the Davidic king says to Yahweh, "My father are you" (Ps. 89:26).

15. Cf. Pss. 132:11, 13; 2:6.

16. Note the echo of Exod. 1:14, *ʿᵃbōdāh qāšāh*, "hard service," "harsh servitude."

17. "Good" is used as a technical term for the substance of a political relationship as for its happy results: both loyalty and consequent blessing. Cf. chap. 4, n. 19. At the end of this quotation (v. 16), note the covenantal use of the term "know."

18. Cf. chap. 5, n. 38.

19. "Sons of the prophets": members of the prophetic group. Cf. above, chap. 2, n. 9.

20. Hebrew *sōd:* the word means both a deliberative group and what is discussed in it, with the nuance of something secret. It is Yahweh's privy council.

21. Prophets "run," as messengers are "runners."

22. William McKane, *Prophets and Wise Men*, SBT 44 (London: SCM Press, 1965) brings to life the conflict between the prophets and the kings' counselors or "wise men."

23. On the covenant curses proclaimed by the prophets, see Hillers, *Covenant* (cf. above, chap. 4, n. 21), chap. 6; and idem, *Treaty Curses and the Old Testament Prophets*, BibOr 16 (Rome: Pontifical Biblical Institute, 1964).

The prophetic motif of the "day of Yahweh" deserves a word, especially since it provides a subtext for much of NT thought. On that day, Yahweh would "judge": make his *mišpāṭ* a reality. He would "come" as warrior god, with cloud and fire, to effect vengeance and vindication, and establish his kingship. The motifs of storm theophany, Holy War, panic, and *ḥērem* are especially prominent in this prophetic scenario of the *Dies Irae*. See Amos 5:18–20; Isa. 13:4–16; Zeph. 1:7–18.

CHAPTER 7. DEUTERONOMY AND THE DEUTERONOMISTIC HISTORY

1. Cf. above, chap. 4, pp. 61–62.
2. Cf. above, chap. 3, n. 37.
3. Cf. chap. 4, n. 19, chap. 6, n. 17.
4. Chap. 5, n. 32.
5. And which is shaped by that allegiance.
6. Dedicated: the root is *ḥnk,* as in the word Hanukkah. In effect the verb means "taking up residence."
7. Harvested: the root *ḥll* means both to defile and to inaugurate or begin. Plucking the grapes is "defilement" of the vine.
8. Hillers, *Treaty Curses,* 28–29, 36–40.
9. "Have made for me this wealth": more literally, "have done for me this *ḥayil.*" "To do *ḥayil*" means to put forth effort in an efficacious and successful way. In other passages the expression is translated "do valiantly," as in Ps. 118:15–16, "The right hand of the Lord does valiantly." (Cf. also Num. 24:18; 1 Sam. 14:48; Ps. 60:14 = Ps. 108:14; Prov. 31:29; Ruth 4:11.) *Ḥayil* is "force" or "substance." A "man of *ḥayil*" or (as in the famous passage in Proverbs 31) "woman of *ḥayil*" is someone of substance and worth. The word can mean, concretely, "army" (e.g., Exod. 15:4, "Pharaoh and his force"), and also "wealth." Ezek. 28:4, the taunt against the king of Tyre, shows the semantic link between "doing valiantly" and "making wealth":

> By your wisdom and understanding
> you have done for yourself *ḥayil*
> and have gathered gold and silver into your treasuries.

RSV translates the second line "you have gotten wealth for yourself." What Deut. 8:17–18 has in mind is not the specific achievement of "getting wealth" so much as acting efficaciously.

10. Conventionally, "Deuteronomic" refers to the Book of Deuteronomy, "Deuteronomistic" to the larger historical work Joshua-Kings. Cross has analyzed the themes of Dtr in "The Themes of the Book of Kings and the Structure of the Deuteronomistic History," in *CMHE*, 274–89.
11. In the study mentioned in the previous note, Cross has shown how the Deuteronomistic History (Dtr) was composed in two editions, which Cross terms Dtr^1 and Dtr^2. Dtr^2 revised an earlier effort, in order to take into account the failure of the hopes reposed in King Josiah and the tragedy of the exile.
12. Cf. above, chap. 6, pp. 103–5.

CHAPTER 8. EXILE AND APOCALYPTIC

1. Cross has shown how the "second edition" of the Deuteronomistic History, the updating of the work abbreviated Dtr^2, tried (somewhat lamely)

to account for the exile by reference to the "sin of Manasseh," the southern counterpart of the "sin of Jeroboam" which was to Dtr[1] the font and prime analogue of the infidelity of the North. *CMHE*, 285–89.

2. The exile in question could have been the exile of the Northern Kingdom. To date the book to the seventh century, in the aftermath of Israel's fall, is attractive, given its connections, to be discussed, with the Deuteronomistic corpus.

3. "Though I am just [the root *ṣdq*], my mouth would make me wicked [the root *rš'*, 'wicked']."

4. The root *rš'*, "to be wicked."

5. The following discussion of Job and Second Isaiah I derive from Cross, *CMHE*, 343–46.

6. Isaiah 41:22–23, 26–27; 42:9; 43:9, 18–19; 44:7–8; 46:9–11; 48:3, 6–8, 16; in effect also 51:1–3 and 54:9.

7. In view of the central motif of the "way" and the use of the verb *'br,* "cross" (as in 51:9–11), this lament contains a delicious pun: "passes away" *('br).*

8. Isaiah 43:22–28; 48:8–10, 18–19; cf. 44:22 and 54:6–8.

9. Cf. Isaiah 42:1–4; 49:22–23; 51:4–5.

10. Chap. 6, under "Prophecy."

11. The Hebrew expression translated "the end of days" is an idiom for "later on." Hebrew *'aḥ^{a}rît hayyāmīm* means (though this translation is not English) "temporal posteriority": *'aḥ^{a}rît* is not so much "end" as "afterwardsness," and the "of days" part of the expression is adjectival for "time." The expression could be translated "in time to come."

12. In the Greek translation of the Hebrew Scriptures, *eschaton,* "end," renders *'aḥ^{a}rît.*

13. Elias Bickerman, *From Ezra to the Last of the Maccabees* (New York: Schocken Books, 1972), is the classic survey of this period.

14. Cf. above, chap. 6, pp. 107–8.

15. "One like a son of man": as we have seen since chap. 2 (n. 9), the expression "son of man" means "member of the genus 'man' "—simply, "human being," "man."

16. Dan. 7:22, 27.

17. Dan. 10:13, 21; 12:1.

CHAPTER 9. THE NEW TESTAMENT

1. Cf. the reminiscences of the nazirite vow in Mark 14:25, "Amen, I say to you that I will no more drink of the fruit of the vine until that day when I drink it, new (wine), in the kingdom of God." Jesus is dedicating himself for the imminent struggle, whose outcome will be the coming of the kingdom, on the Day of the Lord.

2. Following NT usage, by "Scripture" and "the Scriptures" I mean the Hebrew Scriptures ("Old Testament").

3. G has "accursed of God is everyone hanged upon a tree." Cf. Max Wilcox, " 'Upon the Tree'—Deut 21:22–23 in the New Testament," *JBL* 96 (1977): 85–99. The NT passages Wilcox cites are Gal. 3:13 (cf. below); Acts 5:30; 10:39; 13:29; 1 Peter 2:24. He argues "that the NT use of Deut 21:22–23 and the 'tree'-motif involved formed part of an early Jewish-Christian midrashic exposition of the Akedah [the 'binding' of Isaac, cf. Genesis 22] and was employed for the purpose of facilitating the application of the role of Isaac to Jesus" (p. 99).

4. The Greek word *xylon* means "tree" and also "wood." In the Greek translation of Deut. 21:22–23, *xylon* translates Hebrew *'ēṣ,* which likewise means both "tree" and "wood."

5. Ernst Käsemann, "A Critical Analysis of Philippians 2:5–11," in Herbert Braun et al., *God and Christ: Existence and Province, Journal for Theology and the Church* 5 (Tübingen: J. C. B. Mohr [Paul Siebeck]; New York: Harper & Row, 1968), 45–88.

6. John Howard Yoder, *The Politics of Jesus* (Grand Rapids: Wm. B. Eerdmans, 1972), 135–62. See also G. B. Caird, *Principalities and Powers* (Oxford: Clarendon Press, 1956); A. J. Festugière, O.P., *Epicurus and His Gods* (Oxford: Basil Blackwell & Mott, 1955), 73–77.

7. J. A. Fitzmyer, S.J., "The Letter to the Galatians," *JBC* (Englewood Cliffs, N.J.: Prentice-Hall, 1968), 237.

8. Chap. 6, pp. 87–88.

9. See above, chap. 8, pp. 135–36.

10. The Hebrew root *nḥm* is translated by two words, principally, in the Greek version of Scripture: *metanoein,* "repent," and *parakalein,* "console," together with the corresponding nouns, *metanoia,* "repentance," and *paraklēsis,* "consolation." I am arguing that behind the "repentance" of Mark 1:4 we should see the *naḥᵃmāh* of Isa. 40:1.

11. See Kyle McCarter, "The River Ordeal in Israelite Literature," *HTR* 66 (1973): 403–12. The OT imagery McCarter studies almost certainly formed part of the understanding of the Jewish practice of baptism.

12. *Exousia,* the Old Greek translation of *šolṭān* in Dan. 7:14.

13. The ideas contained in this section, and esp. the paraphrases of the parables, I owe to my friend William P. Sampson, S.J.

14. See John R. Donahue, S.J., "Jesus as the Parable of God in the Gospel of Mark," *Int.* 32 (1978): 369–86, reprinted in J. L. Mays, ed., *Interpreting the Gospels* (Philadelphia: Fortress Press, 1981), 148–67.

15. Cf. Heb. 13:12–13.

Suggestions for Further Reading

"CONTROL," AUTONOMY, FREEDOM, ETC.

Bellah, R., et. al. *Habits of the Heart: Individualism and Commitment in American Life*. Berkeley and Los Angeles: Univ. of California Press, 1985. The well-known sociologist and his colleagues survey the tensions, or contradictions, of our culture, covering much the same ground as George Grant in *Technology and Empire*.

Paz, Octavio. *One Earth, Four or Five Worlds: Reflections on Contemporary History*. New York: Harcourt Brace Jovanovich, 1985. Paz is the "outsider" who shows us ourselves as we are.

Slater, P. *The Pursuit of Loneliness*. Boston: Beacon Press, 1970. Now somewhat dated, this book still serves to point out anomalies within the American "consensus."

ANCIENT ISRAEL: ORIGINS, MONARCHY, PROPHECY

Brueggemann, W. *The Prophetic Imagination*. Philadelphia: Fortress Press, 1979. As always, Brueggemann makes the biblical text come alive. He contrasts royal consciousness and prophetic consciousness, with categories like "criticizing" and "energizing." The treatment of prophetic consciousness includes two chapters on Jesus.

———. "Trajectories in Old Testament Literature and the Sociology of Ancient Israel." *JBL* 98 (1979): 161–85. Brueggemann sets up a typology of "Royal" and "Liberation" streams of thought within the biblical tradition; the article gives us a "map" of the tradition—and of contemporary OT scholarship.

Freedman, D. N., and D. F. Graf, eds. *Palestine in Transition: The Emergence of Ancient Israel*. Sheffield, Eng.: The Almond Press, 1983. The latest word on the Peasant Revolt theory, this collection (containing essays by William Stiebing, John Halligan, Norman Gottwald, Marvin Chaney, and George Mendenhall) is notable for Mendenhall's vigorous objections to Gottwald's elaboration of his seminal work on Israelite origins.

Koch, K., "Is There a Doctrine of Retribution in the Old Testament?" In *Theodicy in the Old Testament,* edited by J. L. Crenshaw, 57–87. IRT no. 4. Philadelphia: Fortress Press, 1983. Koch's strangely neglected 1955 essay, now translated into English, underlies the present volume's treatment of Deuteronomy: Koch answers the question in the title of his article with a clear and convincing no.

________. *The Prophets*. Philadelphia: Fortress Press. Volume 1: *The Assyrian Period,* 1983. Volume 2: *The Babylonian and Persian Periods,* 1984. Detailed treatments of the classical prophets, showing them against their historical background.

EXILE AND APOCALYPTIC

Charlesworth, J. H., ed. *The Old Testament Pseudepigrapha.* Garden City, N.Y.: Doubleday & Co. Volume 1: *Apocalyptic Literature and Testaments,* 1983. Volume 2: *Expansions of the "Old Testament" and Legends, Wisdom and Philosophical Literature, Prayers, Psalms, and Odes, Fragments of Lost Judeo-Hellenistic Works,* 1985. An indispensable collection of texts in translation, with generous and helpful introductions and notes by leading scholars.

Hanson, P. *The Dawn of Apocalyptic.* Philadelphia: Fortress Press, 1975. A very influential (and difficult) treatment of apocalyptic and its origins in the early postexilic period, Hanson's understanding of apocalyptic differs markedly from that presented in this volume.

Klein, R. W. *Israel in Exile: A Theological Interpretation.* OBT 6. Philadelphia: Fortress Press, 1979. A study of sixth-century reactions to the exile (Lamentations, Dtr, Jeremiah, Ezekiel, Second Isaiah, and P).

Koch, K. *The Rediscovery of Apocalyptic.* SBT 2d series 22; London: SCM Press, 1972. A wry and insightful study of how apocalyptic has been treated by biblical scholars and theologians. The first chapter "What Is Apocalyptic?" answers its question along the lines presented in the present volume.

Nickelsberg, G. *Jewish Literature Between the Bible and the Mishnah: A Historical and Literary Introduction.* Philadelphia: Fortress Press, 1981. A wonderful overview of the (mostly noncanonical) writings that came out of Jewish experience from the Greek period to the Second Jewish Revolt: Daniel, Sirach, Enoch, Jubilees, Qumran literature, Testaments, etc.

PRINCIPALITIES AND POWERS

Wink, W. *The Powers.* Philadelphia: Fortress Press. Volume 1: *Naming the Powers: The Language of Power in the New Testament,* 1984. Volume 2:

Unmasking the Powers: The Invisible Forces That Determine Human Existence, 1986. Volume 3: *Engaging the Powers,* forthcoming. A survey of NT and other ancient texts, a cultural and theological interpretation of them, and an attempt to show the meaning of the Powers for our lives. Sure to be a standard source.

Index of Authors

Index of Biblical Passages

Old Testament

NEW TESTAMENT